DATE DUE

DEMCO, INC. 38-2931

D1566966

The South's Tolerable Alien

The South's Tolerable Alien

ROMAN CATHOLICS
in ALABAMA *and* GEORGIA
1945–1970

ANDREW S. MOORE

LOUISIANA STATE UNIVERSITY PRESS

BATON ROUGE

Published by Louisiana State University Press
Copyright © 2007 by Louisiana State University Press
All rights reserved
Manufactured in the United States of America
First printing

Designer: Barbara Neely Bourgoyne
Typeface: Adobe Minion Pro, text; Brioso Pro, display
Printer and binder: Edwards Brothers, Inc.

Library of Congress Cataloging-in-Publication Data
Moore, Andrew S., 1968–
The South's tolerable alien : Roman Catholics in Alabama and Georgia,
1945–1970 / Andrew S. Moore.
    p.   cm.
    Includes bibliographical references and index.
    ISBN-13: 978-0-8071-3212-8 (cloth : alk. paper)
    1. Catholics—Alabama—History—20th century. 2. Catholics—
Georgia—History—20th century. 3. Alabama—Social conditions—20th
century. 4. Georgia—Social conditions—20th century. 5. Alabama—
Race relations—History—20th century. 6. Georgia—Race relations—
History—20th century. 7. Catholic Church—Alabama—History—20th
century. 8. Catholic Church—Georgia—History—20th century. 9.
Alabama—Church history. 10. Georgia—Church history. I. Title.
F335.C3M66 2007
975.0088'282—dc22

                                                    2006015760

for Christie

✥

He who finds a wife finds a good thing,
And obtains favor from the Lord.

—PROVERBS 18:22

Contents

✦

Acknowledgments

In completing this book and the dissertation upon which it is based, just about the only thing I did alone was sit in front of my computer and put fingers to keys. It seems that at every other stage of the process I enjoyed support and assistance that deserve more in return than mere acknowledgment. Alas, that is all I have to offer; so offer it I do with gratitude and humility.

Anthony R. Dees, of the Catholic Archdiocese of Atlanta, was the type of archivist all researchers appreciate but few are fortunate to find. In addition to running a tight ship in the archdiocesan archives, Tony befriended me and took a personal interest in my project. His successor, John Hanley, has been helpful since Tony's retirement. In Mobile, Alabama, Archbishop Oscar H. Lipscomb kindly allowed me access to Archbishop Thomas J. Toolen's and Bishop John L. May's papers. And Bernadette Mathews graciously accommodated me in the chancery and made photocopies for me. Charles Boyle, archivist at Spring Hill College in Mobile, gave me complete access to Father Albert Foley's papers. The late Sister Mary Victory, archivist for the Catholic Diocese of Savannah, was always a delight and never failed to remind me that she was praying for me. Gillian Brown, the current archivist in Savannah, has been helpful since I completed my research. Elisa Baldwin, of the University of South Alabama's archives, graciously accommodated me when I dropped in unannounced one day. At the Diocese of Birmingham in Alabama, Sister Mary Frances Loftin, D.C., permitted me free access to the archives, and Gerry Nabors kindly photocopied transcripts from the Oral History Collection for me. Finally, Carol Ellis, then of the University of South Alabama (now at Rice University), shared Joan Sage's unpublished memoirs with me.

ACKNOWLEDGMENTS

The University of Notre Dame's Cushwa Center for the Study of American Catholicism has been very good to me over the years. During the 1998–1999 academic year, I was awarded a dissertation fellowship by the Center, which brought with it the privilege of being part of the Catholicism in Twentieth-Century America Public Presences working group. I am grateful for Scott Appleby, who was then the director of the Cushwa Center, as well as the advisory committee and my fellow grant recipients in the Public Presences working group, all of whom critiqued my project in its earliest stages. Since then, Timothy Matovina, Scott's successor, and Kathy Cummings have been generous with their time and assistance. The College of Liberal Arts and Sciences and the Richard J. Milbauer Foundation of the University of Florida also provided funding for research.

At the University of Florida, I had the special privilege of working closely with a group of scholars who taught me by word and deed how to be both a scholar and an effective teacher. Bertram Wyatt-Brown, Samuel S. Hill, Jr., W. Fitzhugh Brundage, Robert Zieger, and Thomas Gallant all read this when it was a dissertation. Bert and Sam read it more closely than anyone else, and both have been instrumental in helping me turn it into a book. I am fortunate that two such noted scholars worked so well together in mentoring graduate students and young scholars. Their respect for me and my work, as well as their support and encouragement, helped to convince me that I was a scholar myself. I want to influence students as positively as they have influenced me.

Other people have played crucial roles as I turned the dissertation into a book. John McGreevy, of the University of Notre Dame, read the entire manuscript more than once. This is a stronger, more tightly argued book as a result of his constructive criticism. Louis Haas, of Middle Tennessee State University, and Jeffrey Marlett, of The College of Saint Rose, read excerpts at one time or another. Anonymous readers for Louisiana State University Press provided helpful suggestions for improving the manuscript.

Some of the material here appeared earlier in article form. I want to thank the editors of the *Journal of Southern Religion* and *U.S. Catholic Historian* for permission to reprint material that was published in their journals. Material that appeared in the *Georgia Historical Quarterly* is reprinted here courtesy of the Georgia Historical

Society. Anonymous referees for those journals and commentators at academic conferences, most notably Ralph Luker and Peter Huff, also made helpful comments and critiques.

It has been a pleasure to be associated with Louisiana State University Press. John Easterly's interest in and support for this project have been encouraging. I am a worrier by nature, and his timely responses to e-mail queries and requests for reassurance and guidance eased my doubts and fears.

There is a group of colleagues, friends, and family who have not read the first word of this book, but who have contributed to its completion with their friendship, support, and encouragement. I am proud to have finally found an academic home at Saint Anselm College in Manchester, New Hampshire. As a southern Protestant, I had my doubts about fitting in at this Yankee Catholic institution. But my colleagues in the history department—Silvia Shannon, Beth Salerno, Sean Perrone, Hugh Dubrulle, Phil Pajakowski, Matthew Masur, and Father William Sullivan—quickly dispelled those doubts. Since our undergraduate days, John Truslow has been best friend, fellow Atlanta Braves fan, and (most recently) cycling companion. During research trips to Atlanta, chez Truslow was also a home away from home.

I am humbled by the love and support I have received from my family over the years. Jeff and Amy Moore, Julie and Armando Barraza, and Peggy Young and the late W. J. Young all helped to provide the grounding and security that accompany strong family ties. I will always treasure that. There is much that may be written about my parents, Lamar and Vicki Moore. Generous with all they have, they have unselfishly provided emotional, spiritual, and financial support. They are the people I want to be when I grow up.

By temperament, training, and experience, I am a cynical, withdrawn person. It is no small wonder, then, that there are people who still give me the "warm fuzzies." My wife, Christie, and my daughters, Flannery and Percy-Kate, brighten my life and regularly remind me of the true meaning of joy. They probably hindered more than they furthered the completion of this book, but I would have had it no other way. I thank God for them every day. My wife especially has sacrificed and pinched pennies to make a professor's salary last until month's end. She loved me even when I was distracted by this book. And she is raising our daughters to be the brightest, most beautiful little people I ever expect to know. I love her for that and so much more. I am happy this book will finally appear in print, if for no other reason than so I can tell that to all who read.

The South's Tolerable Alien

Good Catholics and Good Citizens

✠

A 1945 story in the *Catholic Week,* the official newspaper of the Diocese of Mobile, acknowledged that Catholics were "scarce in most sections of the South." And where Catholics maintained a public presence "they know they have to be good Catholics and good citizens if they want to attain the respect of their fellow-citizens. And the majority of them do."[1] That was the dilemma facing white Catholics in the predominantly Protestant South. How to be both good Catholics and good citizens in a region that was divided by race and defined by at least nominal adherence to one of a variety of Protestant denominations? This book's primary task is to explain how white Catholics in Alabama and Georgia resolved that dilemma in the roughly two and a half decades or so after the end of World War II. The answer to how they came to share in the southern mainstream comes in part from considering the issue that dominated and shaped the southern landscape like no other. The late journalist and southern critic W. J. Cash once noted that if there are many Souths, there is also one South. For most of the twentieth century, that one South was preoccupied with race and preserving white supremacy and segregation. Race dictated political, social, and cultural power, and access to power stemmed directly from the degree to which one shared in the region's regnant whiteness.

In explaining how Catholics balanced regional and religious identities, this book makes three interrelated arguments. First, for much of the twentieth century, religion rivaled race as a boundary separating groups in the South. Most of the South's Catholics enjoyed the legal, social, and political advantages of white skin color. But examples of anti-Catholicism—including violence and intimidation—

from the early twentieth century until after World War II suggest that Catholics still flirted with the margins of the South's racialized public sphere. In 1921, for instance, a Methodist minister, Edwin Stephenson, shot and killed Father James E. Coyle, pastor of Birmingham's St. Paul's Catholic Church. Coyle had performed the wedding ceremony of Stephenson's daughter, a recent convert to Catholicism, to a Puerto Rican man, and Stephenson sought vengeance with a gun. Alabama lawyer and future Supreme Court justice Hugo Black led an imaginative defense that appealed to the city's religious and racial prejudices to earn Stephenson's acquittal. As one journalist at the time wrote, anti-Catholicism had grown so bad in Alabama that it "stands second only to the hatred of the Negro as the moving passion of entire Southern communities." At the present rate, Charles P. Sweeney continued, one "might some day expect to see the burning of Catholics at the stake and such other of the monstrous delights of inflamed ignorance as are now practiced on the Negro population."[2] That anti-Catholicism persisted into the second half of the twentieth century and determined the outlines of Catholics' relationship to southern society.

Second, the book argues that the high drama of the civil rights movement provided a stage for white Catholics' acceptance into the southern mainstream. Only when Jim Crow was threatened from the outside did religious prejudice subside. The story of Catholic acceptance into the social and cultural mainstream is in part the story of the South and its white Protestants coming to terms with their modern pluralism. But this is not necessarily the triumph of inclusive liberalism that makes room for welcome divergent beliefs. Instead, it is the story of struggle, exclusion, and a common purpose based on discrimination. Provoked by a crisis atmosphere created by racial agitation, whites—both Protestant and Catholic—sought common cause in trying to fend off assaults on the status quo. The South's religious pluralism—achieved, as it were, in the midst of the South's complete modernization—was rooted in a tacit agreement that bound the region's majority Protestants with white Catholics in the preservation of the racial status quo.[3]

Historians have long treated southern Protestantism as unique and particularly shaped by secular society. Writing in the 1960s, in direct response to the black freedom struggle, Samuel S. Hill, Jr., argued that a "central theme" of an overriding emphasis on the conversion experience and the need to be born again marked southern Protestantism. The "practical fruits" of that central theme included an absence of a Christian social ethic and no concern for social reform. As a result, Protestant Christian culture and "southernness" (slavery and racial segregation) coexisted side by side, two cultural systems sharing space in the hearts and minds of white southerners; when southerners were forced to choose between the two, the argument goes, they almost invariably chose southernness.[4]

Recent research on race and religion in the twentieth century points toward the conclusion that the relationship between religion and southern society—or between religion and race—was much more dynamic and fluid than Hill's "central theme" would allow. Historian Paul Harvey has published two highly regarded studies of white and black religious cultures in the late nineteenth and twentieth centuries. Rather than cultural captivity, Harvey described competing and complementary cultures, black and white, and demonstrated the dialectic in which those cultures were engaged. As a result, the intersection between race and religion defies facile categorization. People guided by religious beliefs could be found on both sides of the racial divide. All white Protestant church people, for instance, were not opposed to racial reform. Indeed, Harvey has argued that there existed a tradition of "social Christianity" (rather than social gospel) that "involves envisioning a public role for Christians in reforming and regulating human institutions, without necessarily seeing this public role as primary." That is, rather than cultural captivity, white southern Christians engaged the secular sphere and applied Christian teaching (or their understanding of that teaching) to public concerns. Mark Newman has described much more fluidity in white Southern Baptists' attitudes toward civil rights and desegregation than was previously acknowledged. The Southern Baptist Convention originally endorsed the *Brown v. Board of Education* decision, and individual congregations struggled with the local implications of desegregation.[5]

Because of such recent scholarship on race and religion, historians now understand better the extent to which the civil rights movement was not, as the "central theme" might lead us to believe, a secular movement versus religion. Rather, the freedom struggle was in many respects a religious movement, infused with Christian meaning, symbols, and structure. David L. Chappell recently argued that the movement succeeded where mid-twentieth-century liberalism had failed precisely because of activists' "prophetic religion." White opponents of the movement lacked a similar theological grounding for segregation, Chappell concluded. Chappell rightfully places religious faith (rather than ministers or the black church alone) at the heart of the black freedom struggle, and his argument that the anti–civil rights movement was primarily political is noteworthy. But he underestimates the impact of religious belief on the anti–civil rights movement. We know that opponents of racial justice often responded as religiously informed people. Historian Charles Marsh has described the conflict over the black freedom struggle as a theological struggle. "White conservatives and civil right activists, black militants and white liberals, black moderates and klansmen," according to Marsh, "all staked their particular claims for racial justice and social order on the premise that God was on their side."[6] The movement then became the locus of religious conflict, the arena for sorting out the social implications of Christian faith. It directly affected religious and social structures, interacted with them, and necessarily subverted many of them.

For Catholics the movement brought into sharp conflict two visions of the Church. In the first, the Church was rooted in a medieval Catholic world; it was institutional, hierarchical, and unchanging. Vertical relationships among laity, priests, and bishops were held together by participation in the Catholic sacraments. This church denounced religious individualism and expressed suspicions of political democracy. In America the argument in favor of the institutional Church over and against the individual can be traced back at least to the mid-nineteenth century. Then converts to Roman Catholicism, most notably Orestes Brownson, wrote against what they perceived as the Americanization of the nation's immigrant Catholic population. American Catholics had become too individualistic. The antidote to that individualism was an insistence on the authority of the Church; the laity must follow the direction of the bishops and clergy. As one historian has described Brownson's argument, "Catholicity was an organic whole in which all the elements logically cohered. From the mystery of the Trinity to the humblest act of worship, every Catholic truth and practice formed an unbroken chain. And the truths in that chain, though often above reason, never contradicted reason."[7] Although Catholic theologians argued otherwise, for most twentieth-century lay white Catholics this understanding of the institutional Church was compatible with segregation. White southerners at least viewed their region's social order, including its system of racial apartheid, as inherently good, even divinely sanctioned. Much like early twentieth-century Catholicism, the South's social order cohered into an organic model that was greater than the sum of its various parts.

In the 1930s, 1940s, and 1950s, the South, of course, was in the midst of a modernization and transformation that paralleled the evolution of the older Catholic model of the institutional Church. A second understanding of the Church emerged in the mid-twentieth century to challenge that older model. Beginning in the 1930s, Catholic thinkers bemoaned the European Catholic Church's close affiliation with fascist governments and sought to link democratic political movements more closely to Catholic doctrine and early Church fathers. The French philosopher Jacques Maritain accomplished this by tracing democratic impulses to Thomas Aquinas and the Christian Gospels themselves. After all, at the heart of Catholic ecclesiology is an emphasis on the collective good; a new emphasis on democracy and individual rights, therefore, worried some Catholics, including Maritain.[8] This "Nouvelle Theologie" proved to be part of the evolution of Catholic descriptions of the Church in the modern world. What emerged by the 1960s was a Church re-imagined as more dynamic and adaptable. This modern Church encouraged more lay involvement and de-emphasized the Roman Church's absolutist truth claims. Horizontal relationships between Catholics became more important, while hierarchical relationships between clergy and laity assumed decreasing significance.

The civil rights events of the 1960s coincided with the Second Vatican Council, convened by Pope John XXIII in 1962 for the purpose of studying the Catholic Church's role in the modern world. Meeting off and on until 1965, the world's bishops encouraged the faithful to read "the signs of the times and [interpret] them in the light of the Gospel."[9] The Council also affirmed the right of individual religious freedom. Catholics could be governed by their conscience and "immune from coercion by individuals, social groups and every human power" so that they would not be "forced to act against their convictions."[10] The *Dogmatic Constitution on the Church*, moreover, announced that "the baptized are consecrated as a spiritual house and a holy priesthood." As a result, the bishops re-imagined the nature of the Church, away from hierarchy and institutions to the "people of God" intended to serve their fellow human beings. In this new Church, according to historian John T. McGreevy, "bishops reevaluated the relationship of the Church with contemporary society, emphasizing the duty of all Catholics to improve, not simply reject, the modern world." To be sure, the Council left in place the formal offices of bishops and clergy, but "the common priesthood of the faithful and the ministerial or hierarchical priesthood are none the less interrelated."[11] As radical and controversial as many of these reforms proved to be, the third argument of this book is that for southern Catholics the civil rights movement brought more dramatic and immediate changes than the Vatican Council. The movement forced Catholics onto a public stage and invited the type of ecumenical interchange that conciliar reforms only promised.

The contest between the two models of the Church also points to an uncomfortable proposition. The understanding of the Church as institutional and unchanging provided important support for opponents of the civil rights movement. They could rightfully be alarmed at the sudden, even radical, changes in their Church. Those changes, moreover, seemed to come from sources outside the walls of the Church rather than from Catholic doctrine. Anti–civil rights activists could agree with Louisiana Catholic and White Citizens Council leader Leander Perez, whom New Orleans Archbishop Joseph Francis Rummel excommunicated in 1962 because of his opposition to desegregating parochial schools. Perez asked: "How come we could have slaves, separate schools and churches for these Negroes for ages and ages and now all of a sudden it's a sin? Seems to me like some Communist got some kinda spell over that man [Archbishop Rummel]."[12] Communism had not seized the archbishop, of course, but his actions did signal a new direction for the Catholic Church. Many white Catholics welcomed the changes; others, like Perez, did not.

By undermining the culture of segregation and the racial hierarchy that had dictated the Church's relationship to southern culture, the movement became for many a white freedom struggle as well as a black one. That is, it enabled more southern white Catholics—primarily clergy, female religious, and prominent laymen—to work outside the long-standing racial order in implementing Catholic social doctrine. At the same time, the civil rights movement often separated white laity from their leadership and set in motion a series of events through which laypeople, especially those whites in the South who saw the world through the same racial lenses as other white southerners, were forced to renegotiate their own relationship to the Church. Authority became a contested issue as activist priests and nuns undermined the respect they had enjoyed from laypeople and lost respect themselves for gradualist or obstructionist bishops. Racial reform and the Second Vatican Council, moreover, revealed fault lines within the Church and left in their wake divisions between white and black, liberal and conservative, prelate and laymen. In addition, they reveal that the Catholic Church's history in the South does not fit neatly into categories of progressive and reactionary. Within the Catholic tradition lay impulses for both types of responses. Indeed, at times liberal and conservative tendencies grew from the same Church traditions.

The civil rights movement drew southern Catholics into the public fray. Catholics' religious identity could not be separated from opposition to or support of racial reform and the black freedom struggle. On the one hand, ecclesiastical authority rooted in a pre–Vatican II hierarchy acquiesced to the southern social order and refused to challenge segregation. Indeed, this hierarchical Catholicism was consistent with Jim Crow's emphasis on place and order and promised to protect racial boundaries. On the other hand, the modern, post–Vatican II Church was forced to sort out the moral implications of a relatively newfound social ethic that undermined racial discrimination. In place of hierarchical authority came the promise of racial equality for black Catholics— the Church as the "people of God"—a notion that many whites refused to acknowledge. Although the nature of bishops' authority became increasingly complicated in the late 1960s, their ability to act unilaterally continued to set the Catholic Church apart from Protestant churches. Southern Baptist congregations occasionally voted whether to admit African Americans to their churches. Votes in favor of retaining strict segregation often were influenced by people who attended that congregation irregularly or not at all.[13] There were no such votes in Catholic parishes. The authority of the bishop over individual parishes was absolute and not subject to the whims and prejudices of parishioners.

Differences between the hierarchical and the communitarian understandings of the nature of the Church notwithstanding, similarities between the two visions are compelling—especially when compared to Protestants' theology of the church. For Catholics the Church is larger than the individual person; instead, God's people acting in community experience the sacred together. God's people achieve salvation by participating in rituals that bind them both to God and to each other. This fact made it difficult for the Catholic Church to ignore the South's black population. As a result, the southern Catholic Church's encounter with race was complicated by the fact that it was in fact a biracial church, and that despite providing separate but equal facilities for black Catholics it did allow a small measure of integration. Religious orders of priests and nuns worked among African Americans in the South, winning a few converts and carving out a niche ministry for an otherwise all-white Church. By employing outside religious orders to evangelize and minister to the region's blacks, southern dioceses were able to acquiesce in the region's racial order and maintain the segregation that was required for the Church to operate publicly in the South. Despite separate facilities, black Catholics' public participation in the life of the Church was unmistakable. In many instances blacks expected to be able to attend otherwise white parishes for mass. This fact put the Church in a unique position vis-à-vis other southern white denominations. On the one hand, it was suspect from the start, as its biracial makeup set it apart from the region's Baptists, Churches of Christ, and Methodists, whose membership was exclusively white. Where there were black Baptists, for example, they had their own, separate denomination, founded in the wake of the Civil War and the end of slavery.[14] There was no institutionally separate black Catholic denomination.

This pattern of race relations within the Church in Alabama and Georgia also made it unique from the Catholic Church in the urban North. In the best book available on the Catholic Church and race relations in the twentieth century, historian John T. McGreevy described a tightly knit northern parish that imbued urban neighborhoods with religious significance. The strength of the parish and the importance of community boundaries dictated how northern urban white Catholics encountered the migration of African Americans into formerly all-white neighborhoods. As black neighborhoods pushed up against those parish boundaries, white Catholics perceived them to be violating sacred space. Northern Catholics, then, viewed race relations through the prism of the parish.[15]

But parish development and church growth occurred differently in the South. And, most importantly, the southern Church's experiences with African Americans and race relations followed different patterns. In the South, the Church itself was the only denomination seriously to attempt to bridge the racial divide. That is, the Catholic Church's universal mission—its belief that there was no salvation outside the Church—compelled it to evangelize whites and blacks alike. In the North, the Great Migration of blacks disrupted a parish system already in place. But in the South, the parish system grew up around blacks and accommodated Jim Crow to begin with. Southern Catholics, then, experienced a more diffuse sense of the sacred. For them, the racial order and social hierarchies within the South themselves were sacred. Blacks may have participated in public ceremonies, but later reactions to the civil rights movement demonstrate that whites believed that blacks had a certain, subordinate place in the racial order. Agitation for racial justice violated that racial hierarchy.

Throughout this book different voices can be heard. First there are bishops and priests, Church leaders whose actions and decisions affected entire dioceses. It is logical that they would be heard, since one theme of this book is that the Church's mission in Alabama and Georgia was to link scattered parishioners to the hierarchy, to draw the boundaries of a Catholic subculture and connect individual members and parishes to the Church universal. Bishops, moreover, were the focal points for complaints from parishioners when the laity believed that civil rights activism had gotten out of hand. Indeed, by the late 1960s it was priests and some diocesan officials—in both Alabama and Georgia—who were most supportive of the fight for racial justice. Hearing from and about those people, then, throws the voices of lay opponents of activism into starker relief. At least prior to the Second Vatican Council and the civil rights movement, many Catholics took the authority of bishops for granted and looked to them for leadership.

The second group of voices that can be heard belong to those white laity. It was prominent white laymen who led the fight against anti-Catholicism and who suffered in the face of prejudice and hostility. White laity, furthermore, rose to the defense of segregation in the Church and expressed concerns over the Church's role in southern society. In Alabama, for instance, the laity unleashed a torrent of letters backing the local bishop when he denounced those priests and nuns who had come to Selma in 1965 to participate in voting rights demonstrations.

Other white laity expressed support for civil rights activism, organized assistance for demonstrations, and encouraged integration of parochial schools and churches. It is the interaction between these laymen and women—both defenders and critics of segregation—and diocesan leadership that constitutes much of the argument about the relationship between the civil rights movement and Vatican II.

A third group of voices is muted, but ever present, much as they were in the Church itself during the period under investigation. The presence of black Catholics, a minority within a minority though they were, helped shape white Catholics' interaction with mainstream southern society. White Catholics tried to ignore African American Catholics, and their parishes existed on the margins of the Church in Alabama and Georgia. When whites did acknowledge the biracial nature of their church, they evinced a spirit of paternalism, speaking of "our Negroes" and "our colored people." Whites expected blacks to respect certain racial boundaries. When they did not, white Catholics were forced to confront the inconsistencies between church social teaching and their own actions. This happened first during the battle over parochial school integration and later over Catholic participation in direct-action demonstrations in the 1960s. African American parishes, moreover, provided important support facilities for civil rights activism in Selma and Mobile. Because of their presence within the Church, white Catholics were forced to engage the battle to preserve segregation on two fronts: in their own Church institutions and in society at large.

The Intolerable Alien

CATHOLICS *as* "OTHER"
in the SOUTH

❖

In 1941, journalist-cum-southern critic W. J. Cash argued that despite the South's fast-rising urbanization and industrialization, white southerners evinced a cultural and ideological continuity between the nineteenth and twentieth centuries. One element of the network of ideas that white southerners shared was a social fear that bred anti-Catholicism. From the perspective of an early twentieth-century resurgence of "a bitterly narrow spirit of Protestantism," according to Cash, Catholics were "the intolerable Alien, the bearer of Jesuit plots to rob them of their religion by force." Cash described the first few decades of the twentieth century, but even in the years after World War II that type of anti-Catholicism that approached religious paranoia persisted and brought Catholics attention disproportionate to their numbers in the South. After World War II, Catholics in Alabama and Georgia expected to take advantage of new national calls for ecumenism and interdenominational brotherhood, but white Protestants in those states continued to marginalize them. Indeed, anti-Catholicism united southern white Protestants and gave them common cause with non-southern Protestants. It allowed them to declare their own nationalism and support for the civil religion that characterized post–World War II religious and public life. Anti-Catholicism became, that is, an identity marker for the region's Baptists, Churches of Christ, Methodists, and Episcopalians, who put aside their own theological differences to celebrate a Protestant heritage that transcended regional identity.[1]

This southern brand of anti-Catholicism differed in source and substance from its northern counterpart. Scholars have drawn a distinction between cultural and theological anti-Catholicism. Theological anti-Catholicism is as old as the Protestant Reformation; it emphasizes the theological distinctives that separate Catholicism and Protestantism. In America, it can be traced to the influence of the Puritans on the development of America's Protestant identity. The earliest English settlers to the American colonies had been reared in a culture that was openly hostile to Catholicism. Removing all vestiges of traditional Catholicism required a powerful and intrusive Protestant state. The Reformation in England was a competitive and hostile struggle for the hearts and minds of the English laity. It replaced Catholicism's vibrant ritual and liturgical practice in England's churches. The outcome of that contest amounted to what one historian has called "the stripping of the altars."[2]

Cultural anti-Catholicism locates its roots in the belief that the Roman Catholic Church's institutional presence and hierarchy threatened American democracy and the autonomy of the individual. According to historian John T. McGreevy, anti-Catholicism was an integral component of northern liberalism in the 1940s and 1950s. Secular liberals such as John Dewey and Paul Blanshard insisted that religion was an entirely private matter and must be kept out of the public realm, where it might threaten national unity. In addition, only an emphasis on individual autonomy—"thinking on one's own"—would sustain American democracy. In the minds of the Church's critics, pervasive Catholic separatism (exclusive beliefs, insistence on natural law, parochial schools, and hospitals) presented problems of integration into American society. Liberals questioned how Catholics could become democrats and hence good Americans. Debates raged over state support of parochial schools versus public schools. Only the latter would teach democratic values and American ideals. Strident anti-Catholicism waned over the course of the 1950s, but only after anti-communism took on increasing significance and diverted liberals' attention in that direction.[3] For southern Protestants, in contrast, cultural and religious anti-Catholicism persisted together much longer. Fears of protecting the separation of church and state, irrational though they may have been, were fears rooted in concern for Protestant churches' dominance of southern culture. The South was the last bastion of Protestant America and the last region to flaunt religious prejudice as central to group identity. In the North, anti-communism became the factor that brought greater Catholic acceptance. In the South the issue would be race.

Southern fears of Catholicism may have been unfounded, given Catholics' small numbers in most parts of the region. But sociologist Andrew Greeley and historian Mark S. Massa, S.J., have suggested reasons those fears may be understood as expressions of competing religious imaginations, or worldviews. Adapting the insights of theologian David Tracy, Greeley and Massa propose that Protestants and Catholics imagine the world differently, and these complementary worldviews—or "conceptual languages," as Tracy labels them—constitute the foundation for religious tensions. Tracy focuses on the theologian's treatment of the "Christ event," Christianity's singularly defining moment. He argues that the Catholic "analogical imagination" envisions God as present and active in the world. The analogical imagination views the incarnation of Christ as the focal point. The physical world, according to Tracy, "is now theologically envisioned as sacrament—a sacrament emanating from Jesus Christ as the paradigmatic sacrament of God, the paradigmatic clue to humanity and nature alike." The sacred, in other words, constitutes a tangible presence for Catholics. God is present in the Eucharistic meal, in those icons and statues that differentiate a Catholic place of worship from a Protestant, and in the very community of believers itself. This language of analogy "is a language of ordered relationships articulating similarity-in-difference."[4] As a result, Catholics experience divine presence in a community that is entrusted to the leadership of a divinely ordained hierarchy. That community, the Church, is the presence of Christ. "The Church is," as the *Catechism of the Catholic Church* attests, "one with Christ." It is "Christ himself."[5] Individual autonomy is necessarily and willingly subject to communal order, and grace received through mediating institutions. Catholics achieve salvation by participating in certain rituals, particularly partaking of the actual body and blood of Christ in the Eucharist.

The complement to this analogical imagination is the Protestant dialectical imagination. This conceptual language negates the presence of God in the world; rather than the incarnation of Christ being the focal point, the focus is on "the proclaimed Word." Instead of similarity in difference, this religious worldview emphasizes the differences between God and the world.[6] There are noteworthy examples of Protestants living in intentional community and cooperating to

achieve racial justice and economic equality. These significant exceptions notwithstanding, the Protestant religious world is devoid of symbols, images, ritual, or liturgy. The physical world does not embody
elements of the sacred. Protestants hear and read the word of God.
Rather than encountering the presence of God in community, Protestants approach the divine as individuals. Salvation for them follows an
individual, spiritual encounter with God. A personal relationship with
Jesus is not only possible; it is mandatory. In fact, for Protestants institutions and hierarchies often hinder instead of enable the approach
to God. Historian Massa has argued that this dialectical imagination
has shaped American culture. It protects the individual against "the
encroaching oppressions of the community and its demands." As a
result, the Catholic hierarchical and communitarian model has often
been at odds with the nation's individualistic Protestant culture. Catholics were in fact different than most Protestant Americans, in part
because they looked at the world through different religious lenses.
For Massa—and, indeed, for Tracy—those differences were complementary rather than competing. But in practice, those worldviews invited disagreement and conflict.[7]

Twentieth-century Protestants and Catholics seemed to share a
visceral connection to Reformation-era hostility. Sincere ecumenical
discussions of theological differences would have to wait until later in
the century. In the 1940s and 1950s, Catholics reacted testily to both
perceived slights and blatant slander. They could be as anti-Protestant
as Protestants were anti-Catholic. They defended themselves against
charges that their church was un-American and opposed to democracy
and religious freedom. Catholics in Alabama and Georgia struggled
to overcome their "other" status and to make themselves be understood and accepted by Protestants. But their marginalization also contributed to the strengthening of their religious identity. Indeed, anthropologist Gary W. McDonogh has argued that "Both Catholics and
Protestants have reified 'the Catholic as Other,' holding dialectic read-
ings of a divisive myth." "Protestants and Catholics, whites and blacks,
natives and immigrants," moreover, "have recognized anti-Catholicism
as a socially constructed fact of life and built identities around it even
as they may have contested (or used) it."[8] In Alabama and Georgia,
those competing identities revolved around struggles to define American liberty and to decide whose tradition best represented the nation's

highest ideals. Both groups defined their expectations for the Christian democracy that the nation should be. That their discussions revolved around American identity demonstrates that the South's white Protestants were making attempts in the post–World War II era to bridge the gap between themselves and northern Protestants and to link themselves with the American mainstream. In response to anti-Catholicism, Catholics reluctantly accepted their outsider status and appealed to a rich Roman Catholic tradition and drew clear boundaries around their own religious subculture. Diocesan officials concentrated on increasing central authority and linking scattered parishes to the Church hierarchy. At the same time, they maintained what they understood to be a steadfast devotion to American religious liberty and political democracy.

One factor that set Catholics apart was their numbers. They were overwhelmingly in the minority, but they did experience some growth in the twentieth century. Catholics had long lived in the Mobile and Savannah areas. Their ancestors had arrived during colonial contact, and they predated the Baptists and Methodists who came to predominate during the antebellum era. The growth of the Church in Alabama and Georgia in the twentieth century depended on outside agents that reminded southern Catholics of their marginal status in the region and their relationship to the larger denomination. Financial assistance for parish construction and liturgical accouterments often came from mission organizations based in northern dioceses. Southern Catholics also engaged in organized evangelization. Those duties often fell to religious orders, like the Paulists, who specialized in parish missions or open-air evangelism. Finally, the growth of the Church in Alabama and Georgia can be attributed to in-migration of non-southern Catholics following the end of World War II.[9]

The Diocese of Mobile was created in 1829, with Michael Portier the first bishop. Bishop Thomas J. Toolen, Mobile's sixth prelate, arrived from Baltimore in 1927 to a diocese that claimed just forty thousand Catholics in the entire state of Alabama plus a segment of northwest Florida. That number had increased to seventy-one thousand in 1950. By 1964 there were 128,603 Catholics in the Mobile-Birmingham Diocese, representing 32,206 families. More than twenty-four thousand (24,236) of those individuals lived in the Pensacola, Florida, area, which until 1968 was under the administrative care of Mobile. In 1950 there were one hundred parishes in the diocese, and sixty-two mission stations. In 1960 there were 126 churches that had reached parish status, and still sixty-two missions. In 1964 there were nineteen churches with sixteen hundred or more Catholics on the rolls, and almost twenty-five thousand children in Catholic grade or high schools.[10]

The story was similar for Georgia. In 1950 the Diocese of Savannah-Atlanta (which covered the entire state of Georgia then) contained forty-one parishes and thirty additional mission stations. In 1951 there were just over thirty-one thousand Catholics in the state, an increase of twenty-three hundred in two years' time. In 1956 church officials created the Archdiocese of Atlanta out of the Diocese of Savannah-Atlanta, assigning seventy-one counties of northern Georgia to the see city. At that time, those seventy-one counties contained 23,695 Catholics. Within six years that number increased almost 83 percent, to 43,342 in the 1963 diocesan census. Approximately thirty-six thousand of those were located in the five-county metropolitan Atlanta area. By 1960 the Diocese of Savannah consisted of between twenty-five and twenty-nine thousand Catholics. In the eighty-eight counties in the diocese, there were thirty-three parishes and nineteen mission churches. In 1968 the entire state of Georgia contained 84,032 Catholics, who worshiped in seventy-one churches. That placed them third in size, behind Southern Baptists and United Methodists, among white denominations. By 1975 their numbers had reached 98,666, the fourth largest number behind the Baptists, Methodists, and African Methodist Episcopal churches.[11]

Statistics reveal that Catholic growth far outpaced the rest of the region. Over the course of the 1950s and early 1960s, the Catholic population in Alabama and Georgia increased more than 80 percent. The general population only doubled between 1940 and 1980. As in the North, the Catholic population in Alabama and Georgia congregated in the urban centers. In 1963 more than 80 percent of the Catholic population of the Archdiocese of Atlanta was located in the Atlanta metropolitan area. The Diocese of Mobile-Birmingham's 1964 census demonstrated that Mobile, Birmingham, Montgomery, and Pensacola, Florida, contained the overwhelming majority of Catholics in the diocese. Metropolitan Birmingham registered 39,712 Catholics, Mobile had 38,116, Pensacola 24,336, and Montgomery 13,762. That left between twelve and thirteen thousand in other cities and rural areas of the state. Industrial and technological growth, the advent of cities like

Atlanta as a commercial and transportation hub, and federal investment in the form of military bases and defense contracts attracted this surge in population.

Other, more important, factors besides numbers reinforced Catholics' outsider status. Most importantly, Catholics could not escape their ties to the larger Roman Catholic Church. Protestant prejudice forced Catholics to paper over any internal differences and focus on the religious ties they had in common. So anti-Catholicism became for Catholics their own identity marker; they accepted their outsider status out of necessity and drew on the traditions and doctrines they shared with Catholics everywhere to reinforce their religious identity. They also confronted Protestant attacks and made their own appeal to American ideals and a shared national identity. Just as anti-Catholicism provided Protestants the opportunity to express support for the national civil religion, so too did it give Catholics a similar occasion.

In the middle decades of the twentieth century, southern Protestants reacted to postwar changes that increasingly brought the South into the national mainstream by reaffirming a national civil religion and support for certain American ideals. Catholics as the "intolerable Alien" served as an easy target of hostility and a favorite way of affirming those ideals. Anti-Catholicism took several forms. The most prominent was political. That is, for southern Baptists, Methodists, and Churches of Christ, the Roman Catholic Church constituted a real threat to democracy, liberty, and the constitutional separation of church and state, staples of the American way of life. In the mid-twentieth century, for example, the rest of the nation understood the Cold War to be between only two powers, the good and noble "us" versus the evil "them" of Soviet communism. But at least white Southern Baptists, according to historian Andrew Michael Manis, understood the global conflict to be a three-way battle, with the Vatican assuming equal villain status with the Kremlin in the struggle for freedom. This Cold War religious mentality was one of the integral components of the southern version of the post–World War II American civil religion. The communist and Catholic menaces were threats to America's soul and, if left unchecked, would undermine the United States' divinely ordained mission as a "Christian democracy."[12]

In addition to the political challenge Roman Catholics posed, Protestants also decried Catholicism's religious idiosyncrasies and mystery;

its "sinister wonders," in Tom Watson's words, suggested an evil counter-culture, comprised of people whose peculiarity simply could not be truly American. Its alleged aversion to strict biblical authority, more-over, made the Catholic Church antithetical to the Protestant main-stream that had founded and built the nation. Reformation Days and annual celebrations of a common Protestant heritage provided plat-forms to single out Catholics for public scorn. Those occasions gave the South's white Baptists, Methodists, Churches of Christ, Presbyte-rians, and many other denominations and sects the opportunity to coalesce around a common Protestantism and to define themselves in opposition to Catholics. This type of identity making also gave these white Protestants further opportunities to align themselves with non-southern ideals that transcended regional concerns. Newspaper edito-rials and advertisements and circular pamphlets, furthermore, decried the mystery of Catholicism and denounced Catholic interpretations of Scripture and revelation. Finally, alleged former priests or bishops made regular tours of southern Protestant churches and drew curious crowds eager to be horrified by tales of the evils of the Roman Catholic Church. Each instance of anti-Catholicism was intended to exclude and marginalize Catholics, denying them access to mainstream ac-ceptance.[13]

As World War II drew to a close, the National Council of Christians and Jews (NCCJ) sponsored, and many of America's churches recog-nized, an annual Brotherhood Week in February that was intended to address a perceived need for national unity. For at least that one week, the nation's religious groups were supposed to downplay denomina-tional differences and promote interfaith dialogue. This was especially important during World War II, when Americans sought common pa-triotic ground. Catholics participated in the annual events, but, despite their good-faith efforts to cooperate, those in Alabama and Georgia found themselves maligned by Protestants. Catholic and Protestant reaction to Brotherhood Week revealed the breadth of the gap sepa-rating them at mid-century. The *Catholic Week,* the official newspaper of the Diocese of Mobile (later Mobile-Birmingham), devoted spe-cial issues to Brotherhood Week, and editorials and special articles on ecumenism promoted the annual event to laity. For Alabama's Catholics, Brotherhood Week presented the perfect opportunity to teach tolerance for and promote understanding of Catholicism among

Protestants. An editorial in the *Catholic Week* noted that prejudice and bigotry do not come naturally to children. Echoing President Roosevelt's comments on the importance of Brotherhood Week in uniting Americans of all faiths behind the war effort, the *Catholic Week* proposed that the NCCJ event provided the perfect opportunity to maintain "at home the same degree of understanding and cooperation that our soldiers and sailors are manifesting on the battlefronts. We must match this devotion and this teamwork on the home front. No sacrifice is too great, no discipline too severe, for us at home if we do our part to win the war."[14]

Despite the good intentions of the sponsors of the ecumenical week, however, Alabama's Protestants could not translate the desire for interfaith unity into sensitivity to Catholic feelings. In fact, the 1940s and 1950s witnessed the institutionalization of anti-Catholicism. That is to say, Protestant church organizations themselves became more active in discrimination and expressions of prejudice and bigotry. Alabama's Methodist newspaper, the *Alabama Christian Advocate,* urged its readers to "make the world a real brotherhood. This cannot be done unless we get men to live in the spirit of Christ and establish a social order in which the high ideals of brotherhood shall become the high standards of human relationships." The *Catholic Week* lauded the Methodist organ for its "noble sentiments," but expressed dismay at what appeared to Catholics to be a double standard. In the same issue, the *Christian Advocate* covered the 1945 statement signed by some sixteen hundred Protestants opposing any Vatican role in the postwar peace process. Taking the periodical's coverage as an endorsement of that document, the *Catholic Week* interpreted this as Methodist anti-Catholicism.[15] This incident illustrates the degree to which Catholics and Protestants were still far apart on ecumenical issues. It also illustrates, from the Catholic perspective, one source of anti-Catholic sentiment. Many Protestants—and most Americans—adhered to a clear double standard. They spoke the language of ecumenism and brotherhood but often failed to practice those high ideals. For them, uniting behind a shared Protestant identity proved more valuable than true interdenominational inclusiveness.

Anti-Catholicism has been central to Protestant identity, most often without their realizing—or at least acknowledging—that fact. Because it was so central to Protestant identity, it contributed to Catholic identity as well. Above all else, Catholics were not Protestant, and they drew on the full Catholic tradition to construct their own subculture. That is, they identified with Rome—its traditions, its history, its teachings, and its liturgy—to set themselves apart in a hostile environment. They also appealed to American ideals, for in their estimation, anti-Catholicism was un-American and just plain unpatriotic. Catholics took a couple of different approaches when responding to prejudice. They appealed to a sense of fairness and American patriotism, and they sought to ensure that their attacker and his potential audience were well informed about the tenets of Catholicism. In fact, Alabama and Georgia Catholics attributed most anti-Catholic sentiment to misinformation. And if Baptists, Methodists, or Churches of Christ did not know any better, then they could not be expected to act any differently.

Separation of church and state was the central issue for many mid-century Protestants, who feared that Catholics presented a formidable threat to that treasured American principle. For Protestants, the Roman hierarchy, "which also claims temporal authority," as one Atlantan phrased it, posed a direct threat to democracy. Catholics had long sought public support for parochial schools, moreover, which Protestants opposed ostensibly on constitutional grounds. And when President Harry Truman reappointed Myron Taylor to be his personal representative to Pope Pius XII, Protestants fought hard to reverse Truman's decision. Despite the United States' and the Vatican's mutual opposition to the Soviets, Protestants deluged the White House and State Department with letters. In such an atmosphere, and with cries of concern over church-state issues, the Truman administration failed to establish diplomatic relations with the Vatican.[16]

Accompanying alarmist cries for the separation of church and state were accusations that the Catholic Church was authoritarian and undemocratic. In 1948 an Atlanta man expressed his anti-Catholic fears to Hugh Kinchley, executive director of the Catholic Laymen's Association of Georgia, a group founded in 1916 following the passage of Georgia's convent inspection law. He equated his "democratic church" with a democratic government. And "some of us who are in a free church cannot see why anyone so situated will not read the bible for themselves and see that the hierarchy of your church is without the slightest authority of scripture and was invented after apostacising [sic] in the union of church and state under Constantine."[17] In September

1951 an anti-Catholic pamphlet that began as a column in the *Christian Index*—the official organ of the Georgia Baptists—circulated Georgia. The broadside quoted Father Patrick Henry O'Brien, who spoke on behalf of "We the Hierarchy of the Holy Roman Catholic Church" and warned Americans that "We are going to have our laws made and enforced according to the Holy See and the Popes and the canon law of the Papal throne." The Catholic Laymen's Association found no evidence of there being a priest by that name, but such "Romish Aspirations"—the pamphlet's title—sparked alarm among Georgia's Protestant population.[18]

Catholics often responded to Protestant attacks with their own prejudices, even as they shared southern Protestants' civil religion and central beliefs about America's foundational Christian values. For them, separation of church and state was a Protestant issue that opened the door for communist infiltration of America. Catholics drew what they perceived as separation of church and state's logical conclusion, namely, wholesale secularization of American society. In Catholics' minds, Protestantism equaled secularism and therefore was bad for America. A group calling itself Protestants and Other Americans United for the Separation of Church and State sprang up in the late 1940s. Catholics took particular affront at POAU's agenda and, in their defense, pointed to their own faithfulness to constitutional principles. In 1949 POAU came to Alabama, with chapters opening in Mobile and Birmingham. Alabama's small Catholic population expressed alarm at that development, even as they downplayed the group's significance. After all, the *Catholic Week* suggested, this was but "a very small group of bigoted Protestant ministers and a few other Americans who have proved themselves ready to go to any extent, even to that of leaning away over towards communism, rather than acknowledge the true worth of American Catholicism." And that "true worth" came with impeccable credentials in church-state issues. Indeed, a separate *Catholic Week* editorial placed Catholics in the category of "the other Americans" mentioned in POAU's title.[19]

When POAU opened its Birmingham branch in 1949, the *Catholic Week* anticipated "its inevitable and most vicious attacks on the Catholic Church and on Catholics." The Alabama organ reprinted an article from *Our Sunday Visitor,* a national Catholic weekly, defending the Church against predictable charges that Catholics oppose democracy and would seek unduly to influence the American political process. The column pointed to the Church's diversity to support its contention that "the Catholic Church is the most democratic institution in the world." The periodical obviously confused diversity with democracy, but the point was clear. In Catholics' minds, their church was perfectly compatible with American ideals and institutions. In addition, simply because the headquarters of the National Catholic Welfare Conference was in Washington, D.C., "does not mean at all that it operates a lobby." The newspaper was sure that an informal poll of congressmen and senators would reveal that Catholic clergy sought to influence public policy less than clergy from other denominations did. In short, POAU's fears were at best unfounded. At worst, they were vicious attempts to draw other Protestant organizations into the anti-Catholic fight.[20]

An Edmundite priest, Father Francis Donnelan, attacked POAU from a different angle. To him the organization failed the tests of true Christianity and true patriotism. Separating church and state would "give us an atheistic state, for only an atheistic government could meet the standards they have set." Protestants and Other Americans United, then, would "lead the United States into communism." In 1949 Donnelan entreated 250 members of the Catholic Men's Breakfast Club of Mobile "to fight this menace to Christianity and country by living Christ-like lives." The Edmundite asserted the Catholic belief that Catholicism more truly represented American ideals and was better capable of re-inforcing the nation's Christian heritage. Not only were Protestants responsible for opening the door to communism; their influence on American society had led to "materialism and secularism."[21]

In a 1948 letter to an Atlanta Protestant, Georgia's Hugh Kinchley linked "recent decisions by the Supreme Court" to "a spirit of secular-ism that is seeking a complete separation of church and state in this country." This was not an achievement the founding fathers wanted, Kinchley concluded. Kinchley did not specify which cases he had in mind, but it was in 1947 and 1948 that the Court defined the "the wall of separation between church and state" as constitutional dogma. In 1947 Justice Hugo Black first used that phrase in his majority opinion for *Everson v. Board of Education*. That decision declared that a New Jersey township could reimburse Catholic parents for bus expenses to parochial schools. A year later, however, the Court applied Black's "wall" test in *McCollum v. Illinois* and ruled that it was now unconstitutional to provide "released-time" for religious instruction of public school students in the classroom. These cases together reinforced popular opinions about Catholic designs on public revenue and control of government.[22]

Both Donnelan and Kinchley sounded a theme common to Catholic activists and thinkers in the first half of the twentieth century. American society had moved too far away from its Christian roots; it had indeed become too secular. In response, Catholic intellectuals turned to the medieval writings of Thomas Aquinas to further their efforts to use Catholic doctrine to reform American society. According to this neo-Scholasticism, reason itself could lead to awareness of God and the supernatural. It also would reveal the existence of a natural law, which in turn would point to universal moral truths. Needless to say, for these neo-Scholastic philosophers the Catholic tradition alone was best situated to lead American society away from the secularizing trend and back toward those moral truths. In a discussion of Jesuit theologian John Courtney Murray, one of the leading neo-Scholastic thinkers of the mid-twentieth century, historian Jay P. Dolan explained how Catholics could conclude that American society was, as Murray put it, "the quintessence of all that is decadent in the culture of the Western Christian world." According to Dolan, "American culture denied the primacy of the spiritual over the material and the social over the individual, as well as the reality of the metaphysical."[23] That emphasis on the collective good over the individual often prompted the charge that Catholics could not be committed democrats or loyal Americans. What passed for public debate over communism in the 1940s and 1950s left little room for nuance or reasoned explanation. No one could afford to express sympathy for any ideas that smacked of communism.

In 1950 the threat of communism cast a sinister pall over a nation that should have been relishing a rise to global prominence following its victory in World War II. Just the hint of communist association tarnished bright careers, and anti-communism became a national pastime. At Mobile's 1950 Protestant Heritage Day celebration, Dr. Frederick C. Grant, an Episcopalian professor at New York's Union Theological Seminary, once again coupled Catholicism with communism, claiming that both shared similar totalitarian roots. Catholics did not respond in kind publicly, but privately Monsignor Joseph E.

Moylan offered an ironic interpretation of the source of public attacks against his church. Rather than the Catholic Church being in league with communists, as Grant and others maintained, it was Protestant churches that were loyal to foreign political systems. In August 1950 Moylan expressed to Hugh Kinchley his conviction that "Very much of these attacks upon the Church are Communistic inspired, they have infiltrated the Protestant pulpits to a serious extent." Church of Christ clergy did not receive high salaries "and it is not impossible that [J.A. Dennis, editor of Georgia's bitterly anti-Catholic newspaper *The White Horse*] is obtaining money from sources outside Christianity. The madness and fury of his words . . . should prove his undoing."[24] Moylan privately acknowledged, furthermore, that the problem was much more serious than just renegade Protestant preachers. Savannah's vicar general suspected "members of the New Deal, particularly those in the State Department," of being "more un-American in selling the Country out to Russia than the Knotty Knobs of the KKK, who, whatever their private depredations, have never completely betrayed the Nation nor delivered millions of people into the slavery of Communism."[25]

At mid-century, a fear of communists made most of the nation patriotic Americans. One's patriotism depended on the degree to which one denounced Stalinism and the secular evils of communism. That anti-communism provided Catholics with a natural entrée into middle America comes as no revelation. Anti-communism provided the language used by many American Catholics to understand changing social and demographic circumstances in the 1950s. But in the South anti-communism was more than a patriotic offensive against Stalinism. It was the defense of a way of life. Along with opposition to the civil rights movement and racial integration, anti-communism formed the very essence of white southern identity in the decade or so after the end of World War II. In the minds of the white South, outsiders had the potential to undermine the racial status quo. According to historian Wayne Addison Clark, among southern whites "sectionalism and racism merged with nationalism to form a political and social overview that equated agitation for racial change with treason." White southerners had good reason to fear communism. Beginning in the 1920s, the Communist Party had tried to exploit the "Negro question" to its political advantage and had made racial equality a primary component of its mission. The party also defended the nine black young men falsely accused of raping a white woman on a train bound for Scottsboro, Alabama.[26] Southern Catholics asserted their patriotism and regularly trumpeted their impressive anti-communist credentials. And their commitment to segregation was reflected in the existence of separate church facilities and organizations for blacks and whites. Nevertheless, Catholics spent more time asserting their right to belong than Protestants spent heeding the Catholic cry. Despite maintaining segregated facilities, the Catholic Church included some African Americans, making it difficult for them to escape the close association between communism and the threat of outside racial agitation.

Also on the local level, Protestants acted out a public ritual of separation. Annual celebrations of Protestant culture—in the form of Reformation Days or Protestant Heritage Days—consistently reinforced for Catholics that they were an embattled minority that needed to be constantly vigilant. Responding to those public rituals also gave Catholics the opportunity to assert their patriotism and the Catholic Church's compatibility with American liberty. Between the late 1940s and early 1950s, cities in Alabama and Georgia alike set aside special days in which they celebrated the region's Protestant heritage. These celebrations were curious reminders of the common bond linking the area's non-Catholic churches. Despite the appearance of a singular Protestant culture in the South, there were wide theological divides between, say, Baptists and Churches of Christ, and between Methodists and Presbyterians. The label Protestant means little apart from the presence of a Catholic other. Yet Baptists, Methodists, and Churches of Christ in Atlanta, Savannah, Mobile, and Birmingham chose to emphasize that shared identity.

These Reformation and Protestant heritage celebrations reveal that southern Protestant churches, following almost one hundred years of virtual isolation from the American mainstream, had begun to share once again in the national religious culture. The coming decades would see American evangelicalism returning to acceptability and a position of respect. Anti-Catholicism provided the linchpin for Protestant identity, as well as one element that drew North and South together. At Mobile's 1950 Protestant Heritage Day, for example, the principal speaker was New York seminary professor Dr. Frederick C. Grant, and Methodist bishop G. Bromley Oxnam of Washington, D.C., was a fixture at Atlanta's celebrations and a leader in POAU.[27] Regional chauvinism disappeared in these celebrations. In at least this instance, religion became one factor in the reintegration of the South into the national mainstream.

These celebrations of Protestantism often became deliberate invitations to bash Catholics. Atlanta's 1949 Reformation Day Rally brought four thousand participants to hear Congressman Graham A. Barden of North Carolina, the chairman of the House of Representatives' Committee on Education. Barden echoed the familiar separation of church and state theme. He told the crowd that principle was "far more important than Federal aid to education and if there must be a choice, I, with Protestants over the nation, will give up Federal aid." Barden drew applause when he attacked the Catholic Church in all but name, particularly their campaign for tax support for parochial schools, a perennial issue of concern for Catholics since the nineteenth century. He argued, "there are 256 denominations in America. Only one has attempted to get tax money for church schools—and, so far as I know, the other 255 oppose that one!"[28]

The Savannah Reformation Day celebration that same year featured Methodist bishop Paul B. Kern, of Nashville. Kern gave at least passing reference to the ostensible purpose of the gathering, namely, recalling Martin Luther's nailing of his Ninety-Five Theses to the Wittenberg church door. In a November 7 letter to the editor of the *Savannah Morning News,* the Catholic Laymen's Association's executive secretary, Hugh Kinchley, addressed Kern's mischaracterization of indulgences and church history. Kern had attacked the sixteenth-century pre-Reformation Church for preventing lay access to the Bible and selling indulgences in return for absolution from sin. He also had claimed that the Protestant faith was responsible for individual liberties. In response, Kinchley first pointed to the normally good ecumenical relations in Savannah and the Catholic contribution to the betterment of the local community in the form of schools, hospitals, orphanages, and other welfare. He conceded that some people abused indulgences, but then he defended the doctrine, arguing that they "are not an easy means of obtaining pardon for sin." Instead, no applicant was dismissed "without grace" and those who could not afford the fee "were to give their prayers for the kingdom." Kinchley finally noted the irony in so closely relating the Reformation with the separation of church and state. For, Kinchley maintained, it was European civil powers that spread Protestantism, and Germany, England, and Denmark, for example, all had established state churches.[29]

In 1950 Dr. Frederick C. Grant, the Episcopalian anti-Catholic spokesman, told several thousand Mobile Protestants that "Romanism and Communism are fundamentally totalitarian." Both also encouraged overpopulation, he lectured, and contributed to high poverty levels. Communism was "the natural economy of scarsity [sic], while Roman Catholicism makes the patient endurance of poverty a virtue." He then sounded a familiar political warning. Once the Catholic Church reached a 51 percent majority in the America, "it will begin to take over our political institutions." Such a harangue was nothing new from Protestant leaders in the 1950s, but Mobile Catholics were reluctant to believe that Grant spoke for all Protestants. The *Catholic Week* editorialized that of course local Catholics would be "pained" at such an attack. "But such is the foul nature of Dr. Grant's address that even greater must be the pain it caused in the hearts of sincere Protestants, in whose name it was made."[30] Alabama's Catholics, then, appealed to a general sense of Christian fairness and American liberty, the violation of which would also surely shame other Protestants.

Protestant Heritage and Reformation Days were not the only—or even the most common—instances of anti-Catholicism that southern Catholics faced. Examples of prejudice surfaced in publications throughout the region. Newspapers and pamphlets in Alabama and Georgia regularly published anti-Catholic libel, often spreading blatant untruths and unproven rumors about Catholicism. These published broadsides, along with itinerant speakers who billed themselves as former priests or nuns, depicted a Catholic counterculture—if not underworld—that was, from a Protestant perspective, fundamentally weird, whose mystery was necessarily anathema to the liberty and openness of mainstream America. At the very least it was built on a weak spiritual foundation that could not sustain American ideals. These anti-Catholic examples differed little from nineteenth- and early twentieth-century attacks. Members of the laity monitored those publications and rose to the defense of their Church. Indeed, the Catholic Laymen's Association of Georgia was founded expressly for that purpose. In 1949, for example, the *Morgan County (Ga.) News* printed a series of articles written by a Baptist minister which, according to the executive secretary of the CLA, "were anti-Catholic in tone." The

CLA ran an advertisement in the *News* offering free information about the Catholic Church to anyone who requested it. The editor of the paper—"a religious fanatic" to whom "nobody in the county paid any attention"—reluctantly ran the ad, but refused payment for it.

The editor also tried his hand at Baptist-style evangelism. In correspondence with Hugh Kinchley, he attempted to explain "how you could be saved from your sins by accepting the Lord Jesus Christ as your personal Saviour, but you would not hear from me." Maybe ten thousand years in hell would do the trick, the editor surmised; then "you will think how you persecuted Christians. In your heart you know that no priest can save you from hell." In 1952 Kinchley's report to the CLA's annual convention described "a considerable amount of anti-Catholic literature sent us by another woman in Georgia who is pleading with the executive secretary of the Laymen's Association to accept Christ as his Saviour and be saved."[31] The Catholic layman delivered that statement with a smirk, one could imagine, and no doubt elicited at least a few knowing chuckles from his audience. The path of salvation differed for Catholics and Protestants, and the latter's zeal—if not their hostility—probably made many of the former uncomfortable.

The CLA received some response to their newspaper ads, and Kinchley carried on an active correspondence with some of Georgia's Protestant laymen about Catholicism. Some of the exchange of letters reveal both Kinchley's and his correspondents' attempts to define their identity in oppositional terms. Kinchley's correspondents viewed the divisions between Catholics and Protestants in religious terms. Catholics did not hold the proper reverence for the Bible, which led them away from proper worship of God. As a result, Catholics were non-Christians in need of proselytizing. The primacy of the Bible (in Protestant minds) versus Tradition, the 1950 proclamation of the dogma of the Assumption of Mary, and competing interpretations of church history separated the two sides. Following the Reformation tradition's adherence to *sola Scriptura*—the argument that Holy Scripture was the final authority on matters of faith—southern Protestants held special reverence for the Bible. One distinction they drew between themselves and Catholics was the tension (in their minds) between biblical authority and reliance on Tradition. Ann Taves has argued that at least in the nineteenth century the Bible served as a "devotional symbol" for Protestants, an equivalent to the Catholics' Blessed Sacrament.[32] There is ample evidence to conclude that circumstances had not changed in the first half of the twentieth century.

In September 1948 Kinchley responded to an editorial entitled "Priceless Bible" in the *Douglas County (Ga.) Sentinel.* The editorial, according to Kinchley, noted that "'for many centuries the Bible was a closely guarded book, unavailable to the common man.'" The editorial made no explicit mention of Rome, but Kinchley feared that readers of the Douglasville, Georgia, periodical would incorrectly infer that the Catholic Church should be held responsible for that scriptural repression. Kinchley's preemptive defense pointed out Rome's role in establishing the canonical books and the Venerable Bede's translation of Scripture "into Saxon, which was at that time the language of the people of Britain."[33] J. G. Malphurs's initial correspondence with Kinchley has not survived, but the CLA executive secretary's 1950 letter to the Albany, Georgia, resident suggests some of Malphurs's concerns about Catholicism. Kinchley responded to a litany of issues, ranging from parochial schools and teaching religion in public schools, to the pope's temporal power as ruler of a sovereign state, to communism. Kinchley defended the Church's support for the Bible. "No religion holds the Bible in higher regard than the Catholic," Kinchley wrote. In fact, "her sons wrote the books of the New Testament." But the Catholic Church predated the canonical Scriptures, and "most of our separated brethren must depend on Catholic tradition and history" for the foundation of their faith.[34]

Several months later, Malphurs wrote an editorial column for the *Albany (Ga.) Herald* in response to the recent papal proclamation of the dogma of the Assumption of Mary into heaven. Malphurs complained that the new dogma "is absurd, and contradictory to Bible facts." The New Testament mentions the mother of Jesus only a few times, and no relevant passages point to her ascension into heaven. For Malphurs, "this dogma is another proof that Roman Catholics do not accept the Bible as God's complete revelation to man." In defense of Pope Pius XII and Catholics everywhere, Kinchley reiterated that "Christianity did not begin with the Bible," an impossible feat since "millions of Christians . . . lived and died before the printing press was invented." When Kinchley wrote that the "Catholic Church is not dependent upon the Bible for her existence, nor is she limited to it in her teachings," he outlined one boundary of both Protestants' and

Catholics' identity.[35] For Catholics, both church tradition and Scripture together were necessary for the discernment of divine truth. For southern Protestants, the Bible alone was the ultimate spiritual authority, the very words of God.

Malphurs's objection to the dogma of the Assumption of Mary revealed a second religious issue separating Protestants and Catholics. Protestants accused Catholics of worshiping the mother of Jesus and placing her in a position equal or superior to that of her son. Rose Hill Church of Christ in Columbus, Georgia, sponsored advertisements in the local newspaper to denounce Catholic doctrines concerning Mary. Mary was neither without sin nor perpetual virgin, one advertisement charged. And the notion that Mary is the Mother of God "is repulsive to intelligent and enlightened people. God has no mother."[36] Kinchley again drew on Church tradition to support the Catholic belief, but not before wondering what business this was of Malphurs's in the first place. In response to Malphurs and in defense of Catholicism, Kinchley surmised from his letter that Malphurs was "evidently not a Catholic . . . so it seems that he is disturbed about something which is of more concern to Catholics than it is to him." Nevertheless, Kinchley argued that devotion to Mary was almost as old as the Catholic Church itself, founded "more than 1,900 hundred [*sic*] years ago."[37]

The laity in Alabama were not as prepared for the sort of communication with non-Catholics in which the CLA engaged; but priests and lay members of the Knights of Columbus monitored newspapers and attempted to keep the general public in line with what they perceived to be American ideals of liberty and freedom of expression. When the local Churches of Christ sponsored a series of newspaper advertisements that labeled Catholicism as being "Satanic in origin," the Catholic Priests Association in Birmingham wrote both of that city's daily newspapers, the *News* and the *Age-Herald,* in protest. The priests conceded the right of the Churches of Christ to "freedom of opinion and expression in religious matters." But they failed to understand "how the tenor of such articles serves the cause of religion and public well-being. . . . We are appalled at the thought that any Christian group could so stigmatize their Catholic neighbors as to say that they are allied with Satan and engaged in a work essentially evil." The priests believed they were in excellent company, at least. The charges reminded them of an instance from Scripture when Jesus was accused of casting out demons under the authority of Beelzebul, "prince of devils." Since Christ came not from "satanic origins," then neither did they. Instead, the Birmingham clergy appealed to what they believed to be commonly accepted standards of Christian fairness. The priests concluded, "the advertisements are in bad taste, scurrilous, and insulting to the Christian integrity of our Catholic people."[38]

Publicly, Catholics were well behaved and respectful in their responses to instances of prejudice. But in their private correspondence and other times when individuals let their guard down, their true feelings came to light. The Diocese of Savannah's vicar general, Monsignor Joseph E. Moylan, could be particularly caustic. Criticizing the Baptist doctrine of the autonomy of the local church, Moylan wrote to Hugh Kinchley that taking Baptists' problems seriously was difficult for two reasons. "Each one of them is a schismatic," and "none of them knows that he is, even what schism is." Moylan then recalled the popular joke that a Methodist is just a Baptist who can read and write. "I do not question the ability of Baptists to read and to write, but in matters of religion few of them read right or write right."[39]

In July 1950, the *Albany Herald* printed a letter from a local preacher (in Hugh Kinchley's words) "denouncing various an [sic] sundry thinks [sic] Catholic," including the execution of William Tyndale in 1536 for translation and distribution of the Bible and Catholic opposition to public schools. Moylan speculated that the minister must have received help in preparing his complaints. "Somebody must have given him a book of fairy tales which he thought was history," the sarcastic vicar general surmised, "or perhaps somebody read it to him." Moylan concluded that "These tub-thumpers do not disturb me seriously. . . . There is no logic, nor dignity, nor theology, but only raw prejudice. This is not a Southern attack either."[40] Louie D. Newton, an Atlanta Baptist minister and denominational leader and frequent anti-Catholic antagonist, was one of Moylan's favorite targets in private correspondence. In 1950 Moylan described Newton's election to the presidency of the Georgia State Baptist Convention. When Newton proclaimed his support of the separation of church and state, Georgia's Baptists expressed their approval with, in Moylan's demeaning words, "their fervent Amens and other hog grunts of pietistic affirmation."[41] With those expressions of "pietistic affirmation," Baptists affirmed a leader who—more than any other individual—symbolized their Protestant identity. If it did nothing else, their support of Newton confirmed that they were not Catholics. Similarly, Newton offered an easy target for Catholics. If he did nothing else, that is, Newton demonstrated to Catholics what they did not want to be. In their minds, Newton detested their religion's core beliefs and represented the antithesis of American liberty and fair play, in which Catholics believed. Newton, therefore, provided a clear boundary for both Protestant and Catholic identity.

Protestants were suspicious of the mystery of Catholicism and of "secret" Catholic groups such as the fraternal Knights of Columbus—not to mention wary of cloistered nuns and an exclusive, celibate priesthood. Maria Monk's *Awful Disclosures of the Hotel Dieu Nunnery,* published in 1836, alarmed antebellum Protestants with tales of sexual and physical abuse in a Catholic convent. In 1954 the Book and Bible House, a Decatur, Georgia, publishing outfit, distributed a similar pamphlet. "My Life in the Convent" purported to be the story of Margaret L. Shepherd "as compiled by Evangelist L. J. King," who claimed to be a convert from Catholicism. The pamphlet is not in the Catholic archives, and the extant documents do not describe its contents. But the Catholic Laymen's Association of Georgia gathered information about King in an effort to discredit him. John E. Markwalter wrote the Book and Bible House, informing them that at best King was baptized a Catholic as an infant but never made his first communion and, apparently, never went to church. By the age of fifteen, "he had become a bar-room 'bum' and had a reputation for incorrigible immorality." The CLA had ample documentation of King's earlier anti-Catholicism. In the early 1920s he was active in Boston, Massachusetts, where he was accused of blackmail and theft. In Missouri and Ohio he stirred up riots, and one Presbyterian pastor ejected King from his church "after listening to one or two of King's filthy lectures." The Book and Bible House, Markwalter warned, would be better off "praying and hopping [*sic*]" that more young women would enter the convent and "devote their lives to the instruction of youth; to the building of character . . . [and to] the sick and the dying."[42] If the Decatur publishers responded to Markwalter, there is no evidence of that correspondence. But they were not the only group accused of disseminating such inflammatory literature.

Anti-Catholic groups occasionally circulated copies of a purported oath taken by all members of the Knights of Columbus. No documents in the Catholic archives reveal the substance of this "bogus oath." But the *Catholic Week* described the "scurrilous and libelous matter," spread by people "who are susceptible to infection with the virus of intolerance." Elsewhere, the paper labeled it "false and libelous and is part of a propaganda based on bigotry." The broadside claimed that the oath was copied from the 1913 *Congressional Record*. The *Catholic Week,* however, provides the rest of the story. The oath was an exhibit in an investigation of the congressional committee on elections, in which the distribution of the oath figured in the defeat of one candidate for Congress. The oath was not new. It had surfaced in Minnesota, California, and Michigan in the 1920s and in Savannah in 1928. In each of those cases, the person who circulated it was convicted on charges of criminal libel. In 1950 the Savannah woman who served six months in jail for distributing the oath reappeared in Warrenton, Georgia, lecturing against the Catholic Church. The *Catholic Week* drew a direct link between this current instance of prejudice and earlier attacks against the Church. The paper's editor credited "Know-Nothings, A.P.A. and their allies and successors" with creating the "most heinous, ungodly and unchristian 'oath.'"[43]

Even if they did not spout anti-Catholic rhetoric or read the "bogus oath" of the Knights of the Columbus themselves, many of the South's Protestants proved receptive to Catholic impersonators who made periodic tours through the region. Sponsored by both local denominations and Mason lodges, they usually addressed Protestant worship services (often as part of a revival series). These "ex-priests" and "former bishops" drew crowds of inquisitive minds wanting to know more about the secret intrigues of the Roman Catholic Church. They critiqued Catholic doctrine—as far as they understood it—and told tales of priests and nuns being held in the Church against their will. The Catholic Laymen's Association of Georgia maintained a constant vigil across the state for these lecturers and used its resources to expose the itinerants as frauds.

In February 1950 one of the "renegade" priests appeared in Statesboro, Georgia, as a representative of the Christian Mission Organization, an alleged organization of ex-priests. The only account of his visit appears in correspondence between the pastor of St. Matthew's Catholic Church in Statesboro, Father Edward W. Smith, and Monsignor Moylan, the diocesan vicar general. Apparently local Catholics infiltrated the talk. Two Catholic students "asked the apostate the suggested question concerning virginity and acoholism [*sic*]," Father Smith reported. The man was "diabolically clever handling an audience," however. He "heckled" his questioner and dismissed him with the claim that "this was the Catholic answer to anyone attacking the Church." According to Father Smith, the "apostate" began with a customary attack upon the Church's alleged opposition to religious freedom and then touched upon other familiar issues. Protestants in Spain and Italy, the "redeemed" priest claimed, enjoyed no freedom, and there was "no freedom of press, radio, assembly etc. in Cath. dominated countries." The unnamed speaker expressed a fear common to many Protestants at various times throughout American history. As the number of Catholics increased, so would their influence on public life. In the 1950s, the South and the West were the last fortress against Roman power, but even there Catholic assault appeared imminent. As Father Smith recalled the speech, the "Catholic Church will spend millions of dollars to take over the South and the West to finally take over the United States."[44]

Catholics, furthermore, must accept "the Roman Catholic Church or the Bible," because "Nothing in the Bible . . . can support the teaching of the C.Ch." This brought a "big Amen" and then "'That's what I told them'" from the host church's pastor. Contrasting views of the availability of salvation also troubled this "former priest." As Father Smith reported the speech, there could be "*Absolutely* no salvation outside the Catholic Church (this stressed very much). 'If I die outside the Church, I'll go straight to Hell.'" In the pre–Vatican II church, this actually was a correct understanding of Catholic doctrine—*extra ecclesiam nulla salus* (outside the church there is no salvation)—although by the 1950s leaders of the American Church were de-emphasizing its significance. In 1952 the Vatican condemned a Boston group that had made that dictate central to its Catholic identity. But the laity who attended weekly lectures by Father Leonard Feeney, the charismatic Jesuit leader of the group, at Cambridge, Massachusetts's St. Benedict Center, were not as heretical as Rome might have it. According to one historian, the reality was that Feeney "had changed the interpretation of St. Cyprian's dictum far less than had the experience of postwar American Catholicism itself." Still, the importance the unidentified lecturer in Georgia placed on that element of doctrine (which so separated Protestants from Catholics) reveals how Protestants and Catholics continued to define themselves in opposition to the other.[45]

Most examples of anti-Catholicism in Alabama and Georgia were predictable and fit common formulas. Catholics readily linked this most recent period of anti-Catholic bias to earlier eras, to Know-Nothings and convent burnings of the nineteenth century, and the Klan of the 1920s. Catholics were accused of not supporting freedom of religion, and of being anti-democratic, mysterious and secretive, and opposed to the Bible. In the minds of many Protestants, those things equaled opposition to Protestantism itself. Those same Protestants also believed that their opposition to the Catholic Church enhanced their own patriotism and proved their American identity. They evinced the exclusive nationalism that characterized the early years of the Cold War in America, but in Alabama and Georgia, as in the rest of the South, that nationalism remained distinctly religious—indeed, Protestant—in nature. According to this reasoning, by its very nature Catholicism was incompatible with Americanism.

Catholics refused to see the incompatibility. They would wear the "intolerable Alien" badge only so long. Their patriotism and commitment to democracy and religious liberty should be indisputable. Southern Catholics asserted their right to belong and be taken seriously in the larger society. In their minds, they and their message were to be acknowledged and heeded not in spite of their Catholicism but because of it. Protestants should direct their energy toward achieving other goals, instead of defaming a fellow Christian group. Indeed, Alabama's and Georgia's Catholics implied that postwar Protestantism needed Catholicism to save it from itself. This was an inclusive American Catholicism, shaped by peculiarly American notions of religious freedom and tolerance. "What is needed," Hugh Kinchley wrote Albany's J. G. Malphurs in 1950, "is not for representatives of different religious beliefs to debate their differences, but for them to find ways of working together in a spirit of Christian unity for the common welfare of the nation and the freedom of all of the peoples of the world." The preservation of American liberty depended on "the loyal, patriotic devotion and sacrifice of Catholic, Protestant and Jews united against the onslaughts of atheistic totalitarianism."[46] Rather than being tangential to American society, Kinchley was saying, Catholics and their belief system should be central to it.

Catholicism, of course, never became central to southern society, as Kinchley may have wanted. And anti-Catholicism persisted in Alabama and Georgia into the 1960s. For many observers, John F. Kennedy's election to the presidency in 1960 marked American Catholics' coming of age in modern America. But for many Catholics the victory was bittersweet. One of their own could become president, but not without virulent attacks and renewed anti-Catholicism questioning their ability to be true to American democracy. In Georgia, Bishop Francis E. Hyland of Atlanta felt compelled to console the Catholics in his diocese in the wake of the election of 1960. Hyland's November pastoral letter reflected the ambivalence that southern Catholics continued to feel about their relationship to the larger society, despite their good-faith efforts to honor the political expectations of non-Catholics. Hyland wrote before he knew whether Kennedy or Richard M. Nixon had won; indeed, the outcome probably mattered little to people, who were "distressed . . . by these unjust attacks upon the faith, which we cherish above everything else in life, and upon the Church, to which we refer with filial affection as our Holy Mother." Hyland had not written earlier because he wanted to avoid the appearance of playing politics. "There have been no politics in our Catholic pulpits," he wrote, since the "church is the house of God" and not the place "to promote the political fortunes of anyone." To Hyland, that proved Catholics' support for the constitutional separation of church and state, a notion that was "part and parcel of the American way of life, which we cherish with all our hearts."[47]

In December 1963, furthermore, Archbishop Thomas J. Toolen wrote a confidential letter to his priests instructing them to urge their parishioners to vote against a controversial proposed state constitutional amendment that would have required Alabama voters to re-register, with the risk that their registration could be rejected. The proposed amendment came in the midst of increased agitation for an end to segregation and disfranchisement and was not drafted with Catholics necessarily in mind. Toolen recognized that the amendment was aimed at keeping African Americans from voting, but he feared that "it could just as easily prevent any of us." And in 1965 a doctor from Buena Vista, Georgia, a small town in the western part of the state, inquired of Toolen about the feasibility of opening a medical clinic in a rural section of Alabama. Toolen advised against it, noting that he would have a hard time establishing a clinic in small-town Alabama, where there lived few Catholics. "I know you would not just depend upon

Catholics but there is still a terrific amount of bigotry in these small towns in Alabama," the bishop warned.[48] It is noteworthy that a physician would feel the need to seek the bishop's advice before opening a clinic, a sign that Catholics continued to be wary of Protestant attack and suspicious of their good graces. Of course, Toolen confirmed the doctor's fears.

Both Hyland and Toolen wrote to their own people, Catholics who remained under attack. Those attacks had declined by the 1960s, to be sure, but anti-Catholicism, both explicit and subtle, forced a diverse population to unite. They did not shrink from public view, even as they engaged in the rhetorical battle with Protestants over their own American loyalty. They were good democrats, firmly committed to the constitutional separation of church and state, and dependent on American ideals of freedom and religious liberty. Catholics carried on an active contest over public sacred space, which delineated the boundaries of their religious subculture. Their contest, in part, was a contest over religious pluralism and their own public role in the South. They called for the boundaries of the southern religious mainstream to be redrawn to include Catholicism. Although it went unspoken, that religious mainstream was a white, Christian democracy. Catholic contests over public sacred space included evangelism efforts where they engaged Protestants and non-Christians on street corners and in open fields. And public celebrations and worship services sanctified public stadiums and downtown squares. These celebrations were designed to encourage and unify the faithful. They reminded local Catholics what was distinctive about them and served as media for reminding non-Catholics why Catholics should be included in the mainstream.

2

A Group Apart

SACRED SPACE *and* CATHOLIC IDENTITY
at MID-CENTURY

❖

In a 1992 interview, a Childersburg, Alabama, woman reflected on the isolation she and other Catholics experienced in the South fifty years earlier: "But we were a group apart. Just as Catholics have been, in my estimation, everywhere I've been in the South for all the years I've been here. They are a group apart. Even in Birmingham."[1] Amy Winters was from Colorado originally; her husband was from Mobile. Winters expressed in simple language how disconnected from southern society the region's Catholics could feel. Her description of being set "apart" from mainstream southern culture suggests in spatial terms the isolation and prejudice they experienced from the Protestant majority. In many areas of Alabama and Georgia, Catholics had good reason to feel isolated. Not surprisingly, unlike in the North and Midwest by the end of World War II, the area contained few signs of the public presence of Catholics. They remained an overwhelming minority and the targets of anti-Catholic bigotry. But as their sometimes feisty responses to anti-Catholicism demonstrate, many Catholics in Alabama and Georgia were willing enough to engage their critics and not shrink from public view. Despite Protestant opposition, they carried out an active evangelism program and put on massive public celebrations that displayed those distinctive religious features that were so central to Roman Catholics and which placed them on the margins of southern society (e.g., devotions to the Blessed Sacrament and the Virgin Mary). In doing so, they distinguished sacred space from public places to both rally and unify the faithful behind the walls of their religious subculture, even as they made tentative efforts to reach out to secular society and to unchurched southerners.

In the North and Midwest, the urban parish served as the cornerstone of a strong Catholic identity. For those Catholics, the parish identified the neighborhood in which they lived and demarcated the sacred boundaries that gave their environment religious meaning. In effect, for northern Catholics the parish became sacred space and shaped their own religious and cultural identity.[2] Alabama and Georgia Catholics, by contrast, were so few and so scattered that the parish never became the wellspring of identity as it was in the urban North. Spreading the faith and building new parishes in pursuit of an expanding population characterized the southern Church in the middle decades of the century. Even in urban areas where Catholics were most numerous, parish and neighborhood did not always coincide. Instead, southern Catholics constructed an identity based in part on their shared Roman Catholicism. In a sea of Protestants, that is, being Catholic mattered. To be sure, the parish was important. For people with little or no visible symbol of their faith, a new church building was inspiring. And even the smallest mission station could be seen as the house of God. But many counties and towns still lacked a full-fledged parish or a full-time pastor. Many areas built parishes at a time when Church authorities were engaged in concerted efforts to centralize their authority. As a result, church buildings often did little more than connect parishioners to diocesan and—by extension—Roman authority.

The story of each parish in Atlanta and Georgia differs by time of foundation, but the circumstances surrounding the advent of each one can fit into one of several patterns. A few churches in Mobile and Savannah trace their history back to the nineteenth century. Priests were more available there, since those cities were the center of Catholic activity in their respective states. In other districts, a group of Catholics might gather in someone's home whenever a priest made his rounds through several parishes under his charge. When a certain section had a Catholic population large enough, the bishop would then appoint a priest—assuming one was available—and priest and people would locate or build suitable facilities for mass and other services. Obtaining sufficient numbers of clergy proved to be a difficult chore. One statistical report from Savannah circa 1960 pointed to the desperate need: "If we are to bring our holy faith most effectively into the mission areas of South Georgia we must have more priestly personnel."[3]

Parish growth in the mid-twentieth century often followed the example of Huntsville's Holy Spirit Church, whose foundation can be traced directly back to the migration of Catholics into the South following World War II. Diocesan authorities observed Huntsville's postwar growth and anticipated a tremendous expansion of the population due to the advent of the nation's space program. In 1954 they authorized the pastor of St. Mary of the Visitation parish in downtown Huntsville to purchase ten acres of land outside of town near the airport. Between 1950 and 1960, Huntsville's population grew from sixteen thousand to seventy-two thousand, a boom attributable directly to industrial and technological development in the city. Red Stone Arsenal, the army's site for missile-defense research, opened during the 1950s, and NASA added a space flight center in 1960. In 1962 Archbishop Toolen admitted that the diocese did not know how many Catholics were in the city. Before the advent of Red Stone Arsenal, there were approximately two hundred; but since then, the city and its Catholic population had grown too quickly, and diocesan resources were too limited to keep up with the rapid expansion.

According to the 1964 diocesan census, St. Mary of the Visitation was the largest parish in the diocese, with 5,895 Catholics from 1,483 families. In 1959 Visitation began construction of facilities that would become a school and then a mission station of the church. The school opened in 1960, and work on Holy Spirit Church began in 1963. Monsignor John A. McGonegle, pastor of St. Mary of the Visitation parish, first celebrated mass in the new church on April 4, 1965, and Archbishop Toolen dedicated it in October of that year. By 1965 the Catholic population had grown so much that Holy Spirit School had four hundred students, and another eight hundred Catholic children attended public school. The majority of this new population resulted from migration into Huntsville because of the space program and military installations there. The post–World War II South's population growth increased the number of Georgia's Catholics as well. By 1963, for example, Clayton County, located just south of Atlanta, was the fastest growing county in the state. In 1950 its population made it thirty-fourth in the state; in 1960, it was thirteenth. The influx had come so quickly that Jonesboro, the county seat, did not even have a mission chapel by 1963, while the surrounding towns of Griffin, Thomaston, Jackson, McDonough, and Newnan all did.[4]

Because the parish was an unreliable marker for their religious identity, Catholics in Alabama and Georgia evinced a more diffuse sense of the sacred. The parish church was the most important location for providing sacred comfort and protecting Catholics from a sometimes harsh Protestant world. In addition to their local parish church, they claimed street corners, vacant lots, football stadiums, city streets, and public squares as the locations where they asserted their religious identity. Their contests for public sacred space became more than mere assertions of identity. Indeed, they provided the opportunities to craft a secular (both regional and national) identity that would be influenced by their Catholicism and shape their interactions with non-Catholics. Protestant anti-Catholicism—not to mention Catholic anti-Protestantism—suggested that such public claims for recognition and acceptance would not go uncontested. And Catholics participated in these ceremonies and attended parish missions with that bigotry well in mind. But Catholics' claims for public space gave them the opportunity to answer their Protestant critics and invite them into further dialogue on Catholic terms. It was in public that these Protestant-Catholic exchanges mattered. Announcements of special services and public celebrations invited non-Catholics to attend. But Catholic desires to be inclusive only went so far. These were Catholic ceremonies, with peculiarly Catholic trappings, and Protestants were necessarily excluded. As Catholics defined the boundaries around their subculture, they also acted out, through public ritual, their claims to acceptance in the American mainstream.[5]

For most of the twentieth century, the Church considered Alabama and Georgia to be missionary territories. For those Catholics not living in Mobile, Savannah, Birmingham, or Atlanta, the services of the Church were not readily available. And many parishes in both dioceses were not self-supporting. Priests and bishops were forced to appeal to the Catholic Church Extension Society of Chicago, for example, and other groups with headquarters outside the South. Mission priests often took annual fund-raising trips through northern dioceses, and individual non-southern parishes contributed portions of their mission budgets to Alabama and Georgia. For Catholics, such outside assistance provided them with the resources to build and supply mission

chapels and new parishes across Alabama and Georgia. It also reinforced both their relationship to extra-regional organizations and the
influence of outside religious forces.

St. Vincent de Paul Church in Tallassee, Alabama, provides an almost comical study of contrasts between the strength and numbers
of non-southern agents and the small, isolated churches they helped
build. Bishop Fulton Sheen, the nation's most famous and widely
respected Catholic in the 1950s, had helped to convert Mrs. Robert
Blount of Tallassee. The circumstances surrounding Bishop Sheen and
Blount's spiritual relationship are unclear from the available sources.
Sheen had been in Alabama before, as guest speaker for at least one
Birmingham fund-raiser. Perhaps they met then. At any rate, Sheen
was then on the faculty of Catholic University in Washington, D.C.,
and promised her that he would preach the dedication sermon if a
Catholic Church were built in her hometown. Mass was first offered in
the area in 1910, but not until February 1956 did the small Alabama town,
located approximately midway between Auburn and Montgomery,
have the opportunity to invite Sheen to fulfill his promise. And, one
newspaper reported, "with Bishop Sheen on the morrow will converge
on Tallassee the most distinguished array of clergy ever to assemble
in these parts." In addition to Sheen, the archbishop of Chicago, the
Most Reverend William D. O'Brien, blessed the new building with
holy water.[6]

St. Vincent de Paul Church—"the realization of a dream by a good
woman, the hard work of a few faithful families and the generosity of a
non-Catholic husband"—had eight families and sixteen members in a
mission church that would hold a mere one hundred persons. The size
of the parish notwithstanding, more than two thousand were expected
to turn out to see and hear the host of the popular television show *Life
Is Worth Living*, and organizers made arrangements to accommodate
the overflow crowd at the National Guard armory. Sheen's celebrity
certainly was a factor in the turnout, and no other mission dedication
drew such a crowd. But such a spectacle reveals how active Catholic
missionary organizations were in the South, and how proud they were
upon finding, symbolically, the one lost sheep that had strayed from
the ninety-nine.[7]

But Church officials were not content merely to follow their parishioners around building churches. Evangelism was crucial to Alabama

and Georgia Catholics—or at least to their leaders. They were motivated by their conviction that the people of the South needed to hear their message. At first glance, Catholic revivalism might seem self-contradictory. After all, revivalism was the central component of southern Protestantism, the phenomenon most closely associated with the region. But the Catholic Church was no stranger to revivals. The Church in Alabama and Georgia evinced a revivalist pattern similar to what was otherwise common in the region.[8] Catholics evangelized people familiar with a particular religiosity, one that emphasized the centrality of the emotional crisis conversion.

One Georgia Catholic suggested a fundamental difference between the understandings of salvation when he joked about a Jesuit missionary priest who could hold his own against Protestant revivalists popular in the region. In 1952 Hugh Kinchley wrote to the Diocese of Savannah-Atlanta's vicar general, "This Jesuit from India that has been conducting the Novena of Grace at the Sacred Heart Church was one of the best speakers ever to be heard from the pulpit of that church." Using a phrase common to Protestant evangelicalism, Kinchley sarcastically noted that the priest was so good, in fact, that "He has just about 'saved' me."[9] Kinchley's wit reveals a keen awareness of the differences between Catholics and Protestants over understandings of salvation.

Catholic revivalism in the nineteenth century concentrated on effecting an individual crisis conversion similar to Protestant revivalism. Historian Jay P. Dolan has labeled this phenomenon "sacramental evangelicalism."[10] And southern Catholics in the mid-twentieth century continued this tradition, with local parish missions (or revivals) and street preaching. There was much more involved in conversion to Catholicism than in evangelical individual conversion, however. Unlike Protestant revivalism's emphasis on individual conversion, Catholics in Alabama and Georgia were concerned about bringing people into the fold of the Catholic Church—the "one true church." Whereas Protestants invited converts to struggle with the sacred, Catholics invited people to enter into it.

The parish missions that were held at individual churches throughout Alabama and Georgia most closely resembled Protestant revivals. Rather than being held in borrowed or rented public locations or on street corners, which was the case in areas with no established Catholic churches, various parishes hosted these. Intended in part to reach non-

Catholics—they even advertised in local secular newspapers—parish missions primarily served to reinforce the Catholic community, encourage devotional practices, and instruct laity in the faith. Virtually every announcement of forthcoming missions urged Catholics to "bring their non-Catholic friends with them." The Reverend Francis Broome, a Paulist from Winchester, Tennessee, announced that the mission he would conduct at Montgomery's St. Andrew's parish in 1947 would "be conducted in [a] non-controversial manner. . . . The purpose of this mission is to set forth in a clear and understandable way, the position of the ancient Christian church, especially in these days when so many are asking, as did St. Paul, 'Lord what will thou have me do.'"[11]

At mid-century, Catholics recognized that they were competing with Protestants for the unchurched and increased their efforts to reach non-Catholics. A 1948 Jesuit provincial meeting in New Orleans noted the need for mission work in rural areas, where Catholics registered negligible numbers. The minutes of that meeting noted that from one-third to two-fifths of rural southerners belonged to no church. There was work to be done. "Protestants realize the importance of apostolic work in rural areas, and are at work," the Jesuits noted. "A recent article in the Christian Century tells of the work of the National Catholic Rural Life Conference, and urges Protestants to do likewise." Included on the list of tasks Jesuits should undertake to offset Protestant advances was "street preaching in rural areas . . . for the formation of new parishes and mission stations, the reclaiming of fallen away Catholics and making converts."[12]

In 1949 the executive secretary of the National Catholic Rural Life Conference concurred. Monsignor Luigi G. Ligutti lamented the Church's slow growth in the nation's rural areas. He claimed that of the 78,177 small towns with a population of less than 2,500, there were only 9,641 Catholic churches and approximately 5,300 resident priests. There were more than 68,000 towns without any Catholic church. Such numerical imbalances threatened Church growth and needed to be corrected with evangelism. White Southern Baptists feared this type of evangelism. In 1950 one Baptist writer fretted over Catholic intrusion into rural areas. Hugh A. Brimm wrote, "Are we going to stand idly by while they build churches and schools in rural areas . . . ? Is it not high time for us as Baptists to turn to our great stronghold, the rural areas of the southland [and] . . . win the countryside to Christ? The time is now—it's later than you think!"[13]

This mission work to non-Catholics elicited many inquiries and a few converts, but it focused as well on strengthening whatever small community of Catholics existed to begin with. The rural South isolated Catholics who migrated ahead of the institutional Church, especially in northern and central Alabama and most of Georgia outside the coastal area. Street preaching enterprises located many of those "fallen aways" and tried to incorporate them back into the fold. In a 1945 pastoral letter soliciting mission funds and encouraging more vocations to the priesthood, Bishop Toolen painted a bleak picture for Catholics. Those isolated co-religionists were suffering discrimination, and as a result the Church suffered. "These are discouraging missions. In going around I find so often that the Catholics are demoralized by the prejudice they have to face. Quite a few of them have joined Protestant churches. I surely am eager for the weather to warm up that I may go out to these places to preach and if nothing else to raise the morale of our Catholic people."[14]

The Dominicans brought their "motor chapel" to places like Crawford, Georgia, where they could locate only three Catholics in the general population. During one particular stop, more than five hundred non-Catholics gathered over two nights in Crawford to hear the Dominican missionaries' message. Probably reflecting trouble such missionaries had experienced in the past, one report indicated that the Dominicans "were well received by the local sheriff," as well as others in the town. Townspeople had even invited the traveling preachers to return. In Colbert, another small Georgia town only a few miles northeast of Athens, two hundred non-Catholics braved cold temperatures—"huddled into 35 parked cars"—"as they witnessed the religious motion pictures and listened to the missionary's sermons." In World War II–era rural Georgia, preaching services such as these no doubt served as local entertainment, which is one possible explanation for the turnout in inclement weather. But such a utilitarian interpretation is ultimately unsatisfying. Southerners were a religious people, even if their behavior sometimes did not validate the sincerity of their commitment. Because of their denominational affiliation, Dominicans may have seemed an oddity to most southerners. But revivals were familiar to them, "religious events that kept alive the hope of salvation," according to historian Ted Ownby. Many non-Catholics were no doubt drawn to the nightly sermons based on that acquaintance.[15]

In the early 1930s, Father Frank Giri established the North Alabama Mission Band, whose assignment was open-air preaching in areas with but a minuscule Catholic population. These "street preachers" served a couple of different purposes. Their primary goal was evangelism, but Catholic "protracted meetings"—to use a nineteenth-century Protestant phrase—also fulfilled a secondary, but equally important, goal. They provided support for the few Catholics scattered across those counties that lacked a priest and regular access to the sacraments, and attempted to draw back into the fold those "fallen aways" who had begun to neglect their Catholic duty. In 1945 the *Catholic Week,* reflecting the optimistic belief that a properly delivered message would alleviate ecumenical tensions in the South, opined that "The work of the Catholic Church in the South is cut out for it. It takes the warming light of the truth to banish bigotry and prejudice. The Church must be known before it can be loved. If the people will not come to the Church, then the Church must go to the people."[16] And go these priests did. But their tasks were not simple.

If they hoped to catch the attention of non-Catholic southerners through their sermons, street and mission preachers had a rich legacy to live up to, for southerners had a taste for rhetoric. Partly because of low levels of literacy and few available books, southern society in general was predominantly an oral culture and marked by the importance of the spoken word. This proved true from the earliest fiery evangelical Protestant sermon through the demagogues of the New South period. In his 1941 study of southern culture, journalist W. J. Cash described the "Southern fondness for rhetoric." This "gorgeous, primitive art . . . . flourishes wherever [the simple man] foregathers." For the southerner, rhetoric became "not only a passion but a primary standard of judgment, the *sine qua non* of leadership. The greatest man would be the man who could best wield it." An anthropologist has argued that for Southern Baptists, ritual is verbal. They create the sacred by speaking "the Word"; that is, by reading the Bible aloud and preaching the sermon, Baptists experience sacred ritual.[17]

Southern oratory frequently reflected the intense emotionalism that characterized the Protestant revival experience. Faithful listeners believed they could discern an evangelist's proximity to the Holy

Spirit based on the manner in which he appealed to the crowd. Historian Randall Miller has written that because a large majority of priests in the South were not native to the region, they had a difficult time mastering southern customs and idioms; therefore, the sermon proved to be a particular problem.[18] For Catholics, moreover, such religious emotionalism could not necessarily be trusted.

One Alabama mission priest, Father Henry Thorsen, recalled that his sermons were often on a favorite southern Protestant topic. "[T]hey liked to hear about sin and hell," although the existence of Purgatory presented problems for Protestants otherwise emotionally involved in concerns about the afterlife. A second priest who began his stint with the mission band in the 1960s pointed out, "you don't street-preach the way you preach in a Catholic church." Instead, Father Paul Donnelly recalled in the 1990s, "You get up and for forty-five minutes, rant and rave about Jesus like a good old Jimmy Swaggart or . . . evangelist type of thing." But when describing his mission band meetings, Father Joseph Durick reported that his listeners' favorite portion of the sermons was "the vast, deep logic of a man's purpose in life." About another mission priest, a reporter noted, "From reason and revelation he proves convincingly that a peaceful and happy life can be attained only by following the direction of God."[19] If the truth were known, the "deep logic" and "reason" portions of the sermons may have been the priests' favorite segment more than the audience's. After all, trying to live up to the South's rhetorical reputation could be a chore. But this demonstrates one obstacle priests faced in their evangelism.

The pattern of Alabama's open-air evangelism varied little from year to year. A group of five or six priests—in the late 1940s and 1950s led by Father Joseph Durick, later auxiliary bishop of the Diocese of Mobile and then bishop of Nashville—traveled through Jefferson, Walker, Talladega, Shelby, and Bibb counties in north Alabama, "teaching Catholic Doctrine on the streets." A separate group covered counties in the southern part of the state. Speaking before open-air gatherings to laity seated on wooden folding chairs, from the back of a bus or trailer with a mobile public address system, or from a willing Catholic's front porch, priests delivered sermons, answered inquiries about the Catholic faith during "question box" periods, and handed out pamphlets. Father Durick later admitted that he and his fellow priests would occasionally "stuff this question box ourselves." They did this in their efforts "to disabuse people of wrong notions concerning the Church." Father Durick also reported attempts to foster devotion to the Virgin Mary and "giving out rosaries to those who promise to say them." In addition, seminarians would canvass neighborhoods and pass out pamphlets. Those with questions could also visit the Catholic Information Center, an office in downtown Birmingham that offered Catholic publications and answers to non-Catholics' questions about the faith. Besides the priests, female religious organized the women and children and taught them Catholic doctrine.[20]

In 1993 one Alabama woman remembered Monsignor Ed Foster's request that her family—the only Catholic one in Minor, Alabama—allow street preaching from their home. "When you're the only Catholic family in a community,—and you have street preaching in your yard. . . . It was very dangerous," Alice Slatsky recalled. One Baptist church in that small town west of Birmingham refused to give the Catholic evangelists easy access to the community. The Baptists issued "long letters against us, and telling people not to even let us in their house. . . . Not to have anything to do with us." During one particular Holy Week, moreover, local miscreants threw rocks through church windows and disrupted services.[21] The small handful of Catholic families in Childersburg, Alabama, also experienced the strain of being a religious minority and the stress of being expected to share their resources with mission teams.

In 1992 Amy Winters feared that the priest who rounded up five Catholic families in Childersburg did not receive enough credit for his work. Few people, she noted, would understand the pressures "unless they lived on the mission and understood the circumstances of living in a bootleg community where Catholics were people you hated, wished to get rid of if you could. . . . You had to meet your religion face to face." The Ku Klux Klan was strong in the area, as well. The post–World War II Klan announced its customary opposition to Catholics—"'Catholics, Jews, Communists, Negroes and northern agitators' [are] the principal threats to the 'destruction of the white heritage,'" the Montgomery Klan proclaimed in 1956—but concerned itself primarily with issues of race and civil rights. Despite one potentially hostile encounter with a Klansmen, Winters remembered no burning crosses. Still, she and her fellow Catholics felt isolated.[22]

The annual reports of the North Alabama Mission Band reveal the pattern of growth and the limited success of the mission band among the Catholic population throughout north Alabama. This mission band included those small churches and stations located in the counties around Birmingham that did not yet qualify as full-fledged parishes. The Catholic population grew slowly but steadily. Churches' contact with a priest and therefore the frequency of services varied. In some instances there were enough families in an area to justify weekly mass, while others saw a priest only a couple of times a month.

In 1944 the North Alabama Mission Band covered 534 Catholics in fifteen church stations. All of these were white, with some thirty-three being converts to the faith and another thirty-six being confirmed that year. A year later that number had grown to 724 white mission Catholics in seventeen stations. Forty-nine of that number were converts. Reflecting the transient nature of portions of the population, the mission at Pell City, for example, had four families—eleven Catholics—in 1944, with mass being celebrated twice a month. A year later, only one of those families remained. Between 1945 and 1950, the Catholic population of the mission stations fluctuated, increasing to as many as 776 in 1946 before dropping to around 300 in 1950. There were fewer mission stations by half in 1950; however, they included over fifty converts. A few of the mission chapels had been raised to parish status, while others disappeared from use when the Catholic families in the area moved elsewhere. Some of the mining villages, like Blocton, where Italian Catholics had labored in the mines since the nineteenth century, simply disappeared when natural resources were depleted.

In the five-year period after 1950, the number of Catholics assigned to the North Alabama Mission Band increased again. The missions covered 1,063 in 1955, and that number remained high well into the 1960s. The most obvious explanation for this increase is that following 1955 the missions appealed to a greater number of "colored" in the area. In 1955 there were 317 African Americans in the missions along with 746 whites. Beginning with the 1957 report, the number of black Catholics assigned to the mission band dropped drastically. The explanation for this sudden decrease probably lies in the creation of a new parish for blacks. By 1956, there were enough African American converts in the Birmingham area to form a new parish, Our Lady Queen of the Universe. When the archbishop disbanded the North Alabama Mission Band in the late 1960s, mission priests were responsible for 1,042 Catholics—768 whites and 274 blacks. There had been fourteen stations in 1965.[23]

The North Alabama Mission Band and its south Alabama counterpart, the missions of Our Lady of the Rosary, reached into the rural and suburban counties of Alabama. Similarly, in Georgia, Glenmary, Redemptorist, and diocesan priests serviced mission stations in rural areas and suburban counties outside Atlanta. As the region's population continued to increase, parish construction continued throughout the 1960s and into the 1970s. In 1963 the *Georgia Bulletin* reported in its annual mission appeal that there were "many parts of the Archdiocese, particularly in Northern Georgia, where tremendous Catholic opportunity is waiting for us." Those opportunities existed "not only in the rapidly growing towns—many of them near Metropolitan Atlanta—but especially where four or five counties are at present being served by one priest and a chapel." As late as 1970, Bishop John L. May, who succeeded Toolen as Mobile's ordinary in 1969, wrote to a colleague in New Orleans that, "As you know, much of this Diocese is heavily missionary, with many of our counties without a single resident priest or a Catholic Church."[24] The majority of the Catholic population lived in the two states' urban areas, but each diocese's mission labors signaled efforts to unite the diverse southern Catholic Church under a single banner.

In 1948 Father John Horgan, the Mobile diocese's director of missions to south Alabama, bemoaned the lack of institutional support for Alabama's rural Catholics and lamented the absence of a public presence of Catholicism in "what is known locally as the Bible Belt of Alabama." Such a public presence provided "the consolations of our Holy Faith" in "a real house of God."[25] Horgan pointed to the importance of a local parish for the spiritual and, no doubt, psychological well being of the region's Catholics. Whereas Baptists reached the sacred through verbal communication, for Catholics a church building was a sacred place, a visible symbol of hope in a potentially hostile environment. But even with these small houses of God throughout the region, the Catholic Church in Alabama and Georgia needed something more to unite the disparate population. Church leaders realized the need to incorporate rural and urban Catholics, newcomers and indigenous population, under one umbrella. Their Roman Catholicism bound them into a subculture and forced them to negotiate boundaries between their Catholic identity and southern culture. During the fifteen years after the end of World War II, Catholic leaders effected reforms that strengthened the Church's institutional presence in the region and increased connections to Catholic organizations outside the region.

Catholics were outsiders in the South, and during—in Father Horgan's words—"continued storms of ignorance and bigotry," Protestants would not let them forget it. Still, Catholics asserted their right to the public domain. Street preachers and mission priests who made direct appeals to non-Catholics staked out claims to sacred space. Public street corners and open fields temporarily became consecrated territory, sites at which Catholics shared their religious vision with southern society. Even larger and more important public demonstrations occurred during annual Christ the King celebrations and venerations of the Virgin Mary. At mid-century, southern society underwent tremendous population growth, economic development, and social and cultural modernization. Catholics played an integral role in that transformation. Their negotiations of the boundaries between their own sacred environment and southern society revealed how blurred those lines had become, in their minds, by the 1940s and 1950s. In their own defense against prejudice, and in their annual Christ the King celebrations and venerations of the Virgin Mary, southern Catholics fashioned a Catholic identity that consolidated their scattered population behind their shared Roman Catholicism and associated themselves with the well-being of southern—and American—society. They assumed, as historian Jay Dolan wrote about American-born Catholics who wanted to shed their immigrant status, "the mentality of the insider, the cultural critic who possessed the confidence and ability to comment intelligently on the welfare of American society."[26]

As Ted Ownby maintains in his book *Subduing Satan,* in the early decades of the twentieth century, Protestants tangled with southern society over boundaries of the sacred. By mid-century, Catholics entered that fray, marking out for themselves sacred space. As the Catholic experience demonstrates, sacred space in Alabama and Georgia was constructed and depended on particular circumstances. The street revivals suggest that their sacrosanct public presence was more diffuse than that of their northern counterparts, but it nonetheless moved them into a more prominent position in southern society. Mission priests claimed street corners and open fields that became, however temporarily, sacred space for the Church. Even in Mobile, Birmingham, Savannah, and Atlanta, where the majority of the Catholic population called home, the parish often was not a strong enough symbol of identity. In lieu of a strong parish, then, Catholics in Alabama and Georgia drew their religious identity from the traditions and doctrines of Roman Catholicism. At several specific opportunities, they were able to assert a public presence and claim common territory as their own sacred ground. During annual Christ the King celebrations and ceremonies in honor of the Blessed Virgin Mary, Catholics claimed public places in Mobile, Pensacola, and Birmingham, and for an afternoon imbued them with sacred meaning.

For Catholics, an inner-directed spirituality centered on family and home was the norm throughout the nineteenth-century and the first half of the twentieth century.[27] But by the 1940s, Catholic leaders in Alabama and Georgia were making concerted efforts to expand the Church's infrastructure in the region, strengthen parish life, and encourage engagement with southern society. This strengthened the Church's presence and enhanced its own authority. Archbishop Toolen established annual diocesan-wide rallies that brought the disparate Alabama Catholic population together in prominent displays of religious pride. Critics might respond that these spiritual activities were only imposed by the bishop and should not be taken as indicative of lay beliefs. But the relationship between hierarchy, clergy, and laity holds the keys to historical significance. Although it is virtually impossible to determine precisely what the laity thought about the bishop's prescription for a stronger Catholic identity, they did participate, often in surprisingly large numbers. Some years as many as twenty or twenty-five thousand marched in Mobile's annual Christ the King celebration. And in Atlanta, five hundred or so men (from six different parishes) marched in annual Holy Name rallies. Approximately that number of women and children gathered to watch. With their participation, the laity accepted these rallies and devotions and made them their own.

In 1931 Bishop Toolen instituted the public Christ the King celebration "as an outward demonstration of faith." In 1925 Pope Pius XI had used the image of Christ as King to emphasize the importance of authority and orthodoxy in countering the social unrest of the early twentieth century. Pius worried about "the plague of anti-clericalism, its errors and impious activities," that characterized the early twentieth century, and he expressed concern over the "decline of public authority, and the lack of respect for the same." He proclaimed that all humans were "under the dominion of Christ," who alone could bring the salvation of society. Any sovereign or national leader who hoped to preserve his authority and increase his country's prosperity, the pope warned, "will not neglect the public duty of reverence and obedience to the rule of Christ." Pius, therefore, instituted an annual feast day in honor of Christ the King. He reasoned that liturgical festivals such as the Feast of Christ the King were effective means of encouraging the faithful "when they were attacked by insidious heresies, when they needed to be urged to the pious consideration of some mystery of faith." The pope hoped that such an annual celebration, furthermore, would remind nations—and the faithful—of their obligations to the teachings of the Church.[28]

Toolen believed that such a public demonstration of faith would rally Alabama Catholics and reinforce their commitment to the Church. The celebration would lend cohesion to a diocese spread thinly across Alabama and northwest Florida, and bring the Church more fully into the lives of the laity and society at large. Celebrations of the Feast of Christ the King on this scale were uncommon elsewhere in the United States, and their popularity in Alabama reveals certain characteristics of the Catholic Church there at mid-century. The Diocese of Savannah-Atlanta lacked anything to rival Christ the King celebrations and had to be content with smaller rallies and annual St. Patrick's Day parades. But Georgia's Holy Name rallies echoed some of the same themes and served similar purposes as Alabama's Christ the King demonstrations.[29]

Alabama's Christ the King observances almost always centered on themes of anti-communism and patriotism and the deleterious impact of modern secular society. But they also suggest how Alabama's Catholics viewed the role of the Church in their lives and the shape of southern Catholic spirituality at mid-century. Such public demonstrations may at first seem out of place in such a Protestant—and potentially hostile—environment, but the celebrations were instances of Alabama's Catholics asserting their right to belong in southern society, even as they instructed laity how to be good Christians. Where the annual events took place was significant as well. Mobile's was the most prominent, and the largest number of the state's Catholics attended that event. Tens of thousands paraded through downtown Mobile and congregated in the public square. In Birmingham, Pensacola, and Florence, crowds of several thousands gathered in local stadiums. None of these public facilities was the exclusive realm of Catholics; but on that one particular Sunday afternoon in October Catholics claimed them as local arenas of the sacred. They consecrated, however temporarily, public facilities and used them to connect themselves to a much larger sacred world. By taking part in such public celebrations, Catholics in Alabama intimately associated themselves with Roman Catholicism. Their participation in a distinctively Catholic ceremony distinguished them from other southerners.[30]

The image of Jesus as a monarch reigning over his church suggests the hierarchical nature of Catholicism at mid-century. There was a power structure in place that the laity were expected to recognize. This referred not only to the authority of the Church, with Rome and the Pope at the head and the laity at the foot. The image of Christ as monarch ruling over the Church also reveals attitudes about the nature of Catholicism itself. When local Catholics participated in the Sunday afternoon parades and ceremonies, they were affirming the hierarchy and orthodoxy that their Church represented. Bishop Toolen's motives may have been purer than this interpretation will suggest. But Christ the King celebrations were attempts to impose unity outward from a common center. They sought to make Alabama Catholics good Catholics, who were defined as those who supported—even acquiesced to—the Church's authority as represented by priests, bishops, and ultimately Rome itself. The Church's authority would become problematic in a few years, as racial justice became a moral issue and left white southern Catholics in an awkward position. Most Church leaders and official teaching supported integration, but many white southern Catholics sought to disregard the racial justice doctrines, or at least ignore their implications for segregation.

Besides the Church bureaucracy's authority, Toolen referred as well to a "hierarchy of values that must be observed by nations and individuals." Things of God took precedence over "material values." Similarly, Father Paul, a Benedictine priest addressing the 1945 Birmingham Christ the King crowd, asserted that Christ was "King and Lord and Master of this world." As such, "we as his subjects owe Him the duties of obedience, loyalty and reverence. Every ruler, even the most benevolent, must exact fulfillment of these duties." The way to satisfy those duties and properly honor Christ the King was through careful obedience, seeking God and bringing him "into our everyday lives." Observant Catholics would accomplish that in part with "frequent reception of Holy Communion and prayer."[31]

In addition to the mass itself, the central component of each Christ the King service was the exposition and benediction of the Blessed Sacrament, during which the archbishop or presiding priest held the communion bread, or Host, high for all worshipers to see. Catholics believe that the "body, blood, soul and divinity of Christ . . . are truly and substantially present" in the Holy Eucharist.[32] Blessed Sacrament devotion and the veneration of the real presence date back to the twelfth century. According to historian Eamon Duffy, English lay Catholics in the medieval era more often encountered the Host visually rather than by directly consuming the bread and wine. During the medieval mass, the priest raised the Host over his head for congregants to view. For Catholics, Duffy has written, "seeing the Host became the high point of lay experience of the Mass." It brought blessings to those who saw it and reinforced the notion that the Church was one with Christ. The doctrine of transubstantiation separates Catholics and Protestants more than any other issue, and in the nineteenth century it took on increasing significance for Catholic spiritual life and community identity. In historian Joseph Chinnici's words, Christ's presence in the Eucharist provided Catholicism "with social identity in a Protestant world."[33]

Catholics in the South, faced with the rapid urbanization and industrial growth amid the changing shape of American society, took solace in the knowledge that Christ remained a stabilizing spiritual force and that his presence could be assured in their religious services. Indeed, literary figures such as Allen Tate embraced the Roman Church because they saw in its doctrines an acceptable antidote to what one Tate biographer labeled "the intellectual and social problems of secular modernity" that contributed to the "dehumanizing trends of modern life."[34] Of course, these Alabama Catholics could not know that their church would soon be undergoing dramatic changes that would undermine their very faith in the institution itself. At the time, the institutional church was the one constant in these southerners' lives.

Alabama's Christ the King celebrations were an interesting mix of patriotism and spirituality that reiterated the southern Catholic eagerness to identify with American society. That identification came, however, with an important qualification. Because of increasing secularism and materialism, American culture had grown corrupt. Only Catholicism provided the spiritual and moral values to redeem the nation. In 1945 the primary concern was the immediate post–World War II society and the fate of American democracy and freedom. Over the course of the late 1940s and the 1950s, the emphasis shifted gradually from the war to the adverse influence of communism and concerns over increasing wealth and materialism. Each year's demonstrations summoned Alabama's Catholics to measure their devotion to Christ and the accommodations they had made with modern society. The format of the ceremonies varied little from year to year. Christ the King became an annual diocesan event that remained popular well into the 1960s. (It continues today, but on a much smaller scale.) Its parades and spectacle made the state's Catholic population unmistakably conspicuous, as did its message.

When the diocesan Holy Name Society made plans for the 1945 Christ the King celebration, it announced that the festivities would serve as thanksgiving for the end to World War II. In addition, the state's Catholics would be expected to pray for "a just and lasting peace through Christ the King." Organizers expected eighteen thousand to attend in Mobile, but an estimated twenty thousand showed up to form a "two-mile-long parade of parishioners and school children," as the diocesan newspaper described it. The region's laity assembled according to the parish or group with whom they would march beginning at 2:00, Sunday afternoon, October 28. A city police escort, followed closely by color guards, a cross bearer, and the bishop, led parishioners, parochial school children, and some twenty marching bands through downtown Mobile to Bienville Square. Similar but much smaller demonstrations occurred in Birmingham and Pensacola on the same day, while in Florence approximately thirty-five hundred (they expected sixty-five hundred) simply gathered (with no parade) in the Coffee County High School football stadium.[35]

According to the *Catholic Week* coverage of the 1945 program, the "blessing of two service flags—one containing a star for each man from the Mobile diocese who fought in World War II and the other containing a star for each man or woman who paid the supreme sacrifice—was one of the most impressive parts of the religious section of the program." Archbishop Toolen praised the worshipers' "loyalty to Christ and loyalty to your country" through their participation in that day's ceremony. He also told them that "true religion and true patriotism always go hand in hand," and loving one's country meant loving God first. Rev. Walter Royer told the Mobile crowd that it had been God's will that the Allies, under the inspired leadership of the United States, would defeat the Axis powers. Since victory had been divine will and America had been blessed by God, Royer argued, then Americans should not turn from him. They must dedicate their nation to Christ the King, "if we believe that our country is 'God's Country.'" Americans must be "One people, pledged to the cause of Christ, the King, the Prince of Peace, Who has promised peace only to men of 'good-will.'"[36]

Although the specter of World War II hovered over the 1945 activities, in later years organizers and speakers continued to echo themes of patriotism and anti-communism. Alabama and Georgia Catholics commonly heard sermons or speeches inviting "loyalty to Christ and loyalty to country" or "spiritual patriotism," wherein "As Catholics . . . we must stand united for God, country and church."[37] The 1950 gathering in Mobile's Bienville Square included a sermon equating "the Kingdom of Satan with Joseph Stalin." The "Star-Spangled Banner" and the pledge of allegiance to the American flag regularly showed up on the annual programs as well. In 1950 the *Catholic Week* compared its Christ the King celebration to that year's Protestant Heritage Day. Instead of the "sermon of hate" that—from a Catholic perspective—characterized the Protestant ceremonies, Catholics presented "sermons of enlightening and uplifting spiritual content, truly Christian in theme and words."[38]

As their responses to anti-Catholic prejudice indicated, in the minds of Catholics, communism was merely the logical outcome of a secular society. According to local organizers of the 1947 and 1948 Pensacola rallies, secularization threatened to promote the spread of communism. Pensacola's Holy Name Society, organizers of the annual Christ the King program, envisioned their October celebration as "an open defiance of the threat of Communism." Public prayer was beneficial, for "certainly God will listen to the prayers of the large aggregation of laity which will be on hand beseeching Him for real, lasting peace." Communism was a spiritual problem for Catholics, the equivalent of godless atheism, "materialism," and "secularism." To correct that problem "in these trying times of ungodliness with Communism threatening the world they should welcome this chance to turn out and give expression of the faith that is our nation's hope." As if to emphasize the relationship between America's future and the hope found in Catholicism, Pensacola's 1948 program began with the "Star Spangled Banner" and the pledge of allegiance to the U.S. flag before moving to the exposition of the Blessed Sacrament. At Birmingham's 1948 rally, the Reverend E. J. Lawlor, the Josephite pastor of Birmingham's Immaculate Conception parish, blamed divorce, "nations distrusting one another," and "people harboring hatred in their hearts" on the fact that most people no longer recognized Christ as King in the increasingly secular postwar world.[39]

At least according to Catholic leaders in Alabama and Georgia, immediately following the end of the war America was vulnerable to the evils of moral decay, materialism, and secularization. In 1945 Toolen had warned the school children participating in the Christ the King celebration, according to the *Catholic Week,* never to "allow themselves to be doped by the opium of materialism." He added "that the great curse of our day was indifferentism, lack of zeal for things high and noble, the tendency to compromise sacred principles and appease pagan minded individuals and nations." For Catholics, the fact that America was in such a compromised position represented a spiritual problem. This type of spiritual reproach was common to religious leaders of all callings, but for mid-twentieth-century Catholic leaders the situation appeared worse because of the demographic, cultural, and economic changes sweeping the national religious scene.[40]

The situation was so tragic because now succumbing to "materialism" and "secularism" meant becoming like the Protestant mainstream. In 1951 Savannah's Monsignor Joseph Moylan worried about the negative influence on Christians of "years of Protestantism, Materialism and Secularism," all of which combine to create a "watered down," generic faith.[41] Moylan's concerns suggest a degree of Catholic ambivalence over their acceptance into the cultural mainstream. In his mind, there was a direct correlation between the dominant Protestantism and this postwar spiritual crisis.

In the 1950s, speakers at the Feast of Christ the King expressed concern over the potential dangers of the decade's prosperity and the temptations of material comfort. In 1955 Father Frank Giri addressed more than five thousand Catholics at the outdoor Birmingham rally. Giri challenged his listeners to identify with Christ's "conquest of these three evils, love of riches, pride and self-indulgence." Christ overcame the love of riches "when He despised wealth and chose to be born in poverty" and to live in poverty. Christ had also conquered self-indulgence, "the human passionate quest for pleasure." Giri encouraged Birmingham's Catholics to emulate Christ's example. A year later Archbishop Toolen acknowledged that no other nation had been "granted blessings as we have in America." This prosperity, however, could be a curse rather than a blessing. He warned the Mobile crowd "against tendencies toward secularism, materialism and the love of wealth." In 1958 Toolen invited his audience to counter those temptations with a "life of poverty and sacrifice," two concepts that secular society neglected. Observance of the tenets of Catholicism, then, counteracted the decline of modern America. Indeed, a Birmingham Josephite priest, Anthony A. Keil, reminded the 1958 Christ the King crowd at Rickwood Field that "the throne of Christ the King is now the Altar of the Catholic Church."[42]

The spirituality encouraged by the Christ the King observances was a masculine one. The Holy Name Society was an association of Catholic laymen founded in the thirteenth century, whose purpose was promoting the spiritual progress of its members and reverence for the name of Jesus. The diocesan Holy Name Society assumed responsibility for organizing the annual celebration of Christ the King. Father D. P. Harnett, pastor of Mobile's St. Catherine's Church, wrote in 1945 that the Holy Name "has developed a virile, virtuous Catholic manhood, [and] its members have always been the shock troops of Christianity," fighting for the rights of God and country.[43] Christ the King programs regularly included men reciting the Holy Name pledge, and members used the special day to recruit new members and encourage those parishes that did not have one to begin their own chapter.

Such a masculine expression of spirituality stands in sharp contrast to the period's Marian devotions. The veneration of Mary in the 1940s and 1950s served some of the same purposes for white southern Catholics as the Christ the King celebrations and Holy Name rallies. Mary was a figure that Protestants did not honor the same way Catholics did, and her prominence in Catholic doctrine was often the target of Protestant attack. Catholics worldwide, moreover, honored the mother of Jesus. So devotion to the Virgin was yet another element of the construction of a Roman Catholic identity among southern Catholics. That is to say, to venerate the Virgin in any of her many manifestations was to link Catholics in Alabama and Georgia to doctrines and spiritual practices that transcended their southern experience. In 1945 in Montgomery, for example, the annual May Day celebration "is for the purpose of uniting all Catholic organizations and all Catholics of the city in homage to the Mother of God."[44]

Mobile, Montgomery, Birmingham, Pensacola, and Atlanta all had their own Marian activities, whose purpose almost invariably was "beseeching the intercession of the Queen of Peace for world peace and the conversion of Russia." In 1948, twenty-five thousand men, women, and children participated in the Mary rallies in the four Alabama cities, once again marking out sacred space in ways similar to the Christ the King celebrations. Ten thousand crowded into Mobile's Hartwell Field, seven thousand into Birmingham's Rickwood Park, three thousand into Montgomery's Cramton Bowl, and five thousand into Pensacola's Legion Field. The programs for the four demonstrations were relatively uniform. There was "a Holy Hour with procession," crowning of a statue of the Virgin Mary, exposition and benediction of the Blessed Sacrament, saying of the rosary and prayers for peace, "prayers for the dedication of the Diocese to the Immaculate Heart of Mary," a sermon, and an address. The program's purpose and the speakers' messages sounded consistent and familiar themes, invariably decrying "atheistic communism" and its concomitant evils.[45]

In December 1947 a statue of Our Lady of Fatima—a replica of one at the shrine of Cova da Iria, Portugal—began its American journey in Buffalo, New York. The statue was one of two replicas being taken from diocese to diocese around the world. The second one moved westward across Europe, and the plan was for the two to reach opposite borders of Russia, bringing with them the prayers and spiritual conviction of millions of anti-communists around the globe. Some two hundred thousand devotees visited the "Pilgrim Virgin" during its three-day stay in Buffalo. The statue's pilgrimage brought it to Alabama in February 1948, where the four major cities of the diocese took turns hosting it. St. Paul's Church in Birmingham was the first stop on the tour. After two days there, a motorcade of Mobile diocesan priests and officials escorted the Pilgrim Virgin to Montgomery. It arrived in Mobile on February 19, after opportunities for veneration in Montgomery and Pensacola.[46]

At least according to diocesan officials, the tour was an unqualified success. One estimate placed the number of Alabamians and Floridians who visited the statue at forty-five thousand over the entire week.[47] That figure might be high, but it would be consistent with the popularity of Marian devotions at their peak in the late 1940s and early 1950s. Regardless of what the actual number was, the Pilgrim Virgin tour provided Alabama Catholics another opportunity to link their cause with that of Catholics worldwide. The Virgin's message was a universal Catholic one, with which Catholics from Mobile to Birmingham could identify. What's more, they believed that what Mary represented in the years after World War II could appeal to more than just Catholics. The news accounts of both May Day celebrations and the Pilgrim Virgin tour regularly mentioned that non-Catholics attended in addition to Catholics. There never appears any indication what percentage of the announced attendance were non-Catholics; indeed, reporters or diocesan officials probably had no idea how many there were. What is significant is the Catholic eagerness to be inclusive. They probably hoped that their inclusiveness would be reciprocated. Again, however, that inclusiveness centered on a figure whose Catholic interpretation was roundly denounced by Protestants. Inclusiveness, then, should come on Catholic terms. The problems which devotion to Mary was supposed to solve, moreover, were not specifically Catholic issues. The Catholic subculture still existed, but their demands for acceptance and claims to a public presence, they could argue, were bearing fruit.

The appeals to non-Catholics also revealed the contested nature of sacred space. The public arena is necessarily open to competing interests, and Catholics' claim to public space as a sacred Catholic domain was in conflict with Protestant designs on the same public territory. Indeed, the desire to be inclusive only went so far. Catholics invited non-Catholics to participate, but the services could not be for them. With mass, exposition and benediction of the Blessed Sacrament, and devotion to the Virgin Mary, the services were explicitly Catholic and by their very nature excluded Protestants. Catholics, however, meant their spiritual message for non-Catholics and Catholics alike. They indicated what was wrong with the world and why Catholics were the ones whose solution other Americans should follow.

Both Christ the King and May Day celebrations declined in popularity in the 1960s. In 1964, for example, seven thousand Mobilians attended the May Day rally (down from ten thousand in 1948), and that same year Pensacola held its rally in the high school gym instead of the larger Legion Field. Speakers still claimed that devotion to the Virgin was of critical spiritual importance, and for Catholic leaders Mary remained the symbol of feminine purity and the guardian of the home. But their rhetoric had lost the fire of the late 1940s and early 1950s. Similarly, by the late 1960s Christ the King celebrations in Mobile had moved to the Municipal Auditorium, with either a much smaller procession or none at all. This change resulted from transformations in the Church and in southern society in general. First, evidence from elsewhere suggests that by the late 1950s, Catholic devotionalism itself was undergoing important changes. In cities such as Pittsburgh, for instance, diocesan rallies on this scale decreased in attendance, as a new individualized spirituality took root, encouraged by the increasing suburbanization and dislocation of the Catholic population.[48] Beginning in the 1950s with the Supreme Court's announcement of its *Brown v. Board of Education* decision, furthermore, defense of the racial status quo became white southerners' primary concern. When white Catholics participated in that defense, they took advantage of an opportunity to lessen Protestants' suspicions of them. To be sure, anti-Catholicism persisted into the 1960s and beyond, but white Protestants had other problems to contend with and white Catholics proved to be welcome, if sometimes uncomfortable, allies.

3

Southern Liberal in the South

FATHER ALBERT S. FOLEY *and*
RACE RELATIONS *in the* 1940S *and* 1950S

⚜

In 1954 the Supreme Court's *Brown v. Board of Education* decision overturned the constitutional protection for the doctrine of separate but equal in the South's most prized institution, its public schools, the very epitome of local control and racial separation. That ruling threw many of the South's—indeed, the nation's—religious people into confusion, as they sought to square their long-standing support of segregation with the new dictates of the nation's highest secular authority. Most Protestant groups endorsed the *Brown* decision but disagreed over what their endorsement meant and what the decision's implications should be. Advocates of racial reform were in the minority, and their status grew ever more precarious as the decade progressed. After the unanimous *Brown* ruling, race relations and the defense of segregation again became of central importance to white southerners. Between the New Deal and the early 1950s, liberal, class-based politics had made significant headway in the Deep South. But the *Brown* decision produced a climate of racial extremism and led whites to fight back against black advance and to draw clear lines in the sand leading to confrontation with "outside agitators" and federal interventionists. A white supremacy "us" versus a liberal integrationist "them" mentality precluded any equivocation about protecting the racial status quo. Faced with organized "massive resistance" to the end of segregation, anyone who advocated integration and supported civil rights was an "outside agitator," an enemy of the South. In such an environment, religious differences were muted in favor of a concerted effort to defend the South from federal intervention to force integration.[1] Indeed, any Protestant attack of a Catholic was more likely to come in protest of support for integration than for Catholicism's sake.

Father Albert S. Foley served most of his career as a professor of sociology at Spring Hill College, a Jesuit liberal arts institution in Mobile, Alabama. Foley came to symbolize, in the mind of white southerners, the evil outside agitator. Through example and his own writings and teachings, Foley advocated equal rights for African Americans. He founded and supported ecumenical groups devoted to human rights and waged a running battle with the Ku Klux Klan. Foley's long-time assistant at Spring Hill, Joan Sage, recalled what she knew of the Jesuit from rumors before she went to work for him. "All native Mobilians, they 'hated his guts.' He was a 'nigger-lover,' a trouble-maker who was trying to integrate the races, and on and on." Sage never shared that general opinion. Nevertheless, a white man, Foley betrayed the white cause. This made him a threat to white southern society.[2]

To be sure, Foley turned out to be more moderate than liberal after he opposed the 1963 civil rights demonstrations in Birmingham. But his social and racial activism in the 1940s and 1950s led even his fellow white Catholics to ostracize him, just as other white southerners did. The opposition he received serves as an example of white Catholics casting their lot with the segregationist white South. Many made that decision with complicated motives, but in the extremist 1950s southern environment it was clear that intense social pressure to conform to the racial status quo placed Catholics in an awkward position. They were forced to choose sides, and few supported Foley's actions. Foley is significant in this case as a symbol of the changing position of white Catholics in southern society. With race and the defense of Jim Crow again the central issue, hostility directed at him came because of his self-described role as a southern liberal, not because he was a Catholic priest.[3]

After early reluctance to get involved in a position he expected to occupy only temporarily, Foley became a prominent community activist. His accomplishments were atypical for the pre–Vatican II era in that he eagerly participated in ecumenical and interfaith—even secular—organizations. Such cooperation would become more commonplace after the Second Vatican Council in the early 1960s, but Catholics who sought involvement in the civil rights movement were forced to branch out and look beyond their Church's organizations. Father Foley was active in the local division of the Southern Regional Council, the Alabama (and Mobile) Council on Human Relations, the National Conference of Christians and Jews, and the Catholic Committee of the South. The enemies he made through his activism reveal much about the changing status of white Catholics in the South. By his own telling, he was a favorite target of the Ku Klux Klan, and members of his own Church often were reluctant to be associated with him. This made him an outsider from two perspectives: from both the white Protestant South's (as manifested in its most extreme forms) and his fellow white Catholics'. The former comes as little surprise. His fellow Catholics' motives are not as clearly defined. On the one hand, his actions invited more persecution, so, especially in the context of the racial extremism of the 1950s, white Catholics were afraid to be associated with him. On the other hand, many of them simply disagreed with him, and ostracizing him was their way of expressing that disagreement.

In the mid-1950s Foley served as chairman of the Mobile chapter of the Alabama Council on Human Relations, which operated under the auspices of the Southern Regional Council. The human relations council, according to Foley, was an ecumenical and integrated "organization for the educational approach to the resolution of inter-racial tension."[4] Among other things, Foley was responsible for adult community education on behalf of the Council, often leading classes that, as one report noted, were integrated both "racially and religiously." Foley was a marginal character in local church politics and government, but his reform efforts reveal how far the Alabama Catholic Church fell short in racial and social justice. More aggressive in opposing segregation than the elder Jesuit John LaFarge, whose interracialism influenced Foley, the Spring Hill Jesuit demonstrated that mere evangelism of blacks was not sufficient. He was part of the next generation of civil rights activists, those whom LaFarge's biographer has described as "younger, bolder, and more action-oriented, ecumenical Catholics." Despite being in such company, however, in Alabama Foley was swimming upstream in a river full of obstacles.[5]

A Louisiana native, Foley was reared in the segregated South and "grew to know the Civil War traditions that were everywhere present in New Orleans." In the Catholic churches of his youth, he could not recall ever hearing a sermon on the race question, "never a bleat out of any of the play-safe pastors." It would have been a small wonder if he had. Foley reached young adulthood during the reign of Huey Long, years when racist demagoguery stirred white lower classes and offered only hollow promises to blacks. Foley's own education in interracialism came slowly. Indeed, he later recalled, "these early convictions and prejudices were not even affected very deeply by my theological studies during the war years, 1939–1943." It was not until he was assigned to teach a course on "Migration, Immigration, and Race" at Spring Hill that Foley gave serious deliberation to the Catholic Church's segregated patterns and to his own racist assumptions and predilections. After preparing for that course, he concluded that the southern Church was not "independent of the prejudiced laity, who hold the purse strings." Therefore, the racial problem in the southern Church (especially in Alabama) was "much more serious and widespread than I had at first realized." He found himself reborn a racial liberal. Rather than ignore the problem and act as if did not exist, which Foley wrote was his first reaction, the Jesuit became increasingly active in discussions on racial justice issues among his peers.[6]

He was not one to back down from a fight or to flee during rough times. "I was able to maintain, as I still hold," he recalled in his unpublished memoirs, "that the place for the Southern liberal is in the South where the action is, instead of holed up in the safety of the anonymous big cities, writing books about the South and enjoying absentee royalties." Foley believed he was particularly well situated to have an immediate impact on southern society. He was a "native Southerner" and, therefore, would be taken more seriously by other white southerners. His Confederate genealogical credentials were respectable, if not impeccable. He was the grandson of a Confederate Army veteran who had named his son (Father Foley's father) after a "Confederate saint, General Albert Sidney Johnston." The traditional Catholic practice would have compelled the Foley patriarch to name his son after an Irish saint instead. Reverend Foley, for his part, shared his father's—and the good General Johnston's—name. With appropriate southern identity intact, Foley was certain he "would not be written off by other Southerners as just another carpetbagger from the North, agitating for Negro causes as an outside disturber of our southern 'peace.'"[7] Foley overestimated any natural relationship he would have with his fellow white native southerners. But his assessment of the situation for outsiders could not have been more accurate. New Orleans native or not, Father Foley was an outsider, a reformer on the periphery of Church power, who was convinced he was in the mainstream of modern Catholicism.

Foley's interracial message confronted a Church that had long balanced the demands of segregation and evangelism. Within the Catholic Church in the South, African Americans were a minority within a minority. Like white southerners, blacks were overwhelmingly Protestant, overwhelmingly Baptist. Despite aggressive evangelism efforts by religious orders and a select few secular priests, African Americans remained relatively insignificant in both the national and southern Catholic Churches. Nevertheless, the southern Church's relationship with the region's black population reveals white Catholics' ambivalence about their own southern identity. On the one hand, racial issues more than any other factors solidified white Catholics' southern identity. For many—if not most—of them, segregation and racism were not moral issues. They were a fact of southern life that had little to do with Christian doctrine. If their belief system had any relationship to the South's racial pattern, they reasoned, it should reinforce segregation, by insuring that boundaries were honored and certain groups of people (primarily blacks) remained in their proper place. From this perspective, the episcopal authority most commonly associated with the Catholic Church could be brought to bear on social relations between the races. Prior to civil rights agitation, blacks and whites could co-exist in the same Church because racial boundaries were firmly in place, respected, and not very often questioned. On the other hand, a handful of Church leaders and marginalized individuals, like Foley, pushed a racial agenda and encouraged Catholic participation in racial and social justice issues. At times this put the Church in an awkward position vis-à-vis mainstream white society. The Church itself never fully resolved this dilemma. The hierarchy and many priests eventually recognized the immorality of racism, but the laity and other priests and a few bishops proved to be reluctant converts.[8]

Despite sometimes open animosity, white Catholic leaders slowly incorporated African Americans into their Church. In Alabama and Georgia, blacks and whites occasionally attended the same parishes. To be sure, these integrated churches were predominantly white, with the number of African Americans often minuscule. St. Joseph's parish in Dalton, Georgia, for instance, had six blacks in a parish of more than three hundred. At Sacred Heart church in Griffin, Georgia, there were four African Americans out of six hundred, fifteen out of six hundred and fifty at St. Joseph's, Marietta, and seven out of almost three hundred at Sacred Heart, Milledgeville.[9] The annual reports give no indication of how comfortably these African Americans fit into parish life, but segregation more than likely characterized the seating arrangements. In 1992 one black Birmingham woman remembered her integrated parish, Our Lady of Fatima (originally Immaculate Conception), wherein blacks sat on the left side of the church and whites on the right. Hattie Bean told an interviewer that "nobody dared use that word [integrated] or even think about it. . . . Now granted, there were definite places to sit." In the 1940s one Josephite priest, Joseph Hennessy, pastor of Montgomery's St. John the Baptist parish, complained to a gathering of fellow priests about signs in Catholic churches that read "For Colored." Father Hennessy also recommended that priests avoid using the derogatory term "nigger." Complaints to Bishop Toolen about diocesan segregation prompted the imperious ordinary to issue a blistering denunciation of the agitating priest.[10]

An unidentified Alabama black man, however, compared favorably his segregated experience with that of his Protestant friends. If any of them questioned his allegiance to the Catholic Church because of its persistent segregation, he responded that he could "go into the Cathedral for Mass whenever I want. I can go to St. Mary's or to any other Catholic Church." His Protestant friends, however, did not enjoy such liberties. "Let me see you just try to stick your nose in the Dauphin Way Baptist Church or in any of the Protestant Churches on Government Street," this man reportedly said to his hypothetical friend. "You know what the usher would tell you right away. 'Get out of here, boy, go where you belong.'"[11]

Southern Catholic leaders often took pride (however false or misdirected) in this type of integration. In a 1959 letter to Archbishop Joseph F. Rummel of New Orleans, Savannah-Atlanta's Bishop Francis Hyland recounted an incident in which a young Catholic African American visited non-Catholic relatives in Detroit. On Sunday morning, an uncle escorted the child to the nearest Catholic church for mass. A white usher refused them entrance and pointed them toward another church, where the blacks would be admitted. Hyland shared with Rummel the comments of the girl's mother to one Georgia priest: "Father, a thing like that would not happen in Georgia." Hyland emphasized, "It would not." Hyland, moreover, conducted integrated confirmation services at that city's Cathedral of Christ the King. In June 1957, for example, Hyland confirmed 208 adults. The newspaper record of the service makes no explicit mention of race, but "more than 80" of the confirmands were parishioners at Our Lady of Lourdes in Atlanta, a predominantly African American parish staffed by Society of African Missions priests. And in 1959 the pastor of Our Lady of Lourdes, Rev. Michael McKeever, S.M.A., assisted Hyland in confirmation services.[12]

Bishop Toolen of Mobile took a different confirmation path. He conducted services in the local parishes themselves, insuring that these special ceremonies remained segregated. Interviewed in the early 1990s, one black woman remembered the implicit racism evinced by even her own ordinary. Mrs. Earnestine Cotton converted to Catholicism at age fifteen, while a student at Immaculata High School in Birmingham. She was a member of Birmingham's Our Lady of Fatima Parish when Sister Rose Sevenich interviewed her in 1992. "I have no fond memories of Bishop Toolen," Cotton recalled. When the bishop administered the sacrament of confirmation "or anything that he had to touch you [Negroes], he would automatically reach to wipe his hands. . . . I don't know why they thought this was going to come off on them [whites]." Toolen's behavior would have come as little surprise to Foley, who rarely had anything positive to say about either the archbishop or his fellow Mobile-area priests. Upon informally surveying black Catholics in the Mobile area, Father Foley learned "they had never heard sermons on the race question or on fair and impartial treatment of their people as Christians and Catholics. . . . I found out that no local priest had ever preached on the race question down here."[13] Foley conducted those interviews in the 1940s, before the *Brown* decision had the opportunity to galvanize white resistance to desegregation. It is probably safe to assume, therefore, that if they had not before, then few priests ventured into that territory during the 1950s either.

His position at Spring Hill College provided a small measure of cover for Foley and his work. Many of his projects fell under the rubric of community education and appeared less threatening than other forms of direct action might have. He sponsored, for example, the formation of the Mobile Students' Interracial Council. The Jesuits

insisted that such an organization required the approval and cooperation of the local ordinary. When Foley, along with an economics professor and Spring Hill's president—all three Jesuit priests—approached
Bishop Toolen about the interracial experiment, the bishop, as Foley
recalled the meeting, "launched into a tirade against the Social Action
Committee of the National Catholic Welfare Conference which had
just published a statement of Negro rights in the field of human relations." Toolen also denounced "other radicals who were agitating
among the Negroes." Mobile's prelate required all priests (who were
exclusively white) working within the black community "to operate
behind the segregation lines and not push the blacks on the whites
in Alabama." Toolen assured the Jesuits that he fully supported "the
religious equality of the Negro and his right to access to the church
and the sacrmanets [sic]." Foley then convinced him that was the sole
purpose of the interracial student organization, "promoting religious
equality and understanding on the part of both black and white students." Toolen permitted formation of the group but warned against
"social equality which led to nothing but trouble."[14]

Foley and Spring Hill's interracial organization proposed a series of
projects that would foster religious equality, but which also promoted
integration. The Interracial Council at least talked about projects that
would require integrated religious arrangements. The student group
called for interracial participation in a variety of spiritual exercises, including mass attendance and prayer groups, Stations of the Cross during Lent, communion and Holy Hours, rosaries and May Devotions,
and novenas to black saints. They also urged the bishop to conduct
integrated confirmation services and planned an interracial pilgrimage to St. Augustine's Seminary in Bay St. Louis. The rationale for this
wide-ranging agenda came directly from Catholic doctrine. For example, that the Catholic Church is the mystical body of Christ, the group
reasoned, should prompt Catholics to attend mass on an integrated
basis. In addition, the belief in the communion of saints—that is "all
saints in heaven [are] united to all Catholics here on earth"—should
encourage white Catholics to offer devotion to black saints as well as
white.[15] Of course, simply because one group proposed such an agenda
did not mean that all students agreed. In 1946 the Mobile Students'
Interracial Council sponsored a survey of Spring Hill students about
their racial attitudes. In general students supported separation of the

races, but an overwhelming majority favored the treatment of Negroes as spiritual equals. Ninety-six percent said African Americans should receive "equal opportunity and equal treatment in law courts," and over 80 percent believed that blacks should receive salaries equal to whites. Seventy percent admitted they would receive communion from a black priest (22 percent did not know), and 75 percent would not be opposed to receiving communion alongside blacks.[16]

The bishop and other white Catholics in Mobile were unhappy with Foley's interracial work, but it was the proposed integrated seminary field trip that prompted Foley's transfer out of the diocese—a move intended to be permanent. A parent of one of the white girls planning to make the "pilgrimmage" learned that his daughter would be on a bus with African American Catholic veterans from Most Pure Heart of Mary high school. In Foley's words, "At that he exploded. He called four or five of his friends and got them to call the bishop to protest my 'forcing' of white girls and black veterans together for an all-day picnic at St. Augustine's Seminary." Toolen complained to Foley's superiors, "urging them to discipline me for having violated the diocesan policy of not promoting integration of whites and blacks." His religious order removed Foley, sent him to do his graduate work at North Carolina, and then assigned him to the Institute of Social Order at St. Louis University "for the rest of my life." Foley enjoyed the drama and conflict that his activism prompted, and he relished the part of uncompromising (symbolic) martyr. His memoirs boast, "I was considered to be too radical to be tolerated in the South."[17] By 1953, however, Foley was back at Spring Hill, a "temporary" reassignment that would last until his death in the early 1990s.

The few decades before what historians now consider the advent of the civil rights movement in the 1950s was for many churchgoers a period of moral and spiritual awakening. Foley was part of a relatively small group of would-be activists who laid the foundation for the later challenge to the South's—no less than the nation's—racial status quo. At least one small group of Catholics took the papal ideals of social justice seriously. In 1939 the Catholic Committee of the South originated when Paul D. Williams, a Virginia layman, sought to establish a social reform group that would serve as an alternative to the Marxist-influenced Southern Conference on Human Welfare. Echoing the ideas of Pius XI, Williams faulted the SCHW and secular groups like it for "neglecting the close tie-up between economics and moral principles."[18] In June 1939 a group of Catholic bishops, priests, and laymen met in Cleveland, Ohio, at the National Social Action Congress and formed the CCS.

The Catholic Committee of the South never amounted to much more than the ten annual conventions it held between its inception in 1939 and its gradual dissolution by 1953. Bishop Toolen supported the endeavor at first, but bowed out only two years after its inception. The bishop had little patience for any movement that advocated civil rights and that was not devoted exclusively to evangelization of blacks. Nevertheless, the CCS's leaders were passionate men and women who took racial justice and labor issues seriously and brought their organization's message home to their fellow churchmen and women.[19]

Bishop Toolen's impatience notwithstanding, the *Catholic Week* continued to publish regularly a CCS column and news about the annual conventions. Indeed, ten years after the Cleveland meeting, the *Catholic Week* praised the CCS for its efforts toward making the "Southland a bulwark of a Christian democracy economically as well as politically." In addition to editorial praise, it was not uncommon for ideas shared by the CCS to appear in the diocese's official organ. In February 1949, for example, one *Catholic Week* column equated those who deliberately hindered racial progress with the Roman ruler who refused to stop Jesus' execution. "The men who stand in the way of social justice and interracial justice today are . . . the many who dip their hands with Pilate's in the water." In that same column, A. J. Jackson also drew a direct connection between the ideals of American democracy and "Catholic teaching that EVERY man is the image of God, and that all men are brothers under the Fatherhood of God." The Catholic respect for human dignity, Jackson concluded, "is the foundation of our civilization."[20]

Through stories in their newspapers and the influence of bishops and certain priests, Catholic laymen in Alabama and Georgia were at least exposed to social justice doctrines, such as those espoused by Bishop William T. Mulloy of Covington, Kentucky. Delivering a sermon at the 1951 CCS meeting, Bishop Mulloy left no doubt that, in light of papal encyclicals, racial justice "is a moral question." What was more, Mulloy understood the Catholic Church to be chosen by God "as the spiritual leaders of the South." As such, "we . . . cannot remain silent," even at the expense of being labeled with "the opprobrious accusation of being 'anti-Southern.'" Mulloy spoke hopefully, certainly too optimistically. The Jesuit Foley shared Mulloy's optimism, as well as his reliance on Catholic social doctrine. In 1954 Foley served on the subcommittee on race for the Catholic Committee of the South and argued in favor of the CCS's issuing a current policy statement on race. In calling for a statement, Foley urged the CCS to reassert the applicability of "clear statements made by the Popes, the Epistles, and the Gospels, on the unity of all Catholics in the Mystical body and the equal rights of all in the Church." Foley argued that a statement by the Catholic Committee of the South could not be dismissed by white southerners, as statements by northern bishops, priests, and scholars had been.[21]

Foley's proposal demonstrated clearly the growing tension between the orthodoxy and hierarchy of the mid-century Catholic Church on the one hand, and its moral authority in racial justice issues on the other. Anticipating the Supreme Court's *Brown v. Board of Education* decision on school segregation, Foley feared that the Church was in danger of losing its moral authority to the Supreme Court. A statement by the CCS in early 1954, Foley maintained, "would reassert the traditional position of the Church as the highest moral authority in these matters of justice and right." Foley was concerned that the CCS reemphasize the Church's "Catholicity . . . the unity of all Catholics in the Church." That unity, the statement reasoned, should nullify the Church's "formerly strict division of the Church's administrative functioning along racial lines." Finally, a declaration from the Catholic Committee of the South would clarify the Church's role in society "as Mother of all the faithful of all races, defender of the oppressed, opponent of injustices, protector of the working classes from exploitation, champion of the poor and unprivileged, and clear proponent of God's truth about relationships between human beings." In such pronouncements, Foley was nothing if not optimistic. He overestimated the CCS's teaching authority in the laity's eyes and inadvertently revealed how impotent activists like him were in convincing "misguided Catholics" of the immorality of their racial prejudices.[22]

The Catholic Committee of the South may never have brought about integration of Church institutions or had any impact on southern society in general, but it was one step in the transition toward the realization that segregation was a moral problem. More importantly, the fact that it was on its way out of existence by the time of the *Brown* decision suggests something else at work among white activist Catholics, for the *Brown* decision changed the southern racial environment, and CCS reformers no longer were marginalized voices crying in the liberal wilderness. Instead, people like Foley were caught up in the extreme racial climate of the post-*Brown* South. They no longer could be so easily ignored, with the understanding that they would simply go away after their annual meeting. Their cries for moral reform had received support and vindication from the federal government, and their influence now had to be countered.

It is within this context that Foley can be most clearly understood, for the best way to assess Foley and his position in both southern society and the Catholic Church (northern and southern) is to judge him by his enemies. His antagonists often had nothing in common, save their opposition to the civil rights movement and the Jesuit's involvement in the fight for racial justice. And even then, there was considerable variance within the enemy camp. For example, some saw integration as inevitable and favored only a gradual march toward that inescapable destination, while others saw no such inevitability and offered violent opposition to desegregation. Both sides were no less opposed to Foley's presence and activism in Mobile. On the one extreme—the former—was Foley's own bishop, Thomas J. Toolen. On the other was the Ku Klux Klan. Not all white Protestants were Klansmen, to be sure, and not all agreed with the hooded order's violent extremism. But the difference between the Klan and the more moderate majority was in degree. That is, most white Protestants opposed civil rights activism and agreed with massive resistance, even if they did not burn crosses or march in hooded hatred.

The Klan's opposition to Foley is perhaps more easily understood. Indeed, the Jesuit seemed to invite the Klan's wrath, even to welcome the attention that the "dunce-cap and bed-sheet brigade" granted him. Foley made it his business, with the help of Spring Hill students, to monitor the KKK and keep tabs on their activities in the Mobile area. According to Foley's accounting of their activities, the Klan had assumed a more prominent public stance in Mobile during the summer of 1956, when a prominent white woman attempted to enroll her black foster daughter in a segregated public school.[23]

In September 1956, Foley and the Mobile chapter of the Alabama Council on Human Relations urged the city commission to pass ordinances against Klan violence. Foley himself drafted the model ordinances and delivered them to Mayor Joseph N. Langan, a fellow Catholic and the most racially liberal member of the city commission. Earlier that year, the mayor had formed a special thirty-member biracial committee to study race relations in Mobile. His fellow commissioners dissociated themselves completely from the committee, claiming, according to the *Mobile Register,* that it was "solely the project of Mayor Langan and do[es] not represent the official views of the City Commission." In September Langan concurred in the model ordinances' substance and agreed to present them to the commission. The first statute would have prohibited police membership in the Klan. The second would outlaw "intimidation by exhibit," a regulation aimed at cross burnings. Other commissioners objected to the ordinances, and a local newspaper reporter identified Foley as the one who initiated the new measures.[24]

Foley later claimed in his memoirs that this publicity was "entirely unsought." The Alabama Council on Human Relations preferred "working behind the scenes." Nevertheless, according to Foley, the Klan took notice. Local newspaper advertisements by the Klan referred to Foley as "a man of large profession and small deeds, a communist and quisling of foreign seed who wants to write new city ordinances." What precipitated their reaction to Foley is unclear from Foley's papers. His memoirs and the above quotation blame the city commission ordinances initiated by Foley. But Foley's response to Elmo Barnard, spokesman and leader of the Mobile Klan, defends a recent survey of local attitudes toward the KKK conducted by Spring Hill College students under the his supervision. Foley's statement was dated the same day (October 13, 1956) that a story ran in the *Mobile Press* about the burning of a cross at the home of a local black man, Allen Travis. Barnard denied any involvement in the burning. Barnard also took the opportunity to denounce the Spring Hill College survey and to defend his organization as "the only true, patriotic, white organization left."[25]

In his response to Barnard, Foley cited the Klan as a "subversive organization" according to the U.S. attorney general. Foley also ridiculed the white knights' patriotism. Failing to hide his venom, Foley snidely suggested that perhaps the attorney general's subversive list had recently been updated "in recognition of the Klan's patriotic activity in stirring up the Tuscaloosa riots of earlier this year, in reward for its 'patriotic' record of arson, killings, and intimidations elsewhere in the South and in our own community." Foley invited Barnard and the Klan to conduct their own "equally impartial survey and find out the facts." Foley was "convinced that the findings they would uncover would be just as damaging to their own self-appointed headship of this community as were my findings."[26]

The "Survey of Attitudes Toward the Ku Klux Klan as a Social Problem" contained five questions, each with a variety of possible answers respondents could select. The survey solicited individual opinions about the Klan (e.g., "How do you estimate it personally?") and what respondents believed should be done about the KKK. Possible responses to the first question ranged from, the Klan is "a harmless group of funmakers engaged in boyish pranks" to "an illegal, subversive organization listed by the U.S. Attorney General as subversive." As to what should be done about the Klan locally, those who answered selected possibilities ranging from "nothing" to "Governor should send in state highway patrol, call out the militia."[27]

Sixty Spring Hill students conducted the survey, polling some six hundred Mobilians. Many of the respondents were of college age (probably at Spring Hill), and not all called Mobile home. Foley reported that 85 percent of those questioned considered the Klan a threat to the community. Catholics were more likely than Protestants to consider the Klan "a grave menace," a "serious, formidable danger," or "an illegal subversive organization." One person contrasted the state of Alabama's position on the KKK with its outlawing of the National Association for the Advancement of Colored People. "It seems completely illogical to me" why a group like the NAACP, which employs "peaceful and legal ways to obtain" their goals, should be banned by state law, when the KKK was "allowed to organize and operate. . . . The KKK is, for my money, the most diabolical organization going." Another respondent labeled the KKK as "very unjust, unchristian, & undemocratic," whose members "would have to be ignorant to a certain extent."[28]

Despite the Klan's anti-Catholic reputation, there were Catholics who perceived it as not only no threat to society, but a positive good. That even a few Catholics could embrace the Klan's mission reveals that by the 1950s race had assumed greater importance than the religious differences that generated considerable anti-Catholic and anti-Protestant sentiment in the immediate post–World War II period. One Mississippi Catholic wrote a personal note to Foley, accusing the priest of being "prejudiced, hopelessly, about the segregation question." This Mississippian reasoned—as many white southerners did in the 1950s—that African Americans must be happy in the South, or else more of them would leave the region for the North. So long as Negroes were in their "place, living in harmony with the whites," then the South would remain peaceful, he concluded. A Catholic New Yorker, evidently in school at Spring Hill, acknowledged that the Klan was "against the Catholics as much as the Coloreds but I am willing to take my chances with them." One Mobile Catholic simply argued that without the Klan, "the negroes will try to overrun the U.S." A second Mobilian refused to answer the survey's questions, but she claimed a need for "more organizations like them [the KKK]. This is the only way we can run the colored people out of Mobile." According to the survey results, such extreme Catholic reaction was not the norm, but it does indicate the extent to which white Catholics tended to identify as southerners when race was a factor. Foley even accused Catholics of being Klan members.[29]

Foley took the Klan's newspaper advertisement attacking him as a personal affront. "They thereby issued a challenge to me that I could not easily walk away from without appearing to be either cowardly or stupid. I, therefore, took up this challenge and decided to go to work to see what could be done about curbing the Klan." Foley began with the Federal Bureau of Investigation, reasoning (optimistically, it turned out) that the FBI would be eager to rid the South of an acknowledged subversive organization. When that tactic proved fruitless, Foley took matters into his own hands. He obtained anonymous financial support and, with unnamed accomplices, hired an undercover man to infiltrate the local klavern. Foley's intelligence man was unable to learn the identities of Klansmen, who wore masks to their meetings. To remedy this, Foley, along with Spring Hill students and faculty, attended Klan meetings and collected license tag numbers of cars at the meetings. This led to more than one dangerous confrontation between the white knights and their Spring Hill opponents. As a result of their snooping, Foley and his Spring Hill cohorts were able to develop a social profile of the local klavern. According to their field work, the local Klan consisted of a "motley collection" of laborers and "petty salesmen," the "grim, tight-lipped, hard-faced, frustrated, Southern poor whites, who individually, are powerless to do anything and who feel important only when they assume the mantle of the fallen dead of the Civil War."[30] Foley suspected two deputy sheriffs of being members, and the sheriff "has come under suspicion as being highly sympathetic and cooperative with the Klan."[31]

Foley perceived himself to be an objective, even scholarly, observer of the Klan, someone motivated by reason and not emotion. He published several articles in national periodicals about the organization, and once prepared a talk for the local radio station entitled "An Evaluation of a Contemporary Local and Regional Social Problem." Foley referred to the proposed radio talk as an "objective and dispassionate statement of fact and history," but radio station owners believed otherwise. Fearing Klan reprisals, they refused to air it. The address may have been an accurate history of the Klan's origins and tactics, but it was nothing if not subjective and passionate. For example, Foley began the talk with a rhetorical question about the Klan's origins and how that group manages "to continue cropping up like a ghost from the grave moving about in a dark night of humanity's soul and haunting the South with a specter from the dead and by-gone past." Foley then traced the "social problem" from its Reconstruction origins to its present incarnation in the 1950s. He concluded his "objective and dispassionate" speech by appealing to his would-be listeners not to "surrender the American ideal of the rule of law for the anti-American reign of terror to which the klan beckons us."[32] Given the Klan's history of violence and intimidation, the radio station's owners probably acted prudently, if not very boldly.

On a couple of occasions, Foley and Spring Hill College became targets of hooded hooligans. One winter night in January 1957, the Klan ended one of its regular meetings by attempting to burn a cross on the campus of Spring Hill. The Klan's caravan to campus comprised two or three dozen cars. Before they successfully erected and lit the cross, however, Spring Hill students converged on them from nearby dormitories and chased the white knights off campus. No doubt embarrassed, the Klansmen returned the next night, with a smaller cross planted outside the main gates. Students retaliated by burning the Klan in effigy a few nights later.[33]

The KKK posed a more serious threat to others in and around Mobile. But not all the reaction to Foley's activism was violent, nor Klan related. Indeed, much of the opposition Foley engendered came from within his own church. He antagonized many white Catholics and showed little respect for the bishop. Not long after his failed radio debut, college authorities tried to halt his public campaign against the Klan. Foley blamed his "bull-dog Irish tenacity" for refusing to back down so easily. Other Catholics did not like Foley's KKK campaign because they feared the Klan would turn on them. Foley recalled that "local Catholic clergy and the bishop" feared a Klan rampage against vulnerable churches and schools. "The chancellor of the diocese told me that I could go ahead and make a martyr out of myself by defending the Negroes, but that I should not continue to endanger the rest of the clergy and laity by making the battle seem to be just a Catholic one." Prior to the height of his activism, Foley occasionally substituted for local pastors during Sunday masses. As he became more critical of Catholics' reluctance to take to heart their Church's teachings on justice, he received fewer invitations to speak and say mass. Eventually, he found himself persona non grata in area parishes.[34]

Father Foley also cultivated a contentious relationship with Bishop Toolen, whom he derisively labeled (privately, to be sure) "Saint Thomas." On more than one occasion, Toolen appealed to Foley's superiors to remove the Jesuit from the diocese. The first came following the Mobile Students' Interracial Council's planned trip to the seminary at Bay St. Louis. A second time, Foley angered the bishop with his role in the mediation—through the Alabama Council on Human Relations—of the desegregation of Mobile's downtown lunch counters. Foley acted at Mayor Joseph Langan's request, but Toolen irrationally feared that Foley was convening blacks "in order to train them in violent tactics for breaking up the lunch counters and causing disorders in the downtown area." Only after Langan intervened with Toolen did the ordinary withdraw his request for Foley's removal.[35]

Foley also acted as leader of the Alabama Advisory Committee of the Justice Department's Commission on Civil Rights, a position that allowed him much public exposure and a platform for his activism. Among other things, the advisory committee monitored local civil rights abuses by public officials and reported them to the civil rights commission. Foley was chairman of, and the lone Catholic on, the committee, whose members came from all over the state, from Mobile to Florence. Under the auspices of the civil rights commission, in 1961 Foley initiated a statewide questionnaire intended to study the application of justice throughout Alabama. He sent the questionnaire to attorneys, judges, and law enforcement personnel across the state. The survey itself, let alone its results, raised the ire of many white Alabamians, Catholic and non-Catholic alike. The report chronicled police brutality and mistreatment of black prisoners throughout Alabama, but particularly in Montgomery and Birmingham. Foley leaked the report to a friend at the Associated Press, and the resulting brouhaha brought condemnation upon the "race mixers" and "integrationists" who had issued the report.[36]

Montgomery's *Alabama Journal* labeled the report "libel" by "well known integrationists," whose only motivation could be "that they hope to receive their reward from the Kennedys, the Humphreys, the Reuthers and all the other crackpot politicians who think they can profit politically by circulating lies about the relations between the races in Alabama."[37] Montgomery's commissioner of public affairs, L. B. Sullivan, threatened to sue Foley and his committee. Foley received assurance from the attorney general's office that the commission on civil rights would be responsible for any legal issues or lawsuits resulting from their involvement with Justice Department projects.[38]

Evidently, a year later Foley undertook a second, expanded study of Alabama's justice system. Prompted by the response to the first report, the American Philosophical Society encouraged further investigation into sentencing differentials based on the race of victims and perpetrators of crimes. This one brought Foley to the attention of the chancery yet again, and precipitated the bishop's complaint to Foley's immediate superior, the president of Spring Hill. Robert C. Garrison, a Birmingham attorney, complained directly to Foley and then forwarded his written grievance to Toolen as well. Garrison described Foley's questionnaire as "so loaded and slanted in the direction of smearing the white people of Alabama as to be revolting." He conceded that some of the "terrible conditions" Foley described existed in "isolated instances," but those were not unique to Alabama. Monsignor Philip Cullen, the diocesan chancellor, appealed on behalf of Toolen to the Very Reverend A. William Crandell, S.J., president of Spring Hill College. Cullen claimed that Foley's questions were "'loaded,' and have caused considerable resentment among the lawyers." Cullen reminded Crandell that the archbishop had requested Foley's removal before, only to relent "because Father Smith pleaded that he be allowed to remain." Cullen urged the president to "take some steps to remedy the situation before it got worse." Crandell later informed the chancellor that "in deference to your wishes and to those of His Excellency," the sociology department had been instructed to cease its study of the administration of justice in Alabama.[39]

Foley remained near the front lines of the civil rights struggle, monitoring the progress of the Student Nonviolent Coordinating Committee and the Congress of Racial Equality's 1961 Freedom Rides in Alabama and hostility in Birmingham. In his dual capacity as president of the Alabama Council on Human Relations and chairman of the Alabama Advisory Committee to the U.S. Civil Rights Commission, Foley "became deeply involved in the Birmingham crisis." Foley's idea of civil rights agitation included "the wise use of the tactics of negotiation, court action, legislation, education, conciliation, bargaining and even direct action where this could be successful." Foley was not a gradualist, like his bishop, but he firmly believed that moral persuasion and an emphasis on human relations would bring about the desired integration. This led to Foley's break with Martin Luther King, Jr., over 1963's Birmingham demonstrations. Foley implored King to postpone demonstrations until Albert Boutwell's more moderate (relatively speaking, of course) mayoral administration could replace that of Eugene "Bull" Connor. When King refused to wait any longer, Foley then criticized the participation of school children in the confrontations with Connor's fire hoses and police dogs. Foley was not alone in his criticism of King and the 1963 demonstrations. Eight white Alabama ministers—including Catholic auxiliary bishop Joseph Durick, who was based in Birmingham—issued an open letter to King asking him to forego demonstrations, wait for negotiations to be successful, and not risk the violent confrontation that Connor was sure to welcome. That appeal from those ministers prompted King's famous "Letter from Birmingham Jail," in which he defended civil disobedience and explained why "waiting" was no longer a viable option for African Americans.[40]

Despite Foley's commitment to the ideal of integration, his moral vision would not expand to include, as he saw it, confrontation for confrontation's sake. The best route to interracial understanding was always through proper understandings of morality and Christian social justice teaching. By the late 1950s and early 1960s, Foley was not so alone in his urgent desire for southern whites to appreciate the immorality of segregation and racism. Racism had become a moral issue for some American Catholics, but even then most laypeople only reluctantly (if at all) recognized the immorality of segregation. The Catholic Church's position on civil rights in the 1950s also reveals a new ambivalence about the source of its authority. The gradual awareness of racism and segregation as moral issues introduced to southern Catholics what, for all practical purposes, was a new concept. For whites, segregation had been an acceptable component of the Catholic Church's mission in the South. But now arguments for spiritual equality before the Church introduced a moral authority in tension with traditional practices. Spiritual equality and the denial of racial superiority within the Mystical Body of Christ would be validated by the convergence of the Second Vatican Council and the civil rights movement in the 1960s. Having outsiders responsible for the black apostolate in the 1950s, however, effectively achieved both spiritual equality and southern segregation goals. It also allowed to go unresolved the tension between the hierarchy and orthodoxy of the mid-century Church and the moral authority of some bishops and popes on racial issues.

Mission work among blacks was not particularly threatening to southern white society, since white southerners typically divorced religious experience from social concerns. That is, individual conversion and a personal encounter with God were good, even desirable, but there was nothing in southern Protestant theology that would suggest such an event should necessarily lead to any change in the racial status quo.[41] So long as segregation remained the order of the day, then, bringing blacks into the Catholic Church was acceptable. Even the small handful of African Americans who attended otherwise "white" parishes probably proved to be little threat to white society. Their numbers were small and seating arrangements were clearly understood. As far as Christ the King celebrations were concerned, moreover, blacks brought up the rear of the procession. It was when Catholic priests and bishops either publicly allowed for the possibility of integration or openly advocated racial reform that the Church veered from the straight and narrow path of white southern society. By the 1950s, an increasing number of priests and bishops were doing just that. Following the lead of Catholic social doctrine, they slowly assumed segregation to be a moral issue. Prior to this, individual Catholics were lone voices—sometimes passionate and prophetic, other times academic and workmanlike—developing theological and moral arguments against racism.

In 1958 the American hierarchy declared segregation a moral wrong that could not be tolerated. The bishops' statement declared that "the heart of the race question is moral and religious" and that "segregation cannot be reconciled with the Christian view of our fellow man." They further recognized that segregation had resulted in "oppressive conditions and the denial of basic human rights for the Negro."[42] In February 1961 the bishops of Georgia and South Carolina issued a pastoral letter condemning racism and segregation. Bishops Francis Hyland (Atlanta), Thomas McDonough (Savannah), and Paul Hallinan (Charleston) proclaimed to their parishioners that "hatred is neither Christian nor American" and that "the Church is moving steadily toward the full Christian solution" to racial segregation. These relatively progressive bishops announced that Catholic schools in their dioceses would be integrated "as soon as this can be done with safety to the children and the schools." This should occur no later than the desegregation of the public schools, the prelates promised.[43] Hyland, at least, acknowledged that the "problem cannot be solved, even so far as the Church down here is concerned, by a few pastoral letters from a few Bishops." Nevertheless, McDonough, Hallinan, and he took an unsteady half step toward preparing their church members for what seemed increasingly like the inevitable.[44]

The 1960s did mark a new era for both the civil rights movement and the Catholic Church. The bishops' statement indicated the direction in which many Church leaders were ready to take their flock. One could argue that such leadership came a decade or more too late. But in fact it was too soon for most white Catholics, who were not prepared to participate in a fully integrated Church or society. For them, papal encyclicals on social justice and the notion that God and the Church showed no distinction between races did not necessarily compel equal treatment of African Americans. Whites could easily point to the evangelization of blacks and argue that the Church was not showing any prejudice based on race. But that did not mean that whites had to treat blacks as social equals. Indeed, that they would be expected to grant blacks full equality was a relatively new concept. The Church had condoned segregation for decades, and slavery since before the advent of Jim Crow. White Catholics could understandably inquire what had changed so suddenly.

By the early 1960s the Church found itself poised at the brink of a new era, prefigured in part by Foley and the Georgia and South Carolina bishops. The image of the Church as institutional and hierarchical, uniting a disparate population under a central authority, was disappearing. In its place appeared the notion of the Church as the "people of God," united by the Mystical Body of Christ and the presence of God among members of that body.[45] The Second Vatican Council, the first session of which Pope John XXIII convened in 1962, would validate this new image of the Church. Not all Catholics readily accepted conciliar changes, however. Southern white Catholics viewed them as threats to their racial status quo. The hierarchy upon which they relied to sustain segregation slowly crumbled beneath them.

Foley and the Georgia and South Carolina bishops also reveal something else about white southern Catholics in the late 1950s and early 1960s. The advent of the modern civil rights movement ensured that their primary concern was no longer defending themselves from anti-Catholic attacks. Anti-Catholicism persisted, to be sure, as the presidential election of 1960 demonstrated. Nevertheless, racial identity assumed increasing importance. White Catholics practiced the politics of exclusion themselves when they joined with other whites in distancing themselves from Foley. It is important to note that Foley was the outsider because of his civil rights activism and not because of his religion. The bishops' announcements that schools would be integrated, moreover, provoked not a few white Catholics who were comfortable with segregation and happy with their separate but equal parochial schools. As the drama of the black freedom struggle intensified in the 1960s, it was more important for many white Catholics that they were white and members of the majority who sought to defend segregation.

4

Practicing What We Preach

The ARCHDIOCESE *of* ATLANTA *and*
LIBERAL RACE RELATIONS

✦

The advent of the modern black freedom struggle created a crisis atmosphere for southern whites, and fostered an environment wherein racial, instead of religious, boundaries were of primary importance. It also aggravated internal divisions among white southern Catholics. A comparison between the Archdiocese of Atlanta and the Diocese of Mobile-Birmingham in the 1960s reveals those divisions. The Catholic Church in Georgia differed fundamentally from Toolen's diocese in Alabama. Bishop Francis Hyland and then Archbishop Paul J. Hallinan fit well with Atlanta's white boosters. Hallinan especially embodied the image that many of them sought to portray (ecumenical, positive, active, youthful, and espousing progressive ideals within the context of his church). Bishops in Atlanta did not have long-standing ties to their diocese, as Toolen did in Alabama. The Archdiocese of Atlanta was created after World War II and included Catholics who were relatively new to the region. As a result, the diocese demanded a more pastoral approach, including a greater openness to lay involvement and a willingness to lead on racial matters. Under Hallinan especially, the archdiocese embodied the notion of the Church as the people of God. Horizontal relationships between Catholics took on unprecedented importance, and bishop and lay leaders emphasized the mutual responsibilities that both whites and blacks shared toward each other. Toolen's vision of the Church continued to be institutional, hierarchical, and authoritative, traits that Hyland and Hallinan could not afford to emphasize.

In Atlanta, regional prosperity demanded at least the appearance of more progressive race relations.[1] In addition to a racially liberal archbishop, the Atlanta Church was led by prominent moderate laymen, attorneys and members of Atlanta's post–World War II business and commercial elite. An untold number of white Georgia Catholics no doubt would have preferred a more conservative approach. But by the mid-1960s, the Church in Atlanta officially endorsed the racial liberalism of Martin Luther King, Jr., and the mainstream civil rights movement. This liberalism was the product of their theology and their understanding of the Church as the Mystical Body of Christ. Church leaders did not necessarily speak for all white laity, to be sure. Indeed, leaders alienated many laymen and women, who struggled with—or opposed outright—the local Church's movement toward integration.

It is important, therefore, to emphasize the ambivalence of many white Catholics. The life and career of Georgia's most famous Catholic, short story writer and novelist Flannery O'Connor, point to the difficulty even some relatively progressive white Georgians had with the looming prospect of racial integration. Writing in the late 1940s and 1950s, O'Connor created main characters who evinced the racist attitudes and language common to many white southerners at the time. Anything less would have rendered those characters even more unreal than O'Connor's grotesque exaggerations already depicted. That same fiction revealed O'Connor's own progressive attitudes toward race and the South's black population, attitudes which were uncommon among white southerners.

The story "The Artificial Nigger," published in 1955 in the collection *A Good Man Is Hard to Find,* offers a compelling example. In that story, a grandfather, Mr. Head, and grandson, Nelson, take a train ride into the city for the ten-year-old boy's first urban experience (his second, he claims, since he had been born there and lived there the first six months of his life). Mr. Head envisions the trip as a moral lesson that the "city is not a great place." For his part, the boy has never seen a black person, but he is fascinated with the prospect of seeing "niggers." The day trip is everything the grandfather had hoped for. Forgetting their sack lunch on the train, the two go hungry for the day; they lose "the direction" and find themselves wandering the "colored" section of town; and the frightened boy collides with and injures a white woman on the sidewalk. That incident causes the grandfather to deny the child is his: "This is not my boy. . . . I never seen him before." That rejection opens a seemingly unbridgeable gulf of shame and horror between them, until they encounter a plaster lawn statue, a crude racist depiction of a black man. Both marvel at the "artificial nigger," forget the distance between them, and board the train for home. The story concludes with the grandfather's awareness of his own sinfulness and need for mercy. "He saw that no sin was too monstrous for him to claim as his own, and since God loved in proportion as He forgave, he felt ready at that instant to enter Paradise."[2]

In a 1955 letter, O'Connor claimed that the statue represented "the redemptive quality of the Negro's suffering for us all." And her work in general reflected her conviction that God's redemptive grace was readily available to even the most offensive and damnable sinners. In this sense, she represents the best of the South's—indeed, probably the nation's—liberal Catholic tradition. Certainly Father Foley believed that Catholic doctrine had much to teach white southerners about treatment of the region's African Americans. But O'Connor cannot be let off that easily. The presence of the word "nigger" throughout her stories and her correspondence is troubling enough. What is more, that correspondence also reveals deep-rooted racist ideas and stereotypes about blacks, as well as hostility toward civil rights agitators and "outsiders." At least one recent biographer has sought to reconcile these two sides of O'Connor. Paul Elie has argued that O'Connor self-consciously styled her fiction "for posterity . . . writing in anticipation of a time when blacks, the equals of whites in the eyes of God, would also be the equals of whites in society."[3] Her private beliefs clashed with her public vocation. Similarly, white Catholics in the South struggled with their church's accommodations to Jim Crow, even as many understood where the Church was leading.

In March 1960 a coalition of Atlanta's black college students launched a series of sit-ins and boycotts of downtown businesses in protest of segregation. They were joined by other civil rights organizations, and on October 19 fifty-one students and Martin Luther King, Jr., were arrested for refusing to leave Rich's Department Store, an Atlanta commercial landmark, and other downtown lunch counters. In December seven Atlanta-area Catholics wrote Bishop Hyland seeking reassurance that their bishop stood for racial justice. They argued, "Catholics living in areas of racial distinctions need to have the spiritual and moral support of a positive declaration of the teachings of Christ." Their concerns resulted from the image their local church presented to fellow Christians. As a religious minority in a Protestant region, they were "constantly under observation." And the image of the Church suffered for a lack of strong convictions on the part of Catholic leaders. One casualty of this negligence would be Catholic "missionary potential." There is no evidence that Hyland responded to the letter. Later that month, however, he signed a holiday pronouncement issued by some thirty white and black city leaders. Read from pulpits throughout the city, the joint statement urged Atlanta's churchgoers to seek peaceful solutions to racial tension and to continue "give and take" conversations between whites and blacks.[4] The ecumenical statement was probably not what Bishop Hyland's correspondents had in mind. Nevertheless, the pastoral letter from Hyland and Bishops McDonough of Savannah and Hallinan of Charleston announcing that Catholic schools would soon be integrated followed just two months later.

That 1961 statement announcing the impending desegregation of parochial schools came after much hand-wringing, soul-searching, and practical weighing of the consequences for the Church in Georgia and South Carolina. Bishop Hyland had at least considered integrating Catholic high schools in the Atlanta area some four years earlier. At the October 1957 meeting of the Archdiocesan Board of Consultors, a group of priests with whom the bishop regularly conferred, Hyland asked the board's opinion about integrating the city's new high school. There were eighty-seven black students of high school age. Two years had elapsed since the Supreme Court had declared that integration of public schools should occur "with all deliberate speed." Perhaps Hyland believed that 1957 was a promising time for the integration of parochial schools. Atlanta certainly would have been one of the earliest dioceses in the South to integrate its schools.[5]

In Atlanta, Bishop Hyland's good intentions never made their way out of the consultors' meeting. His advisers agreed that forcing school integration in the post-*Brown* South would invite retaliation from state officials, "such as taxes and loss of teaching licenses." This fear was not unreasonable for the South in the late 1950s. Politicians and white parents in Georgia were willing to close public schools or use state funds to finance transfers to segregated private schools rather than force integration. Indeed, Georgia legislators made school desegregation illegal until public pressure forced the repeal of those laws in January 1961.[6] Nevertheless, Hyland, McDonough, and Hallinan intended their 1961 announcement to gauge Catholic reaction to possible school integration. Hyland was optimistic and believed that "a substantial number of the people in the South want this issue settled justly as well as peacefully." Despite the pastoral letter, Catholic school integration in Georgia was not immediately forthcoming. Hyland conceded as much in March 1961, less than a month after issuing the school announcement.[7] Indeed, it was not until after Hallinan became Atlanta's first archbishop in 1962 that the archdiocesan schools were integrated.

Compared to the reaction of Alabama Catholics when their bishop issued a similar pastoral letter a few years later, the Georgia response was mild. Atlanta resident Hughes Spalding, a self-described "Cracker, born and bred," did not necessarily welcome the announcement; "but let's say that it is the proper thing to do and that it is inevitable." Spalding's primary concern was the general public's inherent anti-Catholicism, which he feared parochial school integration would only arouse. Others were less circumspect and more appreciative of their bishop's stance. Ferdinand Buckley, another Atlanta attorney and later president of the Archdiocesan Council of Catholic Men, congratulated Hyland "for doing the will of God." He promised that this new "courageous policy" would be supported "by the prayers of your people." A third attorney promised that he and his family were "behind you one hundred percent and will be glad to do anything we can do to help implement your letter." And the Executive Board of the Diocesan Council of Catholic Women "unanimously and enthusiastically approved" the pastoral letter and "wholeheartedly" offered their support in implementing school integration.[8]

But other whites feared potential school desegregation. Mary Bennett was the lone Catholic "in a large office of non-Catholics." Following Hyland's 1961 pastoral letter, she wished that she had been on vacation in order to be "spared the humiliation I feel this morning." Her coworkers, she reported, were "bitter toward" both Catholics and the Negro, but "I have never felt the need to lower my head until this morning." Bennett could appreciate African Americans' efforts to achieve equal rights in public facilities like integrated bus seating and job equality. But in her mind the bishops offered blacks "the churches and schools which have been built and maintained by the present parishioners, without contributions from the colored race." Negroes had their own churches and schools, and they should be content with those, just as whites "of character" were content with the ones they had built.[9] Separate facilities had been acceptable until only recently, and Bennett failed to understand what had changed to make such an arrangement no longer permissible.

For another Atlanta woman, furthermore, the possibility that her seven children might attend school with African Americans undermined her faith in Catholic institutions. Her husband was a Presbyterian, but he had "lived up to the tenets of MY church better than many Catholics do." When they were married, her husband assured the priest that he would help raise any offspring in the Catholic faith, but "Nothing was mentioned about integration. He now for the first time in our 18 years of marriage hears about the 'urgency' of a question never even brought up before." Long assured Bishop Hyland that she did not hate blacks, "but we do hate the many alien forces which are stirring up hatred between our two races." As bad as integration was, it was not the most serious problem facing white southern Catholics, according to Long. She feared that the Church would be unable or unwilling to rein in unbridled social and religious change. Those Catholics who approached integration with a certain nonchalance, in Long's mind, were the same ones who "see no harm in a Catholic girl going with a divorced man since she doesn't *plan* to marry him." Similarly, Long feared that the Catholic Church would not be satisfied with mere token integration. White school children would be forced into intimate situations with masses of "colored classmates." Integration in other Catholic organizations and activities left Betty Long questioning authority figures whom she had trusted all her life. Long informed Hyland that she could no longer tell her children, "Do whatever Father tells you," since "I never know what Father may find 'urgent' to tell them." Both state and national Catholic organizations were integrated; indeed, the year before Long's sixteen-year-old son had found himself seated next to a black girl at a state Catholic Youth Organization dinner. Such racial coeducational mixing went to the gender-based roots of many whites' fears of integration. Long and those white Catholics like her, therefore, struggled with the Church's authority in the 1960s. "We do not want them to go to protestant youth groups and yet we dare not let them go to state CYO affairs."[10] There is no indication how Long eventually resolved her dilemma, but she was not alone in her belief that the Church's about-face on segregation threatened to undermine its moral and spiritual authority on all fronts.

Interestingly, this correspondence occurred before Vatican II had convened. Betty Long associated changes in the Church and crumbling ecclesiastical authority with much larger forces—forces outside the Church and not conciliar ones necessarily. Long and Mary Bennett both—and many white Catholics in Alabama as well—could not understand why things had changed. They were comfortable in the hierarchical pre–Vatican II Church. What had been good for the Church for generations should continue to be acceptable. Anti-Catholicism aside, the Catholic Church of the 1950s and early 1960s had reached a sort of *modus vivendi* with southern society. The Church had focused its efforts on building institutions in the region and accommodating the South's racial norms, even if its members were still ambivalent about the Church's place in society. And in an unsettled and sometimes hostile environment, there was comfort in an unchanging church. But the civil rights movement jolted Catholics out of their insular world and forced an awareness that Church doctrine could be applied to society at large. Catholic acceptance of the spiritual community that movement activists evoked implied that salvation could be available to non-Catholics. The movement also forced Catholics to confront social problems rather than react defensively to prejudice. Theirs now became a positive mission, even if many white Catholics were unhappy about that mission. This 1961 exchange over promised integration reveals an almost inherent racial conservatism that opposed change of any sort. Southern white Catholics were thus predisposed to suspect conciliar reforms that the Vatican Council would promulgate in just a few years, reforms that would mimic changes already introduced by the civil rights movement.

The bishops' joint 1961 pastoral letter acknowledged at least one of the problems inherent in the southern Catholic Church's moving too quickly (relative to the rest of the South) in school integration. The South's racial problems, the bishops cautioned, "must be solved in the wider context of our missionary work." That is, integration must be implemented in such a way as to insure that parochial schools and the Church's position in southern society did not suffer. For his part, Bishop Hyland expressed a deep ambivalence with respect to his episcopal authority over the Church in north Georgia. On the one hand, he wrote to New Orleans Jesuit Louis J. Twomey that his position brought with it the authority to implement Church doctrine and serve unquestioned as "a rule[r] of the Church." On the other hand, though, the bishop should "be a Father in Christ to *all* the people committed to his charge." Hyland was torn between responsibility to his moral authority and his desire not to alienate many of his white parishioners, who comprised 94 percent of the diocese's Catholic population. Hyland defended his and the diocese's record in race relations. A "specialist" like Twomey might disagree, but Hyland concluded that his diocese had "achieved a measure of integration among our Catholic people of which I am rather proud."[11]

A couple of weeks later, Hyland addressed a pastoral letter to the two predominantly black parishes in Atlanta, Our Lady of Lourdes and St. Paul of the Cross. The bishop instructed their pastors to read the letter from the pulpit without comment. Hyland repeated his ambivalence over his episcopal authority, admitting, "I am gravely torn in spirit between these two aspects of the office of Bishop." The Atlanta ordinary promised his African American parishioners that even though he could not "carry on my weak shoulders the causes of the thousands upon thousands of Negro people who" live in north Georgia, he would bear the burdens of "our Negro Catholic people, because they are mine." But the dual nature of his office precluded him from doing anything "to harm spiritually any of our white Catholic people, however wrong some of them may be objectively in respect to proper race relations." Hyland understood it to be his "duty to establish proper race relations among all our Catholic people and I intend to fulfill this duty."[12]

But he requested that Atlanta's black Catholics be patient during the necessary "period of preparation." The challenges of bringing less than two thousand black Catholics into full participation with the diocese's more than thirty thousand whites appeared relatively simple, Hyland conceded. But the sizes of the two populations were irrelevant. The problem required "a change of heart and mind on the part of some. It is a moral and a spiritual problem." But Hyland had additional dilemmas in mind as well. Indeed, he added a third aspect to his dual role as bishop—that of Atlanta booster. Moving too quickly—and too far ahead of the rest of the region—in racial integration threatened to bring unfavorable publicity on the city and, therefore, on the

Church. Hyland recalled the "sad events" prompted in other cities by attempts to desegregate schools. He assumed that the parishioners of Our Lady of Lourdes and St. Paul of the Cross would not want similar disturbances to occur in Atlanta, "and thereby bring nationwide and no doubt world-wide disrepute upon our city." Nor would Catholics want "these unhappy things to happen" to their own properties, which "would injure the good name of our diocese." Hyland contemplated reading the same letter in the rest of Atlanta's parishes a few weeks later, but there is no indication that he did so.[13]

Along with his counterparts in Savannah and Charleston, Hyland had promised to integrate Atlanta's parochial schools "as soon as this can be done with safety to the children and the schools." At the very least, this should occur no later than the desegregation of the public schools, the prelates promised. After five years of court battles, in 1960 Atlanta's public school system finally developed an acceptable integration plan, albeit one that would bring token desegregation at first and only gradual admission of blacks into white schools. Black students would be admitted to white schools one grade per year, beginning with the twelfth grade. Following a one-year delay, nine black students were finally allowed to transfer to four white high schools.[14] But Hyland did not move right away to admit African American students to white parochial schools. That task would be left to Hyland's successor, Paul Hallinan, the former bishop of Charleston and Hyland's co-signatory in the 1961 joint pastoral statement.

An Ohio native and a priest since 1937, Hallinan was a veteran of World War II and a leader in the Newman Apostolate, the Catholic Church's ministry to college campuses. He was consecrated bishop of Charleston in 1958, where he regularly clashed with South Carolina governor Ernest F. Hollings over the state leader's opposition to integration. In South Carolina, the 1961 pastoral letter had met with the predictable resistance, and Hallinan took no subsequent steps to integrate the state's parochial schools. When he arrived as the new Archdiocese of Atlanta's first archbishop in March 1962, Hallinan told the congregation at his installation that the Church must implement its own "clear-cut teaching on racial justice." But he refused to give any firm dates when parochial schools would be integrated. Indeed, that would not be his first priority, he told a local reporter. Echoing the sentiments of his predecessor Hyland, Archbishop Hallinan advised that his first priority was "the good of the Church." Racial problems would be "worked out in that context."[15]

In May, Hallinan announced to the priests on the archdiocesan Board of Consultors that he planned to integrate parochial schools that September. Hallinan had already consulted three prominent Catholic laymen—two attorneys and a superior court judge—former mayor William Hartsfield, and a few of the priests and religious who would be directly involved in implementing school desegregation. The archbishop had obviously planned the announcement carefully, with an eye toward its reception in the archdiocese and by non-Catholics in the city. Hallinan laid out the plan for his consultors. He would issue a pastoral letter to be read in all parishes in June, and a press release would be issued simultaneously. The attention toward the media and how the announcement would be received indicates that Hallinan was keenly aware what the reaction would be. It also demonstrates his willingness to be proactive and tackle the difficult issue straight on, trusting that his ability to control the news could ease its impact among many whites. The archbishop would enlist "key people" in each parish, and the archdiocese would supply each priest with any necessary "background information." Schools would be open to all in September, with efforts to control enrollments "so that no one school is swamped with Negro children." Finally, the archbishop would prepare a *Syllabus on Racial Justice* to be used for instruction in grades seven through twelve.[16]

None of the consultors opposed the plan, but some urged caution. One priest even counseled that "some consideration should be given to the Segregationists." He suggested that a sentence be included in the statement "to ease their consciences." Archbishop Hallinan and a Monsignor O'Connor argued that would only weaken the announcement. Besides, Hallinan noted, the nation's bishops had already declared racism a moral evil. The archdiocese's plan must do nothing to counter that 1958 pastoral. Other consultors expressed concern about their own parishes and about schools outside Atlanta. A Monsignor King wanted parish boundaries to be clarified and students confined to their territorial parish. The minutes of the meeting offer no further explanation, but King's concern probably was rooted in a fear that white students would flee those parish schools that did allow any of the archdiocese's approximately seven hundred black students to enroll. Most agreed that now was the appropriate time.[17]

On June 10, 1962, priests of the Archdiocese of Atlanta read from their pulpits Hallinan's pastoral letter announcing the desegregation of parochial schools in September. Hallinan noted that Atlanta's Catholic churches "have always been open to everyone regardless of race or color." Whites and blacks had attended mass and received sacraments together "for generations." And "excellent schools, as well as pioneer Negro missions, have been established to reach and teach the Negro, not to segregate him." But the Church "has moved forward." Open admission to parochial schools in 1962 was "the logical step," one that "protects the freedom of choice which is the right of Negro parents and children as Catholics and Americans." At a press conference that morning, Hallinan admitted to a reporter that he was worried that the state legislature might retaliate by taking away Catholic schools' tax-exempt status and teachers' licenses. But such state action was "less likely now than . . . a year ago."[18] Indeed, the archbishop had prepared his new archdiocese well. Reaction was relatively mild, and state officials did not intervene.

Hallinan did not have to deal with the very public, and potentially embarrassing, reaction of some prominent white laypeople that announcements of impending parochial school desegregation in other archdioceses often provoked. Hallinan understood that whites would raise questions about the immediacy of desegregation. While Bishop of Charleston, he had appointed a committee to draw up a syllabus on racial justice to be used in the Catholic schools there. He adopted a similar document for teachers to use in grades seven through twelve in Atlanta-area parochial schools. According to Hallinan, Catholics were only indirectly responsible for the legal, political, and economic impact of race discrimination and integration. "But we are directly responsible for the moral course our Catholic people follow." As a result, the archbishop intended the *Syllabus on Racial Justice* "to give our young Catholics fresh insight into the Church's teachings on one of our most urgent social problems." Hallinan's instruction to teachers also reflected the changing nature of authority southern Catholics faced in the 1960s. He instructed teachers to emphasize that the principles taught in the syllabus reflected "a *development, not a reversal,* of traditional Catholic doctrine." But the relatively recent condemnation of racism and segregation as moral evils left many white Catholics uncomfortable with the Church hierarchy's moral leadership. Hallinan recognized this. "Where parents disagree with the practical application of a Catholic truth," the archbishop warned, "it will be necessary to use great care not to lessen the child's honor and obedience." But students were to learn that the "obligation to teach" rested with the bishops of the Church and "decisions issuing from the Bishops can never be ignored."[19]

Three aspects of Catholic doctrine framed the lessons of the syllabus: the universality of the Church, the virtue of justice, and the Mystical Body of Christ. The universality of the Church meant that the Catholic Church's duty was to teach divine truths. The syllabus reminded students that "what the Church teaches is not of human, but of divine origin. The Church teaching, is Christ teaching." And the divine truth was that the Church recognizes the equality of all men. Racial segregation was wrong because the Supreme Court had ruled it unconstitutional and the bishops of the United States had declared it immoral. The syllabus taught, therefore, that "present day segregation is opposed to the full implications of the Universality of the Church."[20]

The sum of the other two doctrines, justice and the Mystical Body of Christ, governed Catholics' relations to others. The Pauline notion of the organic body of Christ, more than any other doctrine, should dictate Catholic attitudes on racial justice, the syllabus warned. Baptism and reception of the sacraments bound all Catholics—white and black—together in communion with the universal Church, "a union far more intimate and real than even the physical union of living members within a physical body." Each member of the Mystical Body of Christ was responsible for all others. "What we do to any member," the syllabus cautioned, "we do to Christ. The application of this to the question of the unity of the races (white and Negro) is obvious."[21]

But in case the answer was not as obvious as Hallinan assumed, the syllabus later spelled out the practical implications of the doctrine of the Mystical Body of Christ. The supernatural union of all members encompassed "every nationality and race" and precluded exclusion or segregation based on race or color. The syllabus then listed specific areas of discrimination wherein "this truth" should apply—employment, housing, education, voting, public services, and a "refusal of honor and respect." The same principles of non-discrimination applied to non-Catholics, "who are admittedly outside the membership of the Mystical Body." Many of those non-Catholics shared "the life of grace" and all were potential members of the Church. By applying the doctrine of the Mystical Body of Christ to society at large, Hallinan and Atlanta Catholic educators reinforced the ecumenical foundation upon which many Georgia Catholics—the archbishop included—relied in their civil rights activism. For those white Catholics who might appeal to the hoary doctrine of states' rights to resist forced integration, the syllabus had an explicit warning. That issue held no weight and "cannot be invoked here to defend Racial Segregation since the State has no power to uphold a law or custom that is unconstitutional and unjust."[22]

Archbishop Hallinan certainly dominated official diocesan policy and expected his parishioners to adhere to Catholic social doctrine. But official pronouncements were formal steps that offered only limited success. The "matter of racial *understanding*," he acknowledged, "is our burden for many a year to come." The archbishop relied on several prominent laymen in the archdiocese to promote racial justice. The St. Martin's Council on Human Relations was a Catholic interracial group devoted to encouraging and demonstrating racial justice. In 1964 the membership roll numbered 104, but only between thirty and fifty of those were active members. Members of the council—along with various priests and nuns—participated in local civil rights demonstrations. But primarily the council continued to be one of the arbiters for the archdiocese's interracial activities. Indeed, a council subcommittee warned members that "our activity must be Catholic activity, since we are not designed for military demonstrations, nor are we a political body." Their goal was to reach the Catholic community. After Hallinan's announcement of school desegregation, for example, the St. Martin's Council sponsored panel presentations to promote racial understanding in individual parishes. Between August 1963 and June 1964, the council's information panel visited every parish and high school in the archdiocese. Panel topics included "A History of Race Relations," "The Origin of Racial Tensions," "Science and Race," "Morality and the Racial Question," "The Church and Race," and "What Can We Do To Ease Racial Tensions." The panel reported that attendance at local presentations "was good in most parishes, especially in those outside of Atlanta." But the larger parishes in the city mustered only disappointing turnouts.[23]

St. Martin's Council on Human Relations served effectively as an interracial example to the city of Atlanta. In 1964 Gerard Sherry, the white lay editor of the *Georgia Bulletin,* was president of the council and participated in the monthly meetings of the Atlanta Negro Summit Leadership Conference. "Our advice has been sought and given to the Leadership group on many pressing problems including housing and education," Sherry noted. He credited St. Martin's with thwarting "the more militant members of the Summit Leadership from taking precipitous action which would cause fruitless demonstrations and increased tensions." In addition, the council cooperated with the Southern Christian Leadership Conference, the Southern Regional Council, and the Georgia Human Relations Council. In fact, Sherry served as director of the latter group in 1963. In 1965, Sherry reported, parishioners of Holy Cross and Immaculate Heart of Mary parishes served on the DeKalb County Human Relations Council.[24]

These laypeople were part of a growing ecumenical movement. Moderate and liberal Catholics were beginning to recognize that they had much in common with Christians of other denominations. Catholic doctrine, they believed, certainly contained all the necessary elements to solve the South's racial problems. Yet Catholics alone could not produce lasting change by themselves. The members of St. Martin's Council on Human Relations who participated in other civic groups demonstrated this same interfaith commitment. Archbishop Hallinan created an environment conducive to such cooperation. His friendships with Jewish and Protestant leaders and with secular civic officials set prominent examples. Also, the *Georgia Bulletin,* the archdiocesan newspaper, under the editorial leadership of Gerard Sherry, regularly engaged secular and ecumenical issues. Through the paper, Sherry and Hallinan demonstrated the boundaries of Christian liberals' support for the civil rights movement. Their uncompromising arguments for racial justice and integration placed them in the company of civil rights activists who saw the movement as a religious event, a redemptive opportunity that would ultimately reconcile blacks and whites in a "beloved community." As early as the mid-1950s, Martin Luther King, Jr., had labeled the Montgomery bus boycott a spiritual movement. Segregation, according to King, "is a blatant denial of the unity which we all have in Jesus Christ." The civil rights movement's goal, then, was reconciliation, a reminder that all were one in Jesus Christ.[25] Sherry and Hallinan embraced the movement's ability to unite blacks and whites in a single godly community. Catholics' "people of God" paralleled the "beloved community" and made greater ecumenism and inclusivity mandatory for Catholics. For Sherry, however, Christian social justice stopped when "extremists" displaced the moral vision of leaders like Martin Luther King, Jr. Those extremists preferred violence to Christian morality and proved more racially divisive than interracially unifying.

Hallinan had founded the archdiocesan newspaper in January 1963. The first two issues described the organ's purpose as "the representative mouthpiece of all Catholic thinking and information. It must protect the vital interests of Catholics in a community . . . [and it] must fight for the reform of any conditions which are a denial of the dignity of man or an obstacle to his progress." One pressing issue, the editorial board noted, was "the problem of race." The nation faced two choices: "being heroically faithful to our country's most ancient and honorable ideals, or being locked in a trap made by money and supported by neurosis." America must be able to rely on the Catholic Church for help, the *Bulletin* warned. Both the "injured man of color" and the "warped man who hates" should be able to turn to the Church. The man of color should find a "helping hand," while the hateful man must not "find fire for his prejudice, but instead the cool balm of reason and the reassuring strength of maturity. By very definition, a Catholic is an integrationist." It was the duty of the Catholic newspaper, and Catholics everywhere, "to make this clear to all who will listen."[26]

The archbishop set the newspaper's agenda and then turned over the reins to Sherry, an experienced journalist, with two priests to assist the layman. The editor wasted little time engaging secular civil rights issues that had ramifications outside the Church. Only a couple of issues into the new organ's existence, Sherry attacked Atlanta's "'Wall' of Shame," a metal and concrete barrier intended literally to block black migration into white neighborhoods on the west side of the city. In efforts to restrict African American movement into previously all-white neighborhoods, the city of Atlanta built new roads or put up other physical obstacles to enforce racial segregation. In late 1962 a black doctor attempted to purchase a house in the Peyton Forest subdivision, an otherwise white development. White residents requested that two roads (Peyton and Harlan) be closed to north-south travel and that barricades be constructed in order to protect the integrity of the neighborhood boundaries. The city, with Mayor Ivan Allen, Jr.'s blessing, complied, until unfavorable publicity threatened to spoil Atlanta's civil rights image.[27]

Sherry saw racial conflict over "The Wall" as yet another element of a perennial problem, the struggle to insure blacks' right to obtain decent housing in nice neighborhoods while dealing with white fears. If one were honest, however, those "White fears" would fall under a different heading—"prejudice. This vice is hidden in all our hearts" and surfaced only when confronted with racial problems. Removing prejudice "requires the fullness of charity and humility." But most whites—"even among Catholics"—lacked an essential understanding of the "unity of the human family," Sherry acknowledged. When the Fulton County Superior Court forced the city to remove the wall two months later, Sherry praised the decision as "the opportunity to show the rest of the country that it [Atlanta] is way ahead in establishing harmonious race relations." Sherry, the racially liberal Catholic layman, supported the right of blacks to "decent housing in decent neighborhoods," but he warned that achieving integrated neighborhoods would take time. "A call for patience in this regard," however, "must not be construed as promotion of the heresy of gradualism."[28]

Indeed, Sherry was not one to show much patience for those who believed that anything less than immediate integration was sufficient. He saw the need for demonstrations and was not surprised that blacks might be impatient at the lack of progress. But Sherry drew distinctions within both the black and white communities and singled out "extremists" who only caused trouble. He favored a type of moral center, based on a commonly accepted natural law that was recognized across denominational divides, by Catholic, Jews, and Protestants alike.

When Klansmen set off a bomb at Birmingham's Sixteenth Street Baptist Church in September 1963, Sherry blamed "extremists" who had been in control "while the so-called moderates have been satisfied with pious clichés unrelated to the basic problem." In that instance, the extremists were white, for whom the Church had made clear the immorality of segregation. White Catholics should stake out the moral center, "rise above the mob, and consciously accept the teaching of the Church." But civil rights activists could be equally guilty of extremism. In 1963 when the Supreme Court reversed the convictions of lunch counter demonstrators in four southern states, Sherry praised the decision but also cautioned that "we must not read into it a mandate

to indiscriminate trespass." Sherry questioned recent Atlanta disturbances in which sit-in demonstrators singled out a restaurant owned
by "a confirmed segregationist." He deplored the restaurateur's "harsh
reaction"; however, "it seemed silly . . . at this stage to goad him with
their actions." Progress would only "be speeded by the calm balm of
reason on both sides."[29]

Sherry and other Catholic liberals favored the moral suasion and
civil disobedience of Martin Luther King, Jr., over the violence and
intimidation of black nationalists. Sherry warned that any attempt to
abandon "the non-violent rule in Negro demonstrations would be fa-
tal. It would assist only the White extremists who desperately seek ways
to avoid general acceptance of the Negro as an equal." Non-violent
demonstrations were necessary components of the moral middle,
efforts "to establish a right which has always been theirs, but which
always has been denied them." According to Sherry, full equality for
African Americans appeared inevitable in 1963. The question was
whether that occurred "through the voice of nonviolent leaders like
Martin Luther King, or through the violent approach of Black Muslims
or other 'white-haters.'" The "Christian conscience cries out against injustice," and the civil rights movement needed Christian leadership.[30]

Fear of extremism, Sherry warned, should not lead to inaction.
"Religious leaders, especially," he explained, "should be careful that
they do not lead their congregation into a state of ennui, simply because to take a strong stand would rock a boat or a congregation."
Instead, "a just and peaceful solution" required ecumenical cooperation and action. That ecumenism should be based on a common
"natural-law morality" which "everybody with a normal human mind
should be able to understand and accept." Catholics had "additional
and deeper reasons for respecting human rights," but both Protestants
and Jews saw the injustice of racial discrimination "as clearly as do
Catholics."[31]

The moral middle that Sherry believed should guide civil rights activism always emphasized the common good over individual rights, a
tenet that the Georgia layman located in Catholic doctrine. According
to the principle of subsidiarity, the purpose of any social organization
"is to help its members and never to destroy or absorb them." Social
functions, according to Catholic doctrine, were always conducted
by the smallest group possible. The principle emphasizes individual

property rights, but many whites, Sherry noted, invoked it "to justify their refusal to allow Negroes to be served on their property." But "individual property rights are not absolute." The common good must always prevail. Sherry used this principle to justify support of the 1964 Civil Rights Act. Initiated in 1963 after events in Birmingham convinced President Kennedy that the federal government should get involved, the act finally passed when President Johnson put the full weight of his personality and political skill behind it. The act was a direct attack on the South's system of de jure segregation and went far toward toppling the racial status quo. Ominously for white southerners, the act created a federal bureaucracy to enforce its provisions and brought the guarantee of racial justice under a federal umbrella.[32]

The public accommodations portion of the bill offended local autonomy southerners the most. That provision banned discrimination in privately owned businesses, including theaters, restaurants, and hotels. George Wallace referred to the act as "the most monstrous piece of legislation ever enacted." When the 1964 bill passed the House of Representatives, Sherry editorialized that it was "an encouraging step in the quest for racial justice." The *Bulletin*'s editor attacked the Atlanta Restaurant Association, whose "trite clichés out of the past" insisted that their property rights had to prevail over equal rights for Negroes. On the contrary, Sherry argued, the common good—which included an end to racial discrimination—justified state intervention. Indeed, the "failure of individuals and groups, including some restaurant owners, to fulfill their social obligations to the community, has made such legislative coercion necessary."[33]

Sherry's editorials elicited a variety of responses from Georgia's Catholics. Some refuted the use of Catholic doctrine to challenge constitutionally protected individual and property rights. Fred T. Humphrey, a Catholic from Smyrna, Georgia, requested that the *Bulletin* no longer be sent to his home, since its "articles are generally fuzzy and without logic or substance." The editorial in support of the Civil Rights Act, moreover, was "a blow to personal freedom." Contrary to Sherry's claim that divine law should serve the general welfare of society, Humphrey argued for a strict separation of church and state. "'[D]ivine law' for each religious denomination has different meanings," he noted, "and for the agnostic and the atheist, divine law means nothing. If this is to be a free country, then it must be guided by civil laws, not divine laws." Humphrey's argument to Sherry reflected the post-*Brown* civil religion of personal freedom that Southern Baptists adopted in response to the Supreme Court's attack on separate but equal schools.[34] More significantly, his rhetoric suggests that he had adopted some of the anti-Catholic rhetoric on church-state issues that characterized earlier Protestant attacks on his church.

Ferdinand Buckley defended the constitutionality of the proposed Civil Rights Act and argued that it was consistent with current Georgia law. Buckley was an Atlanta attorney and president of the Archdiocesan Council of Catholic Men in 1964. He and his wife, Marianne, actively participated in civil rights demonstrations and often entertained African Americans in their home in the 1960s. The lawyerly tone of his letter to the editor belied the passion he and his family would later evince in support of racial justice and equality. He claimed that anyone who based his opposition to the public accommodations section of the civil rights bill "upon constitutional grounds is in danger of stretching the Constitution, if nothing else." Common law, Buckley argued, evolved to delineate the obligations of, for example, both innkeepers and travelers. And the Georgia Code of 1933 spelled out the relationships between proprietors and their customers. The businessperson who advertises his services "'is bound to receive as guests, as far as he can accommodate them, all persons of good character offering themselves, who are willing to comply with his rules.'" The public accommodations provision of both Georgia state law and the 1964 Civil Rights Act "is completely supported by logic and justice," Buckley concluded. Indeed, the common law support for the provision dated to the scriptural account of the Good Samaritan. "Nothing has happened since then to make it or any of the principles embodied in the Civil Rights Bill unreasonable, unconstitutional or un-Christlike."[35]

Editors of the *Georgia Bulletin* agreed. In April 1964 they devoted half a page of news column to an explanation of various aspects of the Civil Rights Act. "Sharing as we do the sense of urgency attached by the Administration" and other agencies, the editors published a summary of the bill and answers to questions about it. They drew the material from a pamphlet published by the Leadership Conference on Civil Rights. They concluded that the "summary correctly points out that the bill does not attempt to abolish prejudice by law." A person had a right to his or her individual prejudices. "But he does not have the right to translate them into actions that deny or infringe on the rights and liberties of others."[36]

When Lyndon Johnson signed the Civil Rights Act in July 1964, Sherry declared its passage "a time of unbridled joy." But there should also be "some sombre reflection on its implications." The act merely reinforced the constitutionality of—and provided legal support for—those rights that African Americans should have already enjoyed. But with the formal recognition of those rights, Sherry argued, came certain obligations and responsibilities. The "Negro community must begin to develop that mark of maturity and stability which many of their critics say they do not possess." In addition, they would be expected "to grasp willingly and diligently the new opportunities of education and jobs in the self-advancement so urgently required." The passage of the Civil Rights Act should be the necessary transition point between "belligerency" and "a more friendly approach" that held no animosity toward whites. Giving up their "belligerency" required a lot from blacks, Sherry acknowledged, "for they have suffered much at the hands of many of us, and for many years." Their "maturity," however, would best be measured "in their being able to forgive." Both white and black Catholics should be able to assist in this transition. Because of Catholics' responsibility to the Mystical Body of Christ, they "must strive for the betterment of [their] neighbors, Negroes included, with the same energy that divine blessings are sought for self."[37]

When Martin Luther King, Jr., won the Nobel Peace Prize in 1964, his hometown stood to suffer a very public black eye if white Atlantans did not acknowledge the award and honor their native son. The city had worked hard in the 1960s to cultivate an image of racial moderation coupled with New South progress, and failure to honor King would have tarnished its national reputation. But most of Atlanta's white leaders proved reluctant to honor the man whom they blamed for causing racial unrest and boycotting downtown businesses. No white businessmen would take the initiative. Archbishop Hallinan joined with three other prominent Atlantans (two white, one black)—Rabbi Jacob Rothschild, Morehouse College president Benjamin Mays, and *Atlanta Constitution* editor Ralph McGill—to sponsor a banquet in January 1965 in honor of the civil rights leader. Racially liberal mayor Ivan Allen, Jr., tried but failed to rally the white business community, some of whom bought tickets at the last minute only to avoid embarrassment.[38]

Governor Carl Sanders neither attended nor sent an official representative. No leaders of the city's white Protestant churches were there either, though the secretary of the Georgia Council of Churches spoke. The archbishop left a hospital stay early to attend the banquet at Atlanta's Dinkler Plaza Hotel ballroom. Two decades later, Mayor Allen recalled that "Archbishop Hallinan was a prime mover in seeing that the business community supported that dinner." And King himself wrote "to express my deep gratitude for your sponsorship of the dinner honoring me." King described Hallinan's brief tribute as "both eloquent and moving and I shall treasure them amongst the storehouse of memories as a light of encouragement for the many dark and desolate days of struggle which are before us." Hallinan praised the civil rights leader as "a pioneer in a new dynamic of peace . . . a creative leader in racial justice, as a man . . . who has raised justice through non-violence from a tactic to a high form of authentic Christian love."[39]

The Atlanta dinner honored King as he and other civil rights activists were intensifying their efforts to highlight voting rights abuses in Alabama. From January to March of 1965, members of both the Student Nonviolent Coordinating Committee and the Southern Christian Leadership Conference had wrangled with local police, election officials, and judges in Selma as they planned and carried out regular voting rights demonstrations. Following the late February death of Jimmy Lee Jackson, who had been shot by an Alabama state trooper during a demonstration, activists decided to undertake a march from Selma to Montgomery, the state capital some fifty miles away. The first attempt, held on Sunday, March 7, met with violent resistance from Alabama state troopers and local sheriff's deputies as demonstrators crossed the Edmund Pettus Bridge out of Selma. Two weeks later, three hundred activists completed the trek and on March 25 held the scheduled voting rights rally at the state capitol. That voting rights campaign prompted white civil rights sympathizers from outside the state to travel to Selma to support the demonstrations. Those white activists included northern priests and nuns, whose presence rankled not a few local white Catholics. Their participation had been prompted by a call from King for white clergy from all over the country to join the demonstrations; and much of it was organized by the National Catholic Conference for Interracial Justice and local Catholic Interracial Councils across the country.[40]

King left Selma to attend the Atlanta banquet and returned there the next day determined to increase the pressure on white officials. The 1965 Selma demonstrations challenged Alabama's social status quo and revealed the extent to which the state's white Catholics separated themselves from their church's moral authority and identified with the South's racial hierarchy. Archbishop Toolen criticized the participation of priests and nuns in the marches, and many whites rallied to his defense and claimed him as their religious spokesman. Even a handful of Georgians turned to him, disgruntled over their own archbishop's liberal stands.[41]

Six Atlanta priests requested permission to go to Selma and participate in the marches. Hallinan first refused the request, fearing for the safety of his priests. Within twenty-four hours, however, the archbishop reversed himself and granted permission. "No priest or laymen was sent," Hallinan wrote a few weeks later in response to critics; "they asked to go with approval—and it was given." Hallinan granted permission on the condition that their parish work not be neglected and that they give only one sermon the following Sunday explaining their participation and the significance of the demonstrations. The participation of Atlanta priests was important, in Hallinan's mind. They were southern priests who "testified to the overwhelmingly good element in the South and this, I feel, was often overlooked by many who came to Selma to demonstrate."[42]

Complicating the social situation for southern Catholics was the convergence of the civil rights movement with the Second Vatican Council in the early 1960s. This union of events presented southern Catholics with a unique, sometimes troublesome challenge. The social order and faith with which most were quite comfortable both underwent unsettling changes. Under the leadership of Martin Luther King, Jr., African Americans asserted their constitutional right to the vote and demanded an end to separate but equal educational and public facilities. Under the guidance of Pope John XXIII and his successor Paul VI, the Roman Church in effect reinvented itself, dramatically altering the liturgy and redefining the very nature of the Church. That these events occurred simultaneously is surely coincidence, but their convergence suggested to many southern Catholics that something was amiss in their world. They believed that liturgical and racial reforms forced them to choose sides: either accept the racial segregation that characterized southern society or embrace the renewed, modern Church.

Catholics were called on to engage secular society and take responsibility for improving social problems, the most important of which in the 1960s seemed to be direct results of racial discrimination. Most white Catholics in Alabama and Georgia only reluctantly supported their church's emphasis on and broader conception of social justice and individual liberty, preferring instead the gradualism of a pre-conciliar Catholicism that made it easier to procrastinate on issues of racial discrimination. Some Atlantans expressed their grievances directly to Hallinan or to the editor of the *Georgia Bulletin,* upset over the changing nature of the Church in the mid-1960s and what they perceived as a lack of properly instituted authority. Still others defended the voting rights demonstrations and either participated or served in support roles.

An Atlanta woman and her family announced their intention to withhold their financial contributions to the Church "as long as members of the Holy Orders make ridiculous public spectacles of themselves in cheap nigger politics." Instead, because their religious leaders had been "mesmerized by a protestant, common rabble-rouser," their money would go to "the white Police fund in Selma and Montgomery, Alabama." Others were not as harshly opposed to civil rights reform in principle, but they expressed discomfort with the tactics employed in Selma. These gradualists eschewed the immediate results demanded by activists in favor of piecemeal reform that might result from moral suasion. Leo E. Reichert, Jr., of Decatur, Georgia, argued that there were Catholics "who believe in the brotherhood of Christ and the dignity and equality of the negro in the eyes of God," but who opposed civil disobedience "and obvious incitements to violence." Archbishop Toolen, Reichert claimed, was in a better situation to evaluate local problems and his authority should have been respected.[43]

Another Decatur resident blamed priests' and nuns' newfound racial justice activism on the Church's recent emphasis on ecumenism. "Isn't ecumenism wonderful?" J. J. Conoley, Jr., questioned in a sarcastic letter to the editor of the *Georgia Bulletin.* Only a few years earlier, nuns would not have been "parading with beatniks on Pennsylvania Avenue" or "arm-in-arm with Negro men in Selma." And priests would not have turned to lawbreaking "rather than to 'render unto Caesar what is Caesar's.'" Those priests and nuns who demonstrated "in a carnival spirit," Conoley argued, took the easy way out. More appropriate would have been working "tireless hours at thankless tasks, such as, teaching Negroes to be qualified to vote." Conoley ignored the main focus of the Selma-to-Montgomery march—the lack of voting rights for Alabama's blacks. But he was quick to sound a theme common to many white southerners at the time. The outsiders should have minded their own affairs back home instead of being allowed "to invade another Diocese."[44]

Official archdiocesan policy was clear, however, and Atlantans did play a role in the demonstrations. One Atlanta woman called her participation in the march to Montgomery "the most deeply moving spiritual experience of my life." Immediately after the march, Janet Rogan went to the chapel of Montgomery's Catholic hospital "to offer my Thanksgiving." She pondered "the solitude of the Blessed Sacrament" and longed for the sacrament to "have been there with us instead of behind those tabernacle doors." Christ had marched to Calvary "to change the political and social order for all men," and the physical presence of his body and blood could have emboldened the marchers. But Rogan inadvertently pointed to one of the theological transitions that resulted from the Second Vatican Council—the reclarification of the Church as the people of God. During the march, she noted being "acutely aware of the Presence of God among His people in an atmosphere of Love and Suffering." For Rogan, then, the civil rights movement provided a concrete example of the conciliar doctrine and an opportunity to practice the ecumenism encouraged by her archbishop.

The priests who participated in the Selma to Montgomery march took their turn among the clergy who led prayers on the "front line" of demonstrators as they confronted Alabama state troopers. In addition to those six priests, one lay member of St. Martin's Human Relations Council went to Selma for the demonstrations. And other laymen assisted from Atlanta. Many would-be demonstrators were left in the lurch in Atlanta's airport en route to Selma. Dr. Joseph Wilbur served as the contact person for them. "Five or six times during the Selma crisis," the president of St. Martin's Council reported, Wilbur picked people up at the airport. One night six priests and six laymen slept in his home, and other council members housed additional stranded marchers.[45]

Gerard Sherry reported from Selma for the *Georgia Bulletin*. His March 11 editorial described the brutality of state troopers against marchers as "reminiscent of the worst days of Nazi oppression." Recent events in Selma were "what we would expect in a Fascist or Communist country where despots survive only by oppression and terror." States' rights was not the issue. "The Alabama brutality is a consequence of the indifference of the majority who have remained silent." Sherry reported tension within the movement participants themselves. Young and "more militant" activists feared that the presence of clergymen would actually be a "restraining hand in the frequent demonstrations" and hinder civil rights progress. But Sherry credited the religious presence in Selma with enabling "the extraction of concessions from the city fathers which they never would have contemplated if they had had to deal only with local Negroes."[46]

Voting rights marchers eventually completed the trek to Montgomery, and later that year President Johnson signed the Voting Rights Act into law. Similar to the Civil Rights Act a year earlier, the Voting Rights Act gave the federal government the authority to intervene in the South in order to insure that blacks were not denied the right to vote. With its passage and that of the Civil Rights Act the year before, civil rights activists essentially achieved their legal goals—equality of opportunity. But the Selma demonstrations carried even greater significance. They helped delineate the boundaries separating Catholic proponents of civil rights from opponents of racial equality and any threat to the status quo. Success in Selma emboldened supporters of the movement and decreased the moral authority—at least among activists—of Church leaders like Alabama's Toolen, whose criticism of demonstrators only encouraged defiance. Archbishop Hallinan, by contrast, increased efforts to use the Church as a tool to improve racial justice.

On July 28, 1965, Archbishop Hallinan convened a three-day conference on "Social Change and Christian Response" in Atlanta. The archdiocese co-sponsored the event with the National Catholic Conference for Interracial Justice, and the St. Martin's Council on Human Relations served as local host for the meeting. The conference brought together five bishops and "several hundred" priests, nuns, and Catholic and Protestant laymen representing twenty-five dioceses and fifteen states to discuss civil rights legislation and the Church's responsibilities in racial and social justice. In addition, representatives of civil rights organizations such as the Southern Regional Council, the Congress of Racial Equality, and the Southern Christian Leadership Conference also led panel discussions and conference sessions.[47]

In his keynote address, Hallinan encouraged Catholics and other religious activists not to abandon the fight for racial and social justice to secular forces. Their moral leadership was necessary. Clergy and nuns in the Selma demonstrations were "not shock troops to be exploited. They are witnesses to justice and love, giving their presence to communities where justice and love have been diminished." They were "co-workers with the Negro in the great social development that is in process." Hallinan then emphasized the recent Vatican Council's "entirely new grasp of what the Church means." Rather than the Church being defined solely as a hierarchical institution, the Council emphasized the notion of the Church as the "People of God." This recasting of that traditional doctrine was based on the Pauline image of the Church as organic Mystical Body of Christ and stressed the servant nature of the Church. For Hallinan, this meant that the Church—that is, those people from bishops to laity who constituted Catholicism—"must initiate and quicken the Christian response as a catalyst accelerates the change in a chemical process."[48]

The substance and timing of the conference point to the relationship in Catholics' minds between the civil rights movement and reforms being issued by the bishops meeting in Rome in the mid-1960s. Hallinan drew an explicit connection between conciliar reforms and the fight for racial justice, but it is important not to assume a causative relationship between the two. In many respects, Vatican Council reforms merely codified what was already happening, at least for American Catholics, who were required to confront a new place for their church in public life. For his part, Hallinan created an environment for the members of his archdiocese to engage in this sort of Christian activism. And he forced upon white Catholics the opportunities—and obligations—to live as the people of God within archdiocesan institutions. Archbishop Hallinan moved ahead of other bishops and Church leaders in encouraging racial justice; but circumstances in secular southern society often dictated the timing and success of Hallinan's initiatives. He did make it increasingly difficult, it would seem, for area white Catholics to ignore the implications of their faith. As the response to threatened parochial school integration and the Selma voting rights demonstrations revealed, however, many whites in Atlanta did not like those implications. Segregation had dictated the makeup of the Church's infrastructure and had guaranteed that black Catholics would remain second-class citizens. The preconciliar hierarchy had protected racial order. Everyone understood his or her place within Jim Crow boundaries, and there were no theological grounds for challenging that status quo. But understanding the Church as the "people of God" reduced that hierarchy and made blacks and whites spiritual and, by implication (at least theoretically), social equals. That was what made Vatican II so threatening to many southern white Catholics.

5

Not Practicing What We Preach

ALABAMA *and* CONSERVATIVE
RACE RELATIONS

✦

As Georgians' reactions to civil rights activism and the reforms of Vatican II demonstrate, the crisis of the 1960s set Catholic against Catholic, and the tension in the South encompassed spiritual and racial issues. In many ways Archbishop Toolen reflected the anxiety within the Alabama Church as the modern South developed. As the spiritual leader of a missionary diocese, he orchestrated a respectable increase in Catholic population and built churches, schools, and hospitals over the course of his forty-two-year reign. Jealous of his authority, Toolen embodied the orthodoxy that so many white southerners craved at mid-century. Firmly entrenched in the pre–Vatican Council Church, Toolen intended his authority to go unquestioned, and many of the Church's white communicants were comfortable in the spiritual and social hierarchy of traditional Catholicism. Toolen provides a fascinating study in apparent contradictions. He was at once racist and paternalistic, and yet mindful of the Church's spiritual obligations to African Americans and aware of the Church's position on social justice policy that was supposed to preclude any racism and unequal treatment of blacks by whites. Bishops Francis Hyland of Atlanta and Thomas J. McDonough of Savannah—and Hyland's successor Archbishop Hallinan—were a younger generation, with few longstanding ties to their dioceses and greater willingness to press the bounds of southern orthodoxy by applying the Church's social ethic to racial justice issues.

Tension over the Church's temporal and spiritual authority was particularly acute in Alabama. With a few exceptions, Church leaders there did not see the need to oppose segregation actively. If they did see that need, their precarious position in southern society made such opposition risky. But as the 1960s unfolded they realized that the civil rights and anti–civil rights movements threatened to upset the region's delicate social and racial balance. From a white Catholic perspective, the threat to social stability was a serious issue. Following Governor George Wallace's infamous "segregation today, segregation tomorrow, segregation forever" 1963 inaugural address, eleven Birmingham clergymen released an appeal for moderation in the state's race relations. Among these clerics was the Diocese of Mobile-Birmingham's Auxiliary Bishop Joseph A. Durick, who signed with the approval of Archbishop Toolen. The statement acknowledged the apprehension over—even hostility to—court-ordered school desegregation but counseled that "defiance is neither the right answer nor the solution." The moderate to liberal clergymen urged respect for law and order and reminded Alabamians that every person is "created in the image of God and is entitled to respect as a fellow human being with all basic rights, privileges and responsibilities which belong to humanity." Later that year Durick signed a similar appeal to the city's African American inhabitants, urging them to forego demonstrations in favor of a "peaceful Birmingham." Speaking in Atlanta, the president of St. Bernard College, a Benedictine institution in Cullman, Alabama, took a less conciliatory tone. Father Brian Egan, O.S.B., attacked the "racial demagoguery which my home state of Alabama is witnessing today." He agreed with the Birmingham ministers that in race relations, "as in all matters of human relations, the place of prudence is of utmost importance."[1]

Other Catholics accepted the need to maintain a properly arranged social order, but disagreed that this should preclude civil rights activism. After all, they reasoned, adherence to Church doctrine should lead one to practice spiritual and social equality. Rev. Roland Inkel, pastor of St. Theresa's of Midfield, Alabama, decried the "vacuum created by our lack of positive action in the present race question." Segregation may continue, Father Inkel averred, but at the very least "the Negro is a person worthy of respect." To be sure, society would always contain "masters and the servants, Officers and the privates,

those in authority and those subject to authority." But most southern whites were "hiding behind the valid sanction of ordered society,"
thereby using laws "which are enacted for the protection of all . . . for
the enforcement of disrespect for the person of our Negro Citizens."
"Respect for the person" would be the foundation for the achievement
of civil rights, Inkel concluded, and would be the means for the peaceful solution to the present crisis. Inkel's claim that "respect" would do
for civil rights what demonstrations and direct action could not was
hardly inflammatory, but his harsh criticism of Catholics' "ostrich-like"
behavior drew a response from Durick. The auxiliary bishop defended
the Church's racial progress and argued that all priests and "informed
laity" knew that segregation was morally wrong. The ecclesiastical exchange revealed much in common between the priest and auxiliary
bishop. Bishop Durick emphasized that any further progress must not
come at the expense of the white community, but he too believed that
"reason and understanding" would ultimately solve the problem.[2]

The Josephites and nuns in Birmingham found themselves potentially in the midst of the coming struggle. The Josephite pastor of
Our Lady of Fatima in Birmingham, Father Paul Downey, prepared
students for potential sit-ins there. He instructed high school students
that the best way they could assist those college students participating
in the sit-ins "and the rest of their people would be by staying away, but
supporting them by prayer." One nun later remembered, "And I do recall we did take time to pray. And it was a very serious and tense time."[3]

On Sunday morning, September 15, 1963, a bomb ripped through
an outside wall of the Sixteenth Street Baptist Church of Birmingham,
where African American church members had already congregated for
the 11:00 service. The blast killed four young girls. Archbishop Toolen
broke his customary silence and issued a pastoral letter condemning
the violence and the detrimental effects it had on Birmingham's business and industry and on the state's image before the rest of the world.
Toolen condemned the "shameful act" and professed disbelief that "a
civilized human being" could hate a person "because a man's color is
different from his own." If there were any Catholics with such feelings, he warned, they should "pluck this hatred out of their hearts
and remember that all men are created equal, all are redeemed by the
precious blood of Christ." In fact, not only was salvation available to
Negroes, but somehow "their souls may be much whiter and more

pure than those seeking to destroy them."[4] Toolen's statement largely ignored the racial situation that prompted the bombings in the first place. He espoused his standard line that all were God's children and should be treated as such. This did not necessarily mean that segregation should come to an immediate end, however. Instead, in his typical paternalistic manner, the archbishop believed that platitudes and doctrinal reminders would gradually break down the racial barriers separating whites and blacks.

Prior to the mid-1960s, Toolen could point with pride to his diocese's record of evangelism among the state's African American population. The extension of the Church outside the boundaries of white society made Toolen vulnerable to white hostility (or so he argued). But the archbishop's concern for black souls resulted from his—and the rest of the Church's—pre–Vatican II conviction that the road to heaven led strictly through Rome. To be sure, including African Americans in the Catholic fold was never meant to imply social equality. But in defense of his diocese's racial progress, Toolen repeatedly alleged that there never was segregation in his diocese and all institutions were ostensibly open to blacks.[5] Toolen's defensive posture reveals how blind he was to the social plight of African Americans and the pressure he was under to use his authority to bring about racial reform. He resisted that pressure, and many Alabama—indeed many southern—white Catholics took their cue from the Mobile prelate.

African American Catholics, on the other hand, were encouraged by nuns and priests who proved to be more sympathetic to their plight. Mary Hill, a Birmingham African American who converted to Catholicism in 1953, enjoyed a few atypical integrated events. But she understood how rare her experiences were. In the late 1950s, Hill participated in an interracial women's retreat in Cullman, Alabama. She traveled to the retreat with "two Caucasian ladies" and even shared a room with one of them. "I know that they had good feelings about me, and I had good feelings about them," Hill recalled. What was more, white nuns treated African Americans with a respect not normally shown blacks in the South. "And the sisters gave us a sense of worth. . . . They would address us as Mr. or Mrs. And here, we just weren't addressed that way. . . . It was either Auntie or Uncle or your first name or whatever. And if you didn't have that innate worthiness within, well, you just didn't feel good about yourself." Hill's positive experiences were isolated, however. "In lieu of the Church's stand on desegrega-tion," she remembered, "I experienced an undercurrent of staunch segregation which was totally alien to church doctrine. In other words, someone was not practicing what they were preaching."[6]

One 1963 incident demonstrates the tension within the Alabama diocese surrounding the Church's official teaching on social justice and equal access to the sacraments and the way in which some Catholics supported the social status quo. That there was tension at all placed the Catholic Church on a different plane than their white Protestant counterparts. On Sunday morning, September 22, Eddie English, "one of our fine colored Catholics here in Mobile," tried to attend mass at the Church of the Immaculate Conception, a white parish in Orrville, Alabama. Some of the male members of the church, however, refused English admission to the mass, which was scheduled to start in less than thirty minutes. According to English, the men stopped him and his party (how many were with him is unknown) with the query, "Where are you going?" "To Mass," came the reply. The men evidently believed the Mobilian had more sinister intentions than worship, for their next question was, "What do you want here[?]" Whatever answer they received was not satisfactory. Again according to English: "They then told us they helped build that church with money of members of the church and we should go 15 miles to Selma to Mass, because we would start a racial incident, if they let us attend that church." English and his group from Mobile missed mass that Sunday when they ar-rived in Selma too late for services.[7]

That English expected to attend mass in the presumably all-white church is noteworthy. Perhaps he anticipated being forced to sit in the back pews and having to wait to receive communion after the white communicants. This was the practice in other white parishes through-out the state. It is also possible that at any other time in the past this church would have admitted English and those with him. The racial climate in the 1960s, however, now made that increasingly difficult. Indeed, the white congregants of Immaculate Conception alluded to that possibility when they expressed their fears about starting "a racial incident," offering that, perhaps, as an explanation of what were un-usual circumstances in trying times. But in 1963 attending a biracial worship service was enough to raise eyebrows in small Orrville, or in any area—rural or urban—throughout the state. Certainly, no group of blacks would have shown up at First Baptist Church of any town in Alabama expecting to be admitted without question.

English expressed his own righteous indignation to Archbishop Toolen in a letter the next day. English's concerns revolved around the image of the Church such an incident presented to non-Catholics. Unlike the white members of the Church of the Immaculate Conception, English's primary consideration was that such racial separation would tarnish the Church's image as a force for integration and racial justice. Toolen himself shared a similar anxiety. He immediately wrote the chapel's priest, instructing Father Thomas Lorigan to "tell the people of Orrville that it is a Catholic Church and belongs to all our people and that if such a thing happens again I will close the church."[8]

Father Lorigan read Toolen's letter during the September 29 mass. The white communicants of Immaculate Conception were surprised at their ordinary's swift, decisive reaction to such a volatile issue. One parishioner complained to Toolen that forcing integration would jeopardize the position in society that the Catholic Church—especially the very small group in Orrville—had worked hard to attain. Whites at the Church of the Immaculate Conception feared that English's attempt to attend mass was a carefully staged event, with worship and reception of the sacraments of less concern than their church's being made an example for all to see. The suspicion that English's visit to Immaculate Conception had been staged to pressure local white Catholics was not unreasonable. Indeed, such efforts to integrate all-white churches were not uncommon, although typically the "pray-ins" involved both black and white demonstrators. Nevertheless, Joseph McHugh, a parishioner at Immaculate Conception, agreed that "we are not altogether right by any means," but in his mind that did not justify being forced to integrate at the expense of community order.[9]

McHugh expressed what was surely on the minds of many (if not most) of the white Catholics in Orrville—indeed, white Catholics throughout the state. They had already suffered for their faith and they worried that if the Church encouraged too much racial progress, their burden would only grow heavier. McHugh wrote to Toolen, "Here we are, born Catholic and raised Catholic in a very small community where we have had to fight poverty, anti-Catholicism, discrimination of our children in public schools, competition with non-Catholic business associates and the general tribulations of being a Catholic in everyday life in an [sic] Protestant atmosphere." A cotton ginner, McHugh's financial security was intimately connected to the area's agricultural economy, and, like other Catholic businessmen in the Protestant South, he found himself in a precarious position. The Klan and Citizens' Council had already pressured him to stay within proper racial boundaries in his business dealings. But McHugh also knew that "there are manny [sic] many colored families dependent on the operation of my business for their livelihood." In McHugh's mind, so long as all parties involved respected racial boundaries, everyone benefited and none suffered adversely.[10]

Archbishop Toolen sympathized with McHugh's dilemma, but in this instance the doctrines of the Church were not to be trifled with, in Toolen's mind. Toolen reiterated his claim that no church in the diocese had ever been segregated and that "all Catholics are welcome in every church in our Diocese no matter what their color." Toolen pointed to the community of faith within which all Catholics were supposed to dwell and expressed shock that a fellow Catholic would turn a man away from the sacraments. As if to console McHugh and make the situation a bit more palatable, Toolen admitted that the early 1960s was "a time of stress and strife" and the situation in Selma was "very bad," a fact that could be partially blamed on one of the Edmundites. But, he argued, that did not change the fact that as Catholics they were beholden to higher principles. Citing Jesus' biblical answer to the question about the greatest commandment—"Love God and Love your Neighbor"—Toolen indicated that "whether we like it or not, the negroes are our neighbors."[11]

Toolen certainly had the authority to close the small Orrville church. Besides the ecclesiastical authority that provided the archbishop with the ability to remove priests from any particular location and to check errant parishioners, in most cases the diocese provided the financial support to build churches and to keep small parishes like Immaculate Conception operating. And the archbishop controlled the purse strings. But the authority of the bishop himself was not at issue.[12] Indeed, whether they agreed with him or not, few people in Orrville would have questioned Toolen's authority over their church. Rather, the Eddie English incident revealed that the issue was the Catholic Church's relationship to southern society. Like most of their white Protestant neighbors, Immaculate Conception's parishioners had made peace with the southern status quo. They had assumed, moreover, that their Church would not challenge that status quo. For English himself, the issue was obviously very different, and the contrast between what whites and blacks expected from their church points to the irony of the Church's position. Both English and the white members of Immaculate Conception worried about the Church's image, although for very different reasons. On the one hand, English saw the Catholic Church as best situated to lead the way in racial reform. As McHugh's letter to Toolen indicates, on the other hand, a long history of prejudice dictated how whites responded to secular issues. Their position in the larger society was always an issue. The Church, moreover, was best positioned to protect the southern way of life and forestall integration.

Probably the social institution most intimately connected with a segregated South was the school system, which whites protected with single-minded zealotry. Indeed, ten years after *Brown* many segregationists believed that they had won that battle and thwarted integration indefinitely. With the election of Governor George Wallace in 1962 and his vow to defend segregation at all costs, white Alabamians were assured that racial boundaries would be protected. White Catholics could be equally as confident. Other Church leaders had become increasingly vocal in their opposition to segregation, and a couple of the bishops of other southern states vowed to integrate parochial schools; but their own bishop, Toolen, could be trusted not to waiver in the face of public pressure to integrate.

But by 1962 demands for integration came increasingly from blacks themselves. That summer Pensacola public schools were on the verge of admitting blacks, a possibility that upset that city's African American Catholic population. In their minds, their church lagged behind the public schools, an embarrassing development for those concerned about the Church's moral and spiritual image. Charles R. Benboe, the president of the Holy Name Society at St. Joseph's parish in Pensacola, wrote the archbishop that he had been "very much humiliated and concerned heretofore about the fact that our Catholic schools were separated because of race." That situation, however, was "tolerable, distasteful though it was, when all the other schools in the area were the same." Benboe implored Toolen to "consider the image of the Church in this community and to do what is in your power to restore the rightful order of things."[13]

Others expressed similar emotions and concern for the image of the Catholic Church among that city's African American non-Catholic population. Lawrence McVoy wrote out of "loyalty and devotion to our church." He decried the local Church's protection of "something which we claim to abhor" and lamented "the comments being made about our silence on the subject of school integration in Pensacola." He noted that white non-Catholics attended parochial schools, while Negro Catholics were deprived of the same privilege. "We say there is no such things as White Catholic and Negro Catholic, but we practice something different." Willie Collins identified himself as "a consciencious [sic], faithful Catholic of Negro parentage," who had "never been a rabble-rouser or a troublemaker." He also referred to the "unfavorable light the Church is in in Pensacola at this time" because of its failure to integrate ahead of the public schools.[14] Handwritten on each of these letters in the archives is the simple word "acknowledged," so Toolen probably made no substantive response to these Pensacola letters, merely admitting that they had been received without addressing the impassioned appeals for racial justice. If he did any more than that, the correspondence has not survived. The archbishop was not one to indulge criticism, but his terse replies could have reflected a growing realization on his part that these black parishioners were correct. He would have to act sooner rather than later.

Pressure also came from some of the religious orders that staffed the Negro parochial schools. In 1962 Toolen reported to the Provincial of the Daughters of Charity that his diocese had already lost two communities "for no reason except they did not want to teach the colored and didn't want a small school."[15] A refusal to teach black students more than likely was not the issue, although Toolen tended to understand multifaceted racial issues that simply. In all probability, those communities (Toolen does not indicate which ones) withdrew for some of the same reasons that the Daughters of Charity considered leaving in 1964. Segregation was quickly becoming outdated, and religious orders devoted to both colored mission work and service to the Church could no longer rationalize maintaining separate facilities for blacks and whites. Sister Mary Rose of the Daughters of Charity wrote Toolen in February 1964 that "our Council feels we should reconsider the wisdom of staffing an all-Colored School." The order hoped to continue serving African Americans, "but with the emphasis on integration from all sources—from the Federal government and civil groups and above all from the Church itself, it seems to us that we would be doing a disservice rather than promoting the over-all good of the Church in this instance."[16]

Toolen expressed shock at the prospect of losing the Daughters of Charity over segregation issues. By that time he undoubtedly saw the inevitability of integration, but he remained unconvinced that more than a few blacks actually desired it and doubted that it would ever be widespread in the South. Ignoring almost every piece of correspondence he had received from African Americans on the subject, Toolen claimed that "the children prefer to go to these schools rather than go to another section of town in a white school. They belong in their own parish school." Toolen conceded that integration "must come and more than likely will come to the Diocese of Mobile in September, but that isn't going to change our colored schools in the least." Parochial schools for African Americans gave them a Catholic education, Toolen explained, although he failed to clarify why integrated schools deprived them of that same opportunity. Toolen concluded his response to Sister Mary Rose by relying on a now familiar refrain: she was an outsider—"from your far off city of St. Louis"—who could not understand the situation in Alabama.[17]

Even before official diocesan-wide integration, at least one parochial school in Alabama opened on an integrated basis. Huntsville's St. Joseph's school differed, however, in its racial composition. It was a previously all-black school with a handful of white students—"reverse integration" of sorts, as parishioners referred to it. St. Joseph's opened in Huntsville in 1952 to serve that city's growing black population. Beginning in the mid-1950s, a few whites attended with the predominantly African American congregation. In September 1963, a couple of days before Governor George Wallace made his infamous stand in the schoolhouse door at the University of Alabama, twelve white students joined 106 black pupils at St. Joseph's school. Father Mark Sterbenz, S.D.S., reported that integration at St. Joseph's progressed "very quietly and very smoothly." The mother of one of the white children recalled that the event was "not just peaceful, but warm, welcoming and comfortable." The impetus for the white enrollment came from parents themselves, and the priest had "no objection whatever." The NCWC news service reported that "the white pupils were enrolled without incident."

The next spring, Toolen wrote Monsignor John L. May (who, incidentally, would become Toolen's successor in 1969) of the Extension Society of Chicago that Huntsville was "a wild place." St. Joseph's had been built "as a colored church but the whites have really taken over." In April 1964 there were approximately fifty white children in the school, "and a great number are going to Mass at the new church."[18]

Bowing to inevitability, on April 26, 1964, Toolen announced—in a terse pastoral letter with minimal explanation—"After much prayer, consultation, and advice, we have decided to integrate all the schools of our diocese in September." The archbishop encouraged Alabama's Catholics to accept the decision "as best for God and Country . . . the common good of all must come first." Admission to diocesan schools would be according to previously published guidelines. That is, for elementary schools, students would apply to the principal for enrollment, and the parish pastor would then review each application and make acceptance or rejection decisions on an individual basis. Students' elementary school record, performance on a placement test, and recommendations of elementary school teachers, principals, and pastors would help determine "that quality of student who would profit most." Such a policy of admitting students on an individual case-by-case basis was standard fare in the educational systems of the post-*Brown* South. This eliminated race as an explicit factor in admission, but it still gave tremendous latitude to white school boards and other officials to exclude black students from formerly white schools.[19] There is no explicit evidence that this is what the Diocese of Mobile-Birmingham intended with their 1964 policy, but it cannot be ruled out. Indeed, given the nature of white southern society, the knowledge that this happened in public school systems throughout the South, and the fact that it took several years for diocesan schools to achieve integration, it appears very likely that this plan was intended to achieve integration slowly and in the process mollify angry white Catholic parents.

If the goal was gradual desegregation, then the diocesan plan was an unqualified success. Diocesan-wide school integration came slowly and depended on local circumstances. It was the late 1960s before Alabama parochial schools achieved even a modicum of integration, but Toolen's announcement prompted the predictable reaction from whites. One "native Mobilian and a Catholic born into the faith" did not "intend to have my children schooled with negroes." Catherine

West was "a segregationist, not a racist," who believed that African Americans could have "equal rights but separate facilities." West was certain she was not alone in her thinking. Parochial school integration violated "the teachings of the past 2,000 years." But given time and "God's will this battle will be won peaceably and our way of life will continue with our Catholic children in Catholic schools."[20]

Another Alabama woman provoked by the bishop's 1964 pastoral letter announced that "As a Catholic I do not approve of the church mixing in politics." Viola Johnson conflated potential school integration with the civil rights demonstrations she watched on television. They were both products of the same alien forces and had no place within the Church. Johnson conceded that "Negroes has [sic] always been excepted [sic] in all catholic churches." But she did not approve of priests and nuns "incouraging [sic] these demonstrations," and she blamed "the head of the church for allowing these things to happen." Despite her displeasure with her ordinary, Johnson's letter sounded a theme that should have been familiar to Toolen—namely, that blacks were not ready to accept the responsibility that accompanied their demands for equal rights. She had no "Quarrels with the negroes," who needed the assistance of whites. She was opposed to what she perceived as African Americans being granted a position in society that they had not earned. "Violence and demonstrations is [sic] not the answer."[21]

Johnson also hints at a spiritual transformation that plagued modern Christianity beginning in the 1950s and 1960s. As her denomination moved further away from what she perceived were its traditional roots, she located her spirituality outside the established Church. Again, she blamed her bishop. "I am sorry to say that the head of the Catholic church is turning me away from my religion, I have always been proud to say that I am a catholic. I hope and pray that God will forgive me, I am sure he will answer my prayer at home if they [sic] are sincere." Dissatisfied with her denomination, she personalized her spirituality and retreated into a sacred world that was more comfortable for her.[22] That sacred world relied on a defense of southern tradition and pre-conciliar understandings of Catholic authority. With her emphasis on an individual's relationship with God and rejection of clerical authority, Johnson inadvertently appropriated elements of the Protestantism that surrounded her.

For white southerners, public school integration broke down cherished barriers and provided the most serious challenge to the racial status quo. Parochial school integration provoked intense reactions, but for most Catholics it turned out not to be an immediate threat. The event that galvanized public sentiment over civil rights and the role of the Church in the South in racial justice issues was the march for voting rights from Selma to Montgomery, Alabama, in March 1965. Until Selma, the Catholic Church had remained on the margins of the civil rights movement in Alabama. Debates over integration had centered on internal Church affairs and not on the Church's interaction with society at large. Support for integration—or at least moderation and "prudence" in opposing the civil rights movement—came primarily from a select few priests and Church leaders. That Father Foley himself was such an isolated example of Catholic activism demonstrates the Church's marginal presence in the movement. But Bishop Toolen's response to the Selma demonstration quickly brought the Church into the forefront and thrust Toolen into a position he did not necessarily want.

Initially, Toolen's voice was a responsible one of moderation. Following violence against demonstrators when the march was first attempted on March 7, the archbishop condemned "without reservation a harsh and brutal exercise of the police power vested in the hands of our public officials as beyond the requirements of present difficulties and unable to effect their solution." He argued that "justice, human decency and Christian brotherhood demand recognition of the real needs of our Negro people." But demonstrations—even those prompted by "justice, human decency and Christian brotherhood"— had limits, in Toolen's mind, and he continued to press for gradual, not radical, methods of dealing with racial strife. In the same statement, he refused to "condone a complete disregard on the part of citizens for statutes legally enacted in the interest of the common good and public safety."[23] The latter statement suggests that Toolen was comfortable with the separate but equal statutes that propped up Alabama society. At the very least, he was reluctant to upset those whites who provided the primary support for his church.

Toolen's moderation gave way to outright reaction a week later when some thirty-five or forty priests and an uncertain number of nuns from around the country joined hundreds of other clergy and activists in defiance of a court injunction to demand equal voting rights for African Americans. In an address before a banquet sponsored by the Friendly Sons of St. Patrick, the Mobile prelate conceded that there were "things that need correcting" in race relations, but he denounced "crusaders" who were little more than "eager beavers who feel this is a holy cause." They were outsiders, he complained. "What do they know about conditions in the South?" Neither priests nor nuns, but especially not the female religious, Toolen asserted, belonged in such an environment. The archbishop revealed an attitude common to white southerners who associated social unrest with the unwelcome intervention of outsiders. With statements like this, the archbishop became a spokesperson for white southern society—Catholic and Protestant alike. Instead of crusading in an unfamiliar environment, according to Toolen, priests' and nuns' "place is at home doing God's work." Toolen conceded that white southerners needed "corrections in our attitudes towards the Negro people," but "sane and sensible Negroes realize we are trying to bring them up to the standards they should have." He and other right-thinking white Alabamians, that is, knew what was best for the state's African American population. The bishop concluded that the "demonstrations are not helping," and Dr. King was merely "trying to divide the people."[24]

Toolen defies neat categorization. He was not necessarily a segregationist, and he was quick to point that out whenever Church authorities or anyone else questioned his spiritual leadership. He complained to Baltimore's Cardinal Shehan that "They made a segregationist out of me and I have never been a segregationist." The bishop claimed that he had always tried to make true separate but equal provisions for African Americans, but blacks refused to appreciate his efforts and their responsibilities to the Church. The diocese also was the first to give blacks papal honors and the first to provide accredited schools for them.[25]

At the very least, his March 1965 speech to the Friendly Sons of St. Patrick reveals a pronounced noblesse oblige. He was a paternalist, who understood himself to be an expert on Alabama's blacks, their friend and protector since his tenure as bishop began in the 1920s. Based on pre–civil rights movement southern white standards, as he wrote Cardinal Shehan in 1965, the archbishop certainly could make a relatively strong case for describing himself as a friend and protector of his state's black population. In the days when integrated institutions were unheard of, he built schools and hospitals for African Americans and recruited religious orders to staff them. Indeed, Mobile's black Catholic hospital was the only place that African American doctors could practice in that city. And he solicited financial help from organizations such as the Church's Indian and Negro Fund and other national Catholic mission sources.[26] Certainly, separate institutions perpetuated racial segregation and stretched Catholic resources even more thinly. But they were necessary for the Church to operate in the segregated South.

The Catholic record in Selma was more complicated than Toolen's reaction to—and nuns' participation in—voting rights demonstrations. For Selma's Catholic African American population in particular, SNCC's 1965 voting registration drive offered the kind of hope that the Alabama Catholic Church had failed to provide. Rachel Ann Nelson was a nine-year-old girl who attended the Edmundites' St. Elizabeth's Mission school in Selma. She participated in the Selma demonstrations and later recalled her role in the march and the way the demonstrations bound the black community together. Her best friend was a Baptist. "But no matter what we were, we all went to the meetings and the rallies at the church, Brown Chapel AME Church. And Catholic priests and nuns were there, too, because the movement was above what faith you were." Nelson's family was one of the first to provide room and board for civil rights workers who came to Selma to plan the demonstrations. The Nelsons even housed a white Presbyterian minister and his family, whose seven-year-old son attended St. Elizabeth's school with Rachel. The white child of such an "outsider" attending a Negro school only served to further marginalize these black Catholics.

They found comfort in at least two places, however. After being attacked for walking home with the white boy, Nelson remembered imploring the statue of the Virgin Mary in her house, "Boy, Mary, if we ever needed help down here, we need it now." The community of activists—Catholics and non-Catholics alike—also provided a sacred respite for Rachel. Brown Chapel AME Church was the central meeting site and rallying point for the voting rights drive. For Rachel, these priests and nuns were in Selma because the civil rights movement itself was far more important than which faith one adhered to. Before the demonstrations began, one of the nuns at St. Elizabeth's told her class to pray for peace in Selma. Rachel innocently inquired "if it would be all right for me to pray at Brown Chapel even if it wasn't a Catholic Church. She [the nun] had smiled at the question."[27]

Following the archbishop's St. Patrick's Day condemnation of the Selma demonstrations, some forty or fifty members of St. Jude and St. John the Baptist Churches—two of Montgomery's African American parishes—signed a letter of protest to Toolen. The presence of those "outside" priests and nuns in Selma made this group feel "for the first time that our Catholic clergy was concerned about the brute force of the local constabulary, and while they did not lead the protests, at least it was apparent that the nuns and priests objected to the injustices." Until then, "we looked in vain [for someone to protest injustices Alabama blacks suffered], for no effort or encouragement had been forthcoming." The members of St. Jude and St. John the Baptist parishes set themselves apart from Toolen and what they perceived as his lack of leadership: "So we will lick our wounds and go on to the job at hand with hope in our hearts, a prayer on our lips, and because of your statements, tears in our eyes, but the tears will not blind us to the real goal of this effort and we will welcome the nuns and priests into our hearts and homes when the pilgrimage from Selma is over."[28]

The parishioners from St. Elizabeth's, Selma, also felt alienated from the mainstream of the Alabama Church. In November 1965, St. Elizabeth's Holy Name Society boycotted that year's Diocesan Holy Name Convention in protest of Toolen's stance on the Selma demonstrations. The president of the parish society, Robert Craig, wrote Toolen, describing his and the group's feeling of betrayal at the hands of their "Shepherd." Evidently, Toolen's history of support for black missions had convinced them that the bishop would come down on the side of civil rights. To their dismay, he did not. In addition, to make matters worse, in the minds of St. Elizabeth's parishioners, Toolen had orchestrated the removal of Father Maurice Ouellet, an Edmundite activist and advocate for racial reform in Selma. In 1963, for example, Ouellet orchestrated a series of civil rights marches by school children, and for a time he enjoyed the reputation of being the only white person in Selma to provide public support for civil rights. He regularly clashed with Selma's white leadership. Selma's mayor wrote Toolen that Ouellet's presentation of black demands to the city were often "to the prejudice of order and tranquility in this community."[29] In 1963 a grand jury investigated Ouellet, looking for someone to blame for recent unrest among the city's blacks. The investigation returned nothing with which to charge the Edmundite. Archbishop

Toolen initially condoned Ouellet's activism, as long as the priest and his fellow Edmundites did not march in demonstrations. By July 1965, however, Ouellet had pushed Toolen and Selma's white population to the limit of any long-suffering with which they had been blessed. The prelate ordered the Edmundite out of the diocese, much to the disappointment of Selma's black population.[30]

Toolen showed no sympathy for St. Elizabeth's men's protest and no remorse for his own actions. Missing the diocesan-wide meeting was their own fault, and "the only ones you hurt by not going . . . was yourselves." What was more, "our negro people were there in great numbers, so you really weren't missed." His response to Craig's letter revealed the strain that was evident between the chancery and religious orders in the diocese who increasingly agitated for civil rights. Although any earlier correspondence cannot be located in the Toolen papers, both Craig and Toolen refer to St. Elizabeth's previous efforts to contact Toolen about racial matters. Toolen ignored those, he said, because they came from a "crowd and I only deal with the people through the priests." But Toolen found the priests in Selma "impossible to deal with . . . for a long time." The fissure between the aging, conservative archbishop and the new generation of activists had widened into a chasm. For his entire tenure as Alabama's prelate Toolen had relied on religious orders to advance the faith among the state's African American population. By the late 1960s, that alliance had given way to open conflict over the application of Catholic racial and social justice.

Despite his opposition to the Selma demonstrations, however, Toolen approved the use of the City of St. Jude, the Edmundites' medical and educational ministry center devoted to African Americans, for marchers to camp at one night en route from Selma to Montgomery. In a statement explaining the decision to allow the encampment, Father Paul Mullaney, director of the City of St. Jude, described the center "as a monument to brotherhood and racial justice." Toolen was in "perfect agreement" that the Catholic property should be used for the marchers. Father Mullaney explained that the City of St. Jude alone had the facilities to accommodate "all of the Sisters and most of the clergy Catholic, Protestant, and Jewish." Instead of being strictly a Catholic-supported organization, Mullaney reasoned, the Catholic compound had national ties that made its mission larger than its ministry to

Selma's African American population. "Many of the demonstrators or their families are benefactors. . . . So really the City of St. Jude belongs to the American people." Mullaney concluded that St. Jude's hospitality would encourage "outside demonstrators [to] bring back to their own communities in their hearts what they witnessed in Alabama in order that it will help them solve their own racial problems."[31]

Toolen's primary sins in the Selma case were poor judgment and a characteristic lack of diplomacy. Wire services ensured that his St. Patrick's Day speech made news nationwide, and his very public stance made him a lightning rod for reaction from groups on both sides of the issue. Staunch segregationists—Catholic and Protestant, from the South, North, Midwest, and West alike—claimed him as their own and rallied around him with their own interpretations of his words. Indeed, in March 1965, Toolen reported that he received "hundreds of letters . . . and most of them are very favorable." He estimated that four out of five—including those that came from outside Alabama—supported his St. Patrick's Day speech. Still others wrote letters to the editor of the *Catholic Week*. A Birmingham correspondent informed the archbishop that "many people not of our faith" had stopped him on the street to express their support for the imperious ordinary.[32]

Many of these people were racists, and opposed to "outsiders" and communists who for whatever reason threatened their way of life. Toolen also was opposed to "outsiders," and he was willing enough to agree that communists were active in the civil rights movement, the United Nations, and quite possibly wherever civic disorder arose. Toolen's Selma opinion stemmed directly from his understanding of the nature of the Church and his authority within the Church hierarchy. He demonstrated a pre-conciliar notion of clerical authority and was at best ambivalent about the changes wrought by the Vatican Council. Indeed, one of his primary complaints about the Selma demonstration was that these priests and nuns did not ask his permission to come to Alabama, a common courtesy usually paid the presiding prelate. Many had gone out of their way to avoid giving Toolen the opportunity to refuse them admission to the diocese. When his own archbishop insisted that he attempt to obtain permission, one Washington, D.C., priest, for example, telephoned the Mobile chancery, knowing that Toolen was out of town at the time—in the nation's capital, in fact—and unable to respond immediately to his request. He left for Selma before Toolen's aides could catch him.[33] At any rate, Toolen believed he had the situation well under control, as far as the Church was concerned, and these religious from outside Alabama were nothing more than interlopers and troublemakers.

The voluminous correspondence between these laypeople and the archbishop reveals the extent to which white Catholics' outsider status had changed since they and Protestants had lumped each other in the same category with communism. Both white Catholics and Protestants muted their oppositional rhetoric toward each other and embraced a new view of outsiders that, temporarily at least, ignored religion. Outsiders were now people who threatened the racial status quo. Race had become more important than religion, but even this fact could not completely comfort white Catholics and remove their ambivalence about acceptance into the southern Protestant mainstream. After all, the presence of many of their own in Selma had prompted Toolen's public statements in the first place. White Catholics who wrote Toolen, moreover, connected the presence of "communist" outsiders in the South with the Church's image in the eyes of non-Catholics. They also worried about the ways in which Vatican II undermined the South's social hierarchy. In the average white Catholic's mind these issues were intermingled and all part of the same problem. Communists supported and staffed civil rights groups, most notably the NAACP, the reasoning went. And when Catholics were associated with such groups, the respect they had worked so hard to earn in Alabama eroded and brought the entire Church under a cloud of suspicion.

Because they came from outside the region, religious orders such as the Edmundites and Josephites assumed most of the work among the South's black population. White laypeople looked on them with a small measure of respect; but, also because of their outsider status, that respect for their devotion and service to the Church at times remained largely masked by periods of suspicion and resentment. Religious orders whose headquarters and superiors were located elsewhere were, in short, outsiders; and according to southern conventional wisdom on racial matters, outsiders could not be trusted. In Selma, for example, Catholic parishioners drew sharp boundaries around acceptable levels of activism among priests and nuns. One white Catholic there acknowledged that the Edmundites' "work is Christian and that the primary purpose of the Mission is the work of God but aren't they getting a little more involved than necessary?" Integration was sure to come, Toolen's correspondent conceded, but when it did, it would be better with "our own colored ones that live here and who have helped us build our Church, not the ones sent here that are looking for trouble." The local Edmundites, in one person's mind, might be better trained in "the doctrines of our Church," but opening the door for "Martin Luther King Jr., Roy Wilkins, Shuddleworth [sic], Shores, etc." was out of the question and abused the "seeming dictatorial power of the Church."[34]

Following the voting rights demonstrations in Selma, one typical Birmingham laywoman noted that this was "a day when Images seem so important," yet "Priests and Nuns who seem to be part time God's servants and part time Anarchists playing into the Communists hands, present a sad picture."[35] In response to a syndicated column of Monsignor George Higgins's, a white Huntsville Catholic also drew explicit connections between civil rights activism and communist influence. William H. Graham was suspicious that Martin Luther King, Jr., would be "concerned about seeing the defeat of Communism." Graham accused King of appointing known communists to positions in the SCLC, and civil rights organizations "are rapidly showing their Red orientation by support of peace rallies, teach-ins, etc." For Graham, Archbishop Hallinan's organizing Martin Luther King, Jr.'s Atlanta Nobel Peace Prize banquet was tantamount to "listening to the Bishop of Havana assure us that Fidel Castro was not a Communist." A second Huntsville man aimed his anti-communist rhetoric at Richard Morrisroe, a Chicago priest who was shot in the back in Lowndes County, Alabama, after participating in a voter registration drive. According to John Francis, Morrisroe, who survived the shooting, permitted "the Communist conspiracy to use him in their sinister take-over of our Republic." The civil rights movement, moreover, had not been infiltrated by communists; "it has been created by them." And diabolical communists had engineered tensions between the races. Exercising acrobatic twists of logic, Francis offered as proof the fact that otherwise good Christians had been forced to hate people of other races. "Let each Christian ask himself how many of another race in his personal acquaintance have the communists succeeded in making him hate, or even dislike."[36]

Toolen's Catholic correspondents were also worried about a second potential problem, namely, the image of the Church in the eyes of their non-Catholic neighbors. This was a serious issue for a group of people who comprised less than 3 percent of Alabama's population. A woman from Montrose, Alabama, Dorothea Brown Miller, applauded Toolen for his "wisdom, understanding and foresight—and the courage in this time of crisis to speak the truth." His words came at an opportune time for Miller, as she found it difficult to handle Protestants' questions about the Catholic presence at the civil rights rally. "Non-Catholic friends have asked me why—also, and it has been hard to answer without condemning the good—perhaps well meaning, misinformed nuns. But today I am so proud of my bishop!" Now, those same friends were praising her bishop as well.[37]

A second woman from Sawyerville, Alabama, who described herself as "inately [sic] religious," expressed a similar sentiment, even as she revealed a perhaps more intimate and troubling concern. As did many other white southerners, Joan Thyson viewed the Selma demonstrations—and civil rights agitation in general—through the lens of sex. Opponents of the civil rights movement had long argued that activists had larger goals than simply the desegregation of public facilities. It was interracial marriage that many whites feared was the ultimate goal of the movement. For Thyson and others, then, the nuns who participated in the Selma demonstration flagrantly violated southern gender boundaries with their open association with African American men. Since there were so few Catholics in the South, nuns, she asserted, "should be above reproach to help us." Instead, much to this letter-writer's consternation, female religious were not "following in the foot steps of 'God's Masterpiece,'—our lovely Blessed Mother. . . . To see pictures of them walking arm-in-arm with Negro men who, even Now, would not dare ask a Southern white lady to do as much . . . shocked me beyond words." Neither blacks nor whites, in her view, could respect sisters who behaved in such a manner. These nuns were "losing souls, and not trying to get voting rights." Toolen agreed about the alleged "immorality in this mob . . . and the priests and sisters were in the midst of it." They were out late every night, "swinging and dancing with the Negroes and shouting and clapping." No place for a sister, he concluded, along with many other white Catholic observers.[38]

White Protestants and other white Alabamians agreed with the Catholic ordinary and his Catholic supporters. The Alabama legislature passed a resolution praising Toolen for "his wise guidance." The resolution outlined the problems facing the state and sounded themes that Toolen's Catholic correspondents recognized all too clearly. The legislature declared that the state's "plight is desperate and our great state is overrun with outsiders who are attempting to change our world and a cherished social order by action calculated to incite turmoil, hatred, and violence." Toolen had sensibly framed the problem as only an insider familiar with that "cherished social order" could do. He served the state well as its spokesman, for he demonstrated "his profound understanding of the root causes of a tragic time." Circuit Court Judge Walter F. Gaillard wrote Toolen that "here is one Presbyterian who is standing with you and for you on your views." "'Peaceful demonstrations,' so called," were not the way to address inequities, and Gaillard appreciated the archbishop's bold stance.[39]

A Dothan, Alabama, Baptist cut straight to the heart of the issues surrounding Catholics' transition from outsiders in the first half of the century to defenders of the white mainstream by the 1960s. William J. Ward acknowledged that the religious differences between himself and Toolen "could be the same difference as color of our skin." But Ward praised Toolen for his "courage to stand up and speak out." Ward conceded that anti-Catholicism was a problem among Baptists, but "this is just as out of place as your Nuns and Priests in Selma." Although the two would never share the same denomination, "the world will never be too small for you and I to live together because we both share an identical belief. The truth needs to be spoken." The truth in this case was not theological or biblical; nor did it have anything to do with church doctrine or ecclesiastical authority. It was racial, and Toolen's "Christian attitude" was what the South needed to preserve the status quo.[40]

If outsider communists running loose in the South threatened to undermine the southern racial hierarchy, at least white Catholics believed their church would forestall the demise of the southern way of life. Indeed, southern literary figures such as Allen Tate had converted to Catholicism in the mid-twentieth century because of the Church's commitment to orthodoxy and hierarchy, which Tate believed could best support the southern social order. Lay reaction to the civil rights movement and to the Vatican Council indicate that the literati were not the only ones with these same concerns, although, to be sure, the lay understanding of these changes was no doubt more visceral than Tate's. The same Birmingham woman who complained of anarchists and communists in the civil rights movement was unexcited about the Council's changes. "The Pope might think all these recent changes resulting from the Ecumenical Council will mean a Great New Day for the Church, but I fear I cannot share His enthusiasm. Frankly, the whole world seems to be in a pitiful state to me." One white Georgia Catholic noted the South's "confused Catholics" and "the pressure of confusion within our own Church."[41]

An Atlanta man expressed his outrage that Catholic priests and nuns "dignified" the "self-professed civil disobedience demonstrations." His reasoning was instructive. Priests' and nuns' "whole life is dedicated to obedience to authority," and in his mind, evidently, their civil rights agitation undermined the authority of the Church in the South. This anonymous Atlantan echoed the concerns of Archbishop Toolen and many other Alabamians. "When priests and nuns are sent in from other dioceses, over the expressed opposition of the local bishop," the man wrote Hallinan, "I am seriously concerned about our newly revised Catholic Church." At the very least, he suggested, those priests and nuns should concentrate on their home parishes and "the alleviation of these political ills" there.[42] A Montgomery woman shared this sentiment and praised Toolen for asserting his authority. "Catholics have been taught that constituted authority is from God, and when we see products of that teaching—especially our religious—join in their ridiculous political and publicity-seeking parade, see them defy and break our laws and set themselves up as lawmakers, thereby encouraging anarchy, we need to know where our spiritual leader stands."[43]

In the minds of these white southerners, the belief system that Toolen symbolized, with its emphasis on certain orthodoxy and divinely established authority, should sustain the white power structure. By the late 1960s, it could not. By 1967 at least one local Catholic, Gordon Abele, complained about "the Vatican engulfed by the Leftist Tide" pressuring the aging Toolen to retire. Abele had a better idea. "It's 'boys instead of bombs' Paul [Pope Paul VI] who should step down." The Church universal had become virtually unrecognizable to many white Alabama laypeople. Indeed, many white southern Catholics resisted Vatican II because it reinforced liberal religious and social changes. These whites became disillusioned with their church because it failed them where they most needed it, namely, in defense of the white southern status quo. They equated this failure with conciliar renewal.

There were also those white lay Catholics who refused to heed Toolen's voice of conservatism and who condemned him for his opposition to civil rights activism in the wake of the Selma demonstrations. These laypersons were very familiar with Catholic doctrine and actively involved in at least some aspect of Church work. One woman from Birmingham compared Toolen to that other Alabamian well known for his reactionary tub-thumping. She argued that Toolen's relationship to the doctrines of Rome were similar to the affinity Governor George Wallace had with the U.S. government. A Cherokee, Alabama, woman concluded that she was forced to abandon any hope of Toolen and the Alabama Church accomplishing anything in the cause of civil rights, especially "since the Alabama Legislature ruled by racist George Wallace has publicly commended you [Toolen] for apparently aligning yourself with his offensive against human rights."[44]

James R. Jackson, of Mobile, converted to Catholicism from the Baptist Church "because we had lost faith with the Baptist people here in the South." Before Toolen voiced his opposition to the Selma demonstrations, Jackson and his family "were a hundred per-cent satisfied with the Catholic faith and with its beliefs." But Jesus Christ himself, Jackson asserted, would have been in Alabama "helping oppressed people," so Toolen's position was completely at odds with the true Catholic position. Another Mobilian, Walter L. Darring, who identified himself as president of a group called Catholic Laymen for Church Reform, agreed that Toolen's position on race deviated from Catholic doctrine. Darring suggested that instead of dividing the people as Toolen charged, King only pointed out the wrongfulness of the separation that already existed. "The only sense in which that may be said to hurt the cause of the Negro is in that it arouses the indignation of those who would suppress him."[45]

By the late 1960s and early 1970s, the leadership in both dioceses had come to accept, if not champion, racial justice as the appropriate Catholic response, and that official position divided Catholic laity. A sermon at 1965's Christ the King celebration in Birmingham revealed those fault lines as they would characterize the Church in the late 1960s. The Right Reverend Francis Wade, editor of the *Catholic Week,* condemned the Klan and groups who "use Christ as a cloak for their violence and hate." He then called on listeners at Rickwood Field to reconsider individual sinfulness in light of Christ's suffering on the cross. Because of personal sins, everyone held responsibility for Christ's passion. Wade called on Catholics to examine their own lives to reveal how they participated in the crucifixion. He first spelled out those wrongdoings commonly accepted by Catholics as sins in need of atonement. This list included sins of personal morality with which few Catholics could quarrel. But then he pushed further. He asked, "And what of the other sins against Christ, the sins we are wont to pass over with clichés and platitudes? The sins of injustice against our fellow man, the denial of personal integrity and dignity to those who differ from us in color or religion or nationality or social standing or birth. The sins of indifference and apathy; the sins of lack of concern for others; the sins of not bothering to become involved; the sins of silence."[46]

Wade stopped short of endorsing recent civil rights demonstrations and full-scale integration and left his listeners to draw their own conclusions about his sermon's practical applications. Not surprisingly, considering 1965's turmoil over civil rights, members of the laity drew the straight line that Wade apparently had in mind. One Birmingham man wrote that there were "plenty of Catholics who don't believe in integration and I'm one of them." He informed Monsignor Wade that his sermon had little impact, other than to "appease a few Negroes and make a lot of other people very mad." Instead of the Klan, it was civil rights organizations like the NAACP and the Congress of Racial Equality that had caused social discord and civil unrest. Frank Brocato concluded his letter with an odd finale that linked the American South with European fascism. "The Church supported Hitler and Mussolini," he wrote, "so I guess they can support Alabama and Southern traditions." His perverse reasoning aside, evidence from the late 1960s suggests that Brocato spoke for more southern white Catholics than leaders like Wade would care to admit. Still, others were more appreciative of the monsignor's message. Gradually, two Selma women acknowledged, Catholics had come to understand that "Christ promoted brotherhood" and that God was "the greatest race mixer of all times." Racial segregation, therefore, was a "grave sin of spiritual pride and vanity."[47]

These Catholics found themselves in the minority, but their support for the civil rights movement symbolized the tension over moral authority within the Alabama Catholic Church. In the former Confederacy, a conservative Protestant hegemony had sanctified strict racial boundaries that kept blacks subordinate to white authority well into the 1960s. Religious differences aside, most white Catholics were comfortable with this racial hegemony. Their church's pre–Vatican II hierarchy protected those boundaries and made it possible for whites to coexist relatively comfortably in a church with black members. Indeed, prior to the Vatican Council, Church leaders did little to challenge segregation. Only a few select individuals and religious orders actively sought racial and social justice for African Americans. But the civil rights movement—reinforced by Vatican II—relaxed racial boundaries and contributed to an unstable southern social order.

6

Race, Vatican II, and the
Catholic Crisis of Authority

⊹

In February 1967, the editor of the *Catholic Week,* Rev. Francis Wade, concluded that "Freedom is a wonderful thing" except when it "degenerates into license" and caused a neglect of responsibility and obligations. Indeed, license "is only another word for free-wheeling, wild-swinging, emotion-packed misuse of freedom." Freedom of conscience, Wade wrote, must always be characterized by "zeal and love for the truth." And it must always maintain "the correct attitude toward the Church's teaching and its magisterium, and the authority of its bishops." Wade echoed language from the Vatican Council's "Declaration on Religious Liberty." Only a little more than a year before, Wade had expressed his support for the black freedom struggle in a sermon at Birmingham's 1965 Christ the King ceremony. From his perspective, however, many Catholics in 1967 misused the conciliar document and placed their own consciences in direct conflict with episcopal authority. "We have more than our share of people, priests and Sisters, as well as members of the laity, tearing things apart in the name of freedom of conscience."[1] It is unclear whether Wade had in mind priests and nuns in the Diocese of Mobile-Birmingham only, or if he wrote based on his knowledge of the American Catholic Church in general in the late 1960s. Either way, as someone concerned about the erosion of ecclesiastic authority, he had much to complain about. In that same vein, he might also have decried the erosion of authority and civility in society at large by the late 1960s. As the local reaction to the Selma demonstrations reveals, many white Catholics certainly equated spiritual and secular crises, and they linked those crises to fallout from the civil rights movement. The black freedom struggle, supported by popular interpretations of conciliar innovations, had released liberty and conscience from their ecclesiastical moorings and set the Church adrift in the late 1960s and early 1970s.

The differences between Toolen and Hallinan notwithstanding, the two dioceses experienced many of the same problems in the late 1960s. The Diocese of Mobile-Birmingham followed the Archdiocese of Atlanta in making racial equality and social justice reform official policy, but that did not necessarily mean that white church people followed diocesan leadership obligingly. Many Catholics still longed for a renewed moral (and concomitant social) order that could maintain proper restrictions on excessive liberty. Race continued to be the issue that divided one Catholic group from another, and restraining license meant primarily stifling racial justice activism wherever possible. Maybe they could not turn back the racial reform clock, but they would have preferred to slow the hands of time in order to preserve as much of the old social order as possible. At the very least, as a comparison between Wade's 1967 editorial and his 1965 sermon suggests, the liberal civic ideals of Martin Luther King, Jr., which official church doctrine supported, had come under increasing assault.

Emboldened by the reforms of Vatican II, priests and nuns nationwide had increased their civil rights activism following the 1965 Selma voting rights demonstrations. They began to identify more closely with the disadvantaged, the marginalized, and the underprivileged. Catholic lay activists followed as the civil rights movement branched out and placed greater emphasis on class as well as racial inequalities. Not all Catholics were comfortable with this increased agitation, however, and the accompanying "freedom of conscience" that reformers seemed to exploit. At the same time, some Catholics in the late 1960s continued to question the Church's moral authority over its own people, let alone over society at large.[2] Racial tension persisted, but by the early 1970s both the Archdiocese of Atlanta and the Diocese of Mobile (the Diocese of Mobile-Birmingham split into two dioceses in 1969) had institutionalized social action and accepted the importance of issues that earlier had split the Church. That is, bishops and prominent priests and sisters took many of the necessary steps toward guaranteeing racial equality within diocesan institutions. But increasing black nationalism, centered in Mobile's most prominent African American parish, and a more confrontational style of activism revealed how far apart official racial justice policy was from agitators' demands, which in effect rejected those civic ideals that Catholic liberals embraced as the solution to injustice.

In Atlanta Archbishop Hallinan had successfully implemented conciliar reforms and at least ostensibly had overcome racial problems within his own archdiocesan institutions. Beginning in 1962, parochial school integration occurred relatively smoothly, and a year later Hallinan announced an open admission policy for Catholic hospitals as well. In March 1963 he declared, with the "full cooperation" of the female religious orders that ran the two local hospitals, that patients would be admitted "without regard to race or color." But an end to de facto segregation did not happen easily. Members of the all-white medical staff at St. Joseph's infirmary, for example, resisted admitting black doctors to practice; and when integration of the staff did occur, some white physicians withdrew and referred patients elsewhere. The number of white patients admitted to St. Joseph's decreased as well immediately following the decision.[3]

In June 1966, however, both Atlanta Catholic hospitals, St. Joseph's and Holy Family, failed to comply with civil rights regulations under the new Medicare program. The Office of Equal Health Opportunity accused both hospitals of admitting patients and referring them to rooms according to race. The federal agency also charged that St. Joseph's limited the opportunities for Negro staff members. Hallinan himself responded via telephone. He summarized the archdiocese's integration history and claimed that hospital desegregation occurred solely because of the "moral imperatives of justice and mercy" and not because of governmental sanction. Both hospitals, Hallinan claimed, had "borne the brunt of integration" and risked "enduring the stigma of some whites that they would probably become de facto 'Negro hospitals.'"[4]

The charges, however, appeared to have sound basis in fact. The availability of qualified African American physicians limited the hospitals' ability to comply with federal standards. Between 1963 and 1966, seven black physicians had applied to work on the staff of St. Joseph's. One was hired. Three of the others were not accredited in their fields, one did not follow up his application, and two applied as surgeons, a department with a waiting list in excess of 150. Since the noncompliance charges arose, moreover, six more had applied. Four of those were board-certified in specializations where the hospital had openings and probably would be hired. At Holy Family Hospital, the nuns had allowed segregation based on race whenever white patients complained. They did this "simply to keep it from becoming a defacto [*sic*] Negro segregated hospital." But if the federal agency insisted, Holy Family would take whatever steps necessary to implement a random room admission policy, "even if it means that this will eventually produce an all-Negro hospital or close its doors and beds." Within a few days, both hospitals took the necessary measures to reach full federal compliance.[5]

The imposition of federal authority marked a new era for civil rights enforcement and reveals the outlines—and continuing ambivalence—of the Catholic Church in Georgia's relationship to secular society. That St. Joseph's and Holy Family Hospitals would feel pressure to placate white patients reveals that Hallinan's and Sherry's initiatives and arguments for racial justice had not convinced everyone. And in the Diocese of Mobile-Birmingham events of the late 1960s revealed a diocese that had accomplished a measure of progress in racial reform and accepted the necessity of the civil rights movement.[6] Toolen softened his own stance against demonstrations, and he accepted (however belatedly) the importance of Martin Luther King, Jr., to the success of peaceful racial reform. At the same time, however, his remained a diocese divided by recent interpretations of conciliar reform and disagreement over appropriate tactics necessary to achieve racial justice. White clergy and sisters followed their consciences and joined direct-action demonstrations for economic and racial equality. Toolen's authority over the priests and nuns in his diocese had declined, and racial divisions in his church persisted despite remarkable progress in just a couple of years. White laypeople continued to complain about nuns and priests who had stepped out of line and were pushing racial justice issues too far.

Following King's assassination in April 1968, Toolen expressed his "deep sense of profound regret" at the violent death of the civil rights leader. Toolen called King "a great leader to his people, [and] a true apostle of Christian charity and human brotherhood." Toolen hoped that the civil rights leader had not "died in vain," and he instructed churches in his diocese to schedule masses and memorial services in tribute to King. Memorial ceremonies—but not masses—could be ecumenical. At first glance, Toolen's sympathy with King and the mainstream civil rights movement marked a radical transformation for a bishop who in 1965 had criticized the Selma demonstrations and accused King of merely "trying to divide the people." It is possible only to speculate, but Toolen's change of heart was probably less complete than it first appears. By 1968 the Mobile-Birmingham prelate found himself in the minority among his fellow bishops, most of whom publicly supported racial justice and the mainstream activism of King. Not issuing a statement following King's murder in 1968, therefore, would have made Toolen as prominent a public figure—for the wrong reasons—as his 1965 denunciation of priests and nuns in Selma had done.[7] King's ideas also were more agreeable given the black power alternatives in 1968. His appeal to inclusive civic nationalist ideals was far more attractive for many whites than black nationalism.

Rev. Richard T. Sadlier, the Josephite pastor of Mobile's Most Pure Heart of Mary parish, remained unconvinced that Toolen had experienced a conversion to racial justice. The priest of Mobile's largest African American parish wrote Toolen, "Your letter on the death of Martin Luther King irked me. I could almost vomit at the hypocrisy in it. I am looking for leadership from you and not a letter filled with nice sounding but empty and deceiving words!" Sadlier then questioned whether Toolen was seriously interested in evangelism among Negroes in the diocese and doubted whether "you have the guts to condemn the cancer of racism and the sick political structure in your Diocese." Sadlier's rebuke did more than challenge the strength of Toolen's convictions. The priest ignored the bishop's episcopal authority and asserted in its place the primacy of Sadlier's own conscience. Sadlier's disrespect for the local ordinary prompted Toolen to complain to the Josephite provincial, the Very Reverend George F. O'Dea. A few years earlier Toolen's petition probably would have brought reassignment for Sadlier—or at least some sort of official reproach. But in 1968, O'Dea refused Toolen's transfer request. The priest's removal, O'Dea argued, would only appear as if he were being punished for his civil rights activism. Toolen reluctantly agreed that such an appearance would damage the Church's image.[8]

By 1968 Sadlier's parish had become—much to Toolen's consternation—the center of racial activism in Mobile. Staffed by a religious order and not secular priests, Most Pure Heart of Mary had educated several generations of black Mobilians. The product of a segregated institution built to evangelize African Americans, Most Pure Heart of Mary nurtured the pride of the black community and prepared many for the city's racial confrontation in the late 1960s.

By 1968 pickets and demonstrations that had characterized the civil rights movement for the entire decade took on a greater sense of urgency.[9] Civil rights organizations became more militant and increased their efforts to achieve both racial and economic justice. An increasing number of Catholics in Mobile openly supported those efforts in south Alabama. But as activists' demands grew increasingly radical and impatient, they illustrated the extent to which the local Church stayed behind the racial curve. Many white laity, even if they did grudgingly admit that blacks were discriminated against and that corrections in their treatment were necessary, could not stomach the radicalism and demands for immediate remedies of late 1960s civil rights agitators. Church leaders themselves, moreover, gradually institutionalized racial and social justice, but impatience with the slow pace of change led civil rights activists no longer to accept the civic ideals on which diocesan reforms were based.

During the 1965 Selma-to-Montgomery voting rights march, Archbishop Toolen had denounced priests and nuns who came to Alabama from other states and forbade those in his diocese from participating in that or any other demonstration. In 1968 he changed his mind. The archbishop recognized that the previous diocesan restriction was "unrealistic and hence it is to be changed." Now priests and nuns would be permitted to participate in public civil rights demonstrations, provided their participation "is just, legal, and in no way conducive to violence, by fomenting or condoning disrespect for law and order." Priests and female religious, furthermore, would participate only "on an 'individual' basis, and not in the name of the Church." They could exercise their legitimate rights "as citizens in keeping with Christian and Catholic principles," but no one could speak for the Church without Toolen's permission. Toolen noted that the new regulation did not excuse those who had demonstrated in the past without the bishop's permission. But now he was prepared publicly to separate himself from those Catholics who condemned priests and religious who felt morally compelled to demonstrate for racial justice. He allowed that "there has never been more need for honest, productive affirmation of the fact of human brotherhood" that participation in legal civil rights demonstrations would bring.[10]

Toolen's announcement more than likely came out of expedience rather than any other reason. With the blessing of Vatican II reforms, clergy and female religious in his diocese had already begun to follow the dictates of their consciences. The change in diocesan regulations reflected the archbishop's attempt to reclaim his authority and keep civil rights demonstrations within proper boundaries. But Mobile's demonstrations and marches left the aging prelate frustrated and out of touch with his priests and sisters. In May 1968 Toolen wrote a California nun that "Things here are much messed up, particularly Toolen High School. They are all wild on the Negro question, and that comes before class, or anything else. I have only been out there once this year, but I do know what is going on and I don't like it."[11]

In 1969 the number and intensity of racial and economic justice demonstrations increased behind the organizational thrust of Neighborhood Organized Workers (NOW). NOW formed in Mobile in 1968 as a nonviolent, direct-action civil rights organization whose purpose was to pressure the city's business and political communities to open up more employment opportunities for African Americans. NOW represented the combination of racial and class-based issues that characterized activism in the late 1960s. In an effort to increase black electoral participation, NOW also conducted voter registration drives and sponsored political fairs to give citizens an occasion to meet candidates. They met every Wednesday night in Most Pure Heart of Mary's school cafeteria.

Compared to other Alabama cities, Mobile had long enjoyed relatively peaceful race relations. In the 1950s and early 1960s, black leaders had cooperated with racially moderate (and Catholic) Mayor Joseph N. Langan to insure peaceful integration of lunch counters and public transportation. But, frustrated with the slow pace of racial reform in the city, NOW broke with Mobile's established middle-class blacks and demanded immediate improvements in employment and housing opportunities for the city's African American population. This new generation of civil rights activists recognized that white-owned businesses reaped abundant profits from black consumers but refused to give them jobs. As a result, NOW sponsored carefully planned—and strategically targeted—boycotts and pickets of the Greater Gulf States Fair, beer and soft drink distributors, local grocery stores, downtown businesses, and the municipal auditorium in order to convince employers to hire African Americans. In July 1968 NOW brought to town Stokely Carmichael, whose "black power" message helped to accelerate the nation's widening racial divide. The group earned its notoriety in 1969 with marches and demonstrations targeted at Mobile's Junior Miss Pageant, one of the city's annual opportunities to perform for a national audience.[12] NOW's presence in Mobile divided the city and the Catholic Church.

Clerical insubordination (from Toolen's perspective) and support for the NOW demonstrations could be located in both secular and religious order priests. Indeed, even Rev. Thomas Nunan, the director of the diocese's Catholic Charities who lived in the chancery with the archbishop, participated in the demonstrations and provoked angry reactions from lay Catholics. In January 1969, John T. Toenes, of Mobile, mailed a check to Catholic Charities to fulfill his 1968 pledge. In an accompanying letter to Nunan, Toenes expressed pleasure (sarcastic, to be sure) at being able to contribute to such "worthy causes" as "the purchase of gasoline and matches by some of your friends, in order to enforce the downtown boycott." Toenes claimed to believe in the importance of charity, but he charged that some members of the clergy "are stretching the meaning of 'charity' too far." The archbishop either missed or ignored Toenes sarcasm. He assured the layman that "no money will go for oil or matches; we need it to [sic] badly for Catholic Charities." James C. Antwerp, Jr., doubted that boycotts were compatible with Catholicism, "even after Vatican II." If they were, then a counter-boycott of Catholic Charities would be acceptable. Instead, Antwerp argued, it would be better for Catholic Charities if Toolen removed Nunan from his post.[13]

In March 1969, James V. Irby, III, claimed to speak for other Catholic laymen when he complained that "It seems to me, to put it bluntly, my Church is publically [sic] aiding and supporting an organization that is responsible for acts of violence and civil disorder. I refer to NOW." In Irby's mind, NOW's boycotts and sponsorship of Stokely Carmichael's visit were serious threats to law and order. And the fact that they were allowed to hold their meetings at a Catholic church served as an "open endorsement" of their lawlessness. The relationship between the Church and the civil rights organization "coupled with the actions of many of the local clergy, is fast making me ashamed" of being a Catholic. Toolen cautioned the layman about condemning the entire Church for the actions of a few and assured him that the Church would never approve of "disorder and breaking the law."[14]

In May 1969, in order to highlight employment inequality in local government, NOW disrupted the Junior Miss Pageant, held annually at downtown Mobile's Municipal Auditorium. NOW demanded that the auditorium acknowledge its dependence on the African American community and hire a black assistant manager. Among the ninety-three arrested the first night of the beauty contest were two white priests and ten white nuns. Police arrested more than 150 the second night. Included in that number were additional Catholic clergy and female religious. The third night of the pageant—and the third round of protests—brought seventy-one further arrests.[15]

Toolen later declared that Catholic participation in the Junior Miss demonstrations was contrary to diocesan regulations established in 1968, but the archbishop resigned himself to an inability to curtail Catholic activism. In a May 5, 1969, letter, Toolen grumbled, "All authority seems to have gone. They are forbidden to take part in these things, but the Bishop's order means nothing." Later he groused to the apostolic delegate that "Most of our trouble is due to our young sisters and young priests who are agitators among the Negroes. . . . They have no respect for anybody's authority, not even God's." He encouraged Mobile resident Glenn R. Sebastian to "keep up the fight and sooner or later, Holy Mother Church will come out on top."[16]

But Toolen's version of "Holy Mother Church" was clearly under assault. The NOW demonstrations could not be separated from Catholic assistance. A Birmingham newspaper columnist reported that without the institutional support provided by Most Pure Heart of Mary parish and the assistance of "some 30 angry priests and nuns," NOW could not have been successful. Indeed, black Protestant churches were reluctant to support the militant organization. As a result, one nun claimed, "'NOW probably would never have gotten off the ground without us.'" Participating clergy and nuns later defended their activism—and their willingness to be arrested—by claiming "Christian commitment and concern" over wage inequity and poor living conditions for many of Mobile's African Americans. They believed that their personal consciences took precedence over Toolen's misguided opposition to direct action and preference for gradual reform. One priest arrested during the Junior Miss demonstrations was Rev. L. Russell Biven, the director of the diocese's Confraternity of Christian Doctrine. Since he held such a prominent position in the diocesan bureaucracy, Biven's arrest contributed to the crisis of authority that plagued many white members of the Church. One mother of four, Mrs. Edward S. Allenbach, threatened to withdraw her four children from CCD classes at St. Mary's parish in Audrey, outside Mobile. As one chancery memo recounted Allenbach's complaint, "she felt that it was high time that something was done about these priests and sisters who hide behind the cloth. What they do on their own time is their own affair, but let it not be done in the garb of religion."[17]

Two Mobile women expressed their support to the editor of the *Catholic Week*. Diane E. Hampton wrote to "praise and thank the priests, sisters and lay people who realized the true mission of the Church and who were willing to stand and support protests against conditions which tear away man's dignity and shroud him in a cloak of bitterness." Lorraine C. Hampton shared a letter she had written to the pastor of her parish, St. Dominic's. Hampton evinced a post-conciliar spirit when she embraced the notion that the Church "is not a building, but is made up of people who are members of the Mystical Body of Christ." She praised her own pastor for his attempts to engender a Christian spirit in his parishioners, "in spite of the fact that members of the congregation have walked out of the church during homilies on the subject of brotherhood." She then separated herself from those disgruntled communicants. Hampton feared that they represented the mainstream of Catholic thought, so she requested that her name be removed "as a tithing member from the roster of St. Dominic's Parish."[18]

Lorraine Hampton's instincts were correct. Not all white laity were pleased with their pastors' commitments to social justice. Coman Dalton was one of the priests who, in Toolen's words, "has really gone wild on this Negro question and will listen to no-one." As one of the group of activist priests, he tried to explain his arrest to his parishioners during one Sunday mass. Some of his parishioners refused to listen. According to Toolen, "a woman in the church got up and told him she came to hear Mass and not to hear why he was arrested, and she and many others left the church." Father Russell Biven met similar resistance when he attempted to explain his involvement during mass at the Cathedral.[19]

In July 1969 several hundred Mobile Catholics petitioned Toolen to cut off NOW's Catholic support. The signatories protested NOW's use of Catholic property and demanded that Toolen order an end to Church assistance of the civil rights organization. "The people in this organization," the petition claimed, "do *not* support the church in any way nor can their evil activities be construed in any way to be beneficial to a progressive Mobile." These anti-demonstrators supported the archbishop's "open criticism of these priests and nuns and offer you our warmest congratulations and highest praise." But they also implicitly critiqued Toolen's 1968 relaxation of the diocesan ban on demonstrating. "We also wish to state that we totally disagree with this business of priests, nuns and other members of the clergy participating in these marches regardless of whether the people involved have a permit or not." The original petition contained over three hundred signatures (with some of those being "Mr. and Mrs."), and a September 4 addendum listed additional supporters. Toolen acknowledged the written protest. "The contents are useful to me not only as an expression of sentiment but also as an index as to the feelings of a large part of our Catholic community."[20]

The NOW activists were participating in that phase of the black freedom struggle which pushed the accepted boundaries of liberal reform. They essentially rejected the authority of the bishop to regulate their racial justice agitation and embraced the "license" that a couple of years earlier Francis Wade had named the chief culprit of the post-civil rights movement. Other priests and nuns, along with a select few laity, pushed the challenge to accepted authority even further. They rejected the exclusive religious claims of the Roman Catholic Church, even in the post-conciliar ecumenical age, in favor of a radical ecumenism that embraced Catholic and non-Catholic, white and black, and male and female. These ecumenical radicals pushed the conciliar notion of the Church as the people of God to its logical extremes. But their initial motivation was not necessarily the documents of Vatican II. Instead, as with those priests, nuns, and laity who participated in civil rights demonstrations in the 1960s, the black freedom struggle had introduced to them a world outside the confines of the established Church. In that world cooperation with other Christian believers and other races was a welcome change from the narrow religious and cultural boundaries of the pre-conciliar Church. Race aligned both liberals and conservatives, and the Second Vatican Council provided the necessary theological foundation for liberal activism as well as the reason for dismay for conservatives.

Father Brice Joyce of Alabama and Atlanta's Rev. Conald Foust began their movement out of the priesthood in the fight for racial justice. They started as members of the mainstream civil rights movement and ended their careers as racial and liturgical renegades. Joyce, a Benedictine priest, had been assigned to Our Lady of Grace Church, an African American parish in the north Alabama town of Sheffield, since 1959. During his tenure, he was a vocal proponent of civil rights and encouraged local demonstrations and racial justice causes. He imposed on the good graces of Toolen and grew increasingly and openly critical of the archbishop and the diocese's civil rights record. In early 1967, the Benedictines, with Toolen's blessing, decided to consolidate Our Lady of Grace with Our Lady of the Shoals in nearby Tuscumbia, which had already been integrated. The move ended Joyce's active pastorate. According to Joyce's immediate superior, Abbot Gregory Roettger, O.S.B., apostolic administrator of St. Bernard Monastery, Cullman, Alabama, the move was carried out for both financial and racial reasons. Our Lady of Grace was in financial trouble, and it was increasingly difficult for the Church to justify using scarce resources to support a segregated parish. Abbot Roettger insisted that Father Joyce had requested the consolidation and transfer from the diocese.[21]

Joyce's racial justice and spiritual journey were not over. From Sheffield, Alabama, Joyce relocated to Wilmington, Delaware, before returning to Alabama to accept the directorship of the Alabama Council on Human Relations, a position he accepted without consulting his Benedictine superior or Archbishop Toolen. His status as a priest was unclear, and Toolen and Roettger repeatedly asked him to clarify where he believed he stood in relation to the Church. Joyce ultimately placed his own authority over that of his bishop and his superior.[22] What started as racial justice activism became something more serious, from a traditional Catholic perspective. According to Toolen, Joyce violated Church laws and procedures. He "was teaching un-Catholic doctrine, tore up the rosary in front of his people, would not obey the orders of his Abbot or his Bishop, and finally took unto himself a wife."[23] By behaving in such a way, he had "made himself the arbiter of what was good, and what was permissible to achieve that good."[24] His priestly career was over. In Joyce's career in Alabama it is possible to discern the intimate relationship between the civil rights movement and the redefinition of the Church's authority in Catholics' lives in the late 1960s. For many activists, the black freedom struggle was the starting point for their movement out from under the Church's authority.

Liturgical and other conciliar reforms of Vatican II, moreover, led to greater experimentation in support of civil rights. Atlanta provided a more serious example of a racial justice and liturgical experiment that got out of hand under the leadership of a priest who eventually questioned his relationship to the Church. In 1967 Archbishop Hallinan launched a bold experiment in parish organization. He authorized the establishment of a new parish, the Community of Christ Our Brother, which would not be defined by geographical boundaries. Instead, its members would come from throughout the city, much like the typical membership of Protestant churches. The Community would devote itself to addressing social justice problems and, eventually, to exploring avenues for liturgical innovations and ecumenical dialogue and cooperation. Alleviating problems of poverty and achieving integration were central concerns. From the start, the Community's participants wanted to locate in a poor (particularly Negro poor) area and make social work a primary goal of the community. They wanted to combine that racial and social justice work with liturgical reform.

The idea for the "open parish" originated with Foust, the administrator of the experimental parish. He argued for the importance of experimentation in keeping the archdiocese modern and relevant. Hallinan agreed. But Foust was already pressing against the boundaries of diocesan authority, and he questioned Hallinan's leadership from the outset. He also included in the exploratory group's first meeting Rev. Kim Dreisbach, an Episcopalian who would have shared pastoral duties with Foust and any other non-Catholic minister who joined the parish. In a letter to Auxiliary Bishop Joseph Bernardin, Foust baldly proclaimed his goal for the new parish: "I envision this as an Ecumenical Church." Bishop Bernardin responded, "Unless more has taken place than I am aware of, I think it would be premature to extend the discussions formally beyond Catholic circles at this time." Hallinan allowed that cooperation could be possible, as long as it followed the dictates of Vatican II's Decree on Ecumenism. For example, Hallinan could support an arrangement that provided for separate liturgical worship services and joint prayer or Bible study services. For now, the parish "should thoroughly absorb the Catholic corpus of faith and moral principles" and "seek its first strength within the Catholic format, not outside."[25]

Early members of the exploratory group disagreed with the archbishop and argued that members of other faiths would not feel as if they were part of the community unless they were included in the planning stages. Non-Catholics did participate from the outset. The first meeting began with mass, celebrated by Father Foust. The second organizational meeting a week later opened with Scripture reading and brief homilies by Rev. Kim Dreisbach and Rev. Austin Ford, both Protestants. Catholics and non-Catholics alike downplayed their denominational differences and emphasized their shared Christian faith. One man, Lee Offen, declared, "Basically we are Christians. This brings the whole community of Christ's Church into one Church." Foust clarified the statement, adding, "regardless of our differences, in different denominations, we are united in Christ." Converts to Catholicism strongly supported Foust and the Community's ecumenical aims. Kay Blair argued, "From my own experience as a convert, I feel we must definitely be ecumenical, not only for those we serve but for us who are serving." As Blair's statement suggests, the group defined ecumenism more broadly than just inter-denominational cooperation; their ecumenism was to include rich and poor, white and black. They sought an integrated parish focused on smoothing the rough edges of poverty in a single community.[26]

Its community action goals may have been consistent with the new social justice aims of the archdiocese, but its implementation pushed the new parish and especially Father Foust to the margins of mainstream Catholicism. After the experiment was officially launched in June 1967, the Community of Christ Our Brother met for Eucharistic services in the Bethlehem Center of the Methodist Church's Gammon Theological Seminary in Atlanta. On Thursday nights, the group conducted "prayer, study, and work sessions" at the center. Throughout the week, they celebrated the Eucharist in individual homes. By July the Community had approximately forty members, ten of whom were

Protestant. In April 1968 there were twenty-eight families who were active in the Community, with approximately forty adults and between fifty and sixty children. The parish operated the Pryor Street School Center on Saturdays that was intended "to encourage Negro leadership." It sponsored programs in drama, arts, crafts, dancing, movies, and physical education. Foust lived in the area that the Community of Christ Our Brother intended to serve, and he himself tutored neighborhood children, played truant officer during the week, and went to court with those residents who were in trouble with the law.[27]

By 1968 any earlier spirit of submission to archdiocesan leadership had evaporated entirely. Foust professed the need to be open to the leadership of the Holy Spirit and the democratic consensus of the Community of Christ Our Brother. That openness to the Holy Spirit led him to further liturgical innovations and open opposition to Pope Paul VI's 1968 encyclical *Humanae Vitae,* which banned the use of artificial contraceptives by Roman Catholics.

In April 1968 Bishop Bernardin, who assumed temporary control of the archdiocese following Hallinan's 1967 death, worried that Foust's insistence on following the leadership of the Holy Spirit, pushed to its logical extreme, "could well lead ultimately to a repudiation of the Church's visible structure and authority."[28] Indeed, Foust became a church unto himself, answering only to the Holy Spirit and the democratic consensus of the Community of Christ Our Brother. In May 1968 Foust "blessed" an interfaith marriage between a Catholic woman and a divorced non-Catholic, a union that canon law of the Catholic Church could not authorize. Foust defended his action by arguing that he was bound by his conscience to validate the marriage to allow the Catholic woman to return to the sacraments. The spiritual good of the person involved should take priority over Church law. Bishop Bernardin conceded that Catholics were responsible for following their conscience, "but we also must have an obligation to form a correct conscience, and to do this we must look to the Church for guidance." Bernardin recognized the larger problem, however. Father Foust's "concept of the Church is different from ours."[29]

Foust continued his vocal opposition to *Humanae Vitae* and urged Catholics to rely on their own consciences. Perhaps most serious, he included non-Catholics in the reception of the Eucharist, thereby violating the exclusivity of the Church's most singular sacrament.[30] Foust

was eventually suspended from his duties as a priest of the archdiocese. The Community of Christ Our Brother stumbled along without
formal leadership before finally dying out. Its members either returned
to established congregations or ceased church attendance altogether.

The Second Vatican Council encouraged Joyce, Foust, and count-
less others, but it was the civil rights movement combined with those
conciliar changes that led them to first challenge and then reject traditional authority completely. Indeed, these incidences illustrate the
crisis of authority created for southern Catholics and Archbishops
Toolen, Hallinan, and Thomas Donnellan—Hallinan's successor—as
a result of Vatican II and the civil rights movement. Most southern
Protestant pastors served at the whim of their congregation. Priests
served at the discretion of their local bishop. Laity who found themselves at odds with their priests had little recourse but appeals to their
bishop. If the prelate refused to remove or reassign recalcitrant priests,
then the laity were stuck with disagreeable leadership. And at eighty-
three, already past standard retirement age and well out of touch with
the Church mainstream, Toolen proved reluctant to discipline his
priests. Circumstances would not improve for white Catholics upset
with the pace of racial and religious reform. Toolen retired in December 1969 and was replaced by John L. May, formerly auxiliary bishop
of the Archdiocese of Chicago. A member of a younger generation
and evincing more liberal sympathies, May reinforced the Alabama
Church's support for racial and social justice and its commitment to
implementation of conciliar reforms.

It would be naïve to assume that Donnellan and Mobile's Bishop
John May succeeded in moving all of their parishioners toward sympathy with civil rights. In fact, both Donnellan and May were forced to
remind white Catholics in 1970 that integration was diocesan policy in
order to keep whites from abusing parochial schools to elude racial integration of public schools. In short, many whites still were not enthu-
siastic supporters of racial justice. But within their respective dioceses,
both Donnellan and May were the ultimate arbiters of integration and
both confronted dissent with the moral authority of Roman Catholic
doctrine. Moreover, by 1970 complaints about racial issues declined
and the crisis of authority that plagued the Church in the late 1960s
shifted to gender issues and disagreement over the Church's ban on artificial birth control. Both the Archdiocese of Atlanta and the Diocese

of Mobile successfully institutionalized social concern and directed resources toward alleviating economic and social inequities that often aggravated racial discrimination.

There remained racial problems to resolve, to be sure, and schools continued to be a source of conflict. Despite Toolen's claims to the contrary, school integration did not immediately follow his 1964 edict. Geographical location most often determined which parish elementary school a student attended; therefore, widespread integration at that level simply did not occur right away. And diocesan high schools were slow to admit racially mixed student bodies. For a couple of years after his pastoral edict, Toolen reported that "All our schools are now integrated," referring to official diocesan policy and not reality. In a 1967 letter to a Wisconsin nun, Toolen explained that, despite being welcome in any diocesan school, few Negroes had applied for admission. "They would rather be with their own and the Negro people all know that Pure Heart of Mary, because of the sisters, is an excellent school."[31]

Diocesan officials initiated integration efforts by pairing white schools with blacks ones and slowly consolidating them. But as late as 1970, both Montgomery and Selma, for instance, still contained two racially separated schools. Indeed, in a 1970 report Bishop John L. May acknowledged that "very little has been done" to overcome geographical boundaries to integration. Nevertheless, he noted, "Almost all schools have some black students. One school has an equal number." And two formerly black high schools had closed and those students attended other diocesan high schools.[32]

In Mobile supporters of desegregation finally won court battles in 1971, and the school system began the court-ordered plan of redesignating schools, implementing new programs, and busing students across the city. The pattern in Mobile and the rest of the South was for private academies to attract white students fleeing desegregation in public schools. For some Alabama parents, Catholic schools promised safe—i.e., segregated—havens for their children. In 1970, however, Bishop May refused to admit those transfer students into parochial schools. "We will not allow our schools to be a refuge for anyone trying to avoid integration in the public schools," May pledged. In a delicious bit of irony, those parents now trying to send their children to diocesan schools were non-Catholics or, according to May, "Catholics who removed their kids from our schools when we started to integrate." By 1972 eighteen of twenty-nine diocesan elementary schools and all four high schools were integrated.[33]

Atlanta was equally as vulnerable to racial unrest in the late 1960s as Mobile. Under Hallinan and his successor, Thomas A. Donnellan, the Church had established its civil rights credentials and promoted racial justice. In 1970 Donnellan reaffirmed the archdiocese's commitment to school integration, but like May, he was forced actually to close parochial school doors to some whites. In a scheme to avoid public school integration, some area whites tried to enroll their children in parochial schools. Hallinan had integrated Atlanta archdiocesan schools, to be sure, but the population of African American Catholics in the city remained small, and that minority was not widely dispersed. Donnellan refused to allow new students to be admitted to archdiocesan schools for the remainder of the year, except for the children of parents who had relocated to a new parish. He announced that admission in the next academic year would be according to regular archdiocesan policy—i.e., open admission, with Catholics within a parish receiving first priority, then other Catholics, followed by all other children, "regardless of race or creed." "Our schools," Donnellan announced, "will always be opened to those who sincerely seek the religiously oriented education that the schools can provide." "Our racial policy will always be the same," the archbishop continued, "to use our schools and our entire educational program to foster racial integration, and understanding and harmony between men of all races and creeds."[34]

When public schools did finally integrate, some white parents often favored integrated parochial schools over public ones. In 1971, for example, when Huntsville integrated its public schools, parents of fifteen white students tried to use St. Joseph's parish elementary school to escape having to send their children to a previously all-black school. In July 1971, Calvary Hill, the formerly segregated public school, had been ordered to admit 30 percent white students for the upcoming school year. St. Joseph's school was 60 percent white. Birmingham diocesan policy required integration and refused admission to white children who were merely trying to escape public school desegregation. An Alabama circuit court ruled that St. Joseph's must accept the students, but in February 1972 the state supreme court overturned the lower court ruling. Birmingham bishop Joseph G. Vath praised the decision and pledged that "in Christian charity . . . the good of these children must be considered." The fifteen white students, therefore, would be allowed to finish the semester at St. Joseph's.[35]

The process of integrating parishes by consolidating black and white churches in the same geographic area began as early as 1968 in Alabama. In Auburn that year, a priest and two laypeople requested that Toolen close a Negro mission and fold the responsibilities for the African American apostolate there into the white parish, St. Michael's Church. The laypeople, Mr. and Mrs. Gerald V. Flannery, a husband and wife who were members of St. Michael's, criticized the "institutionalized racial separation" and "spiritual and physical isolation" created by separate parishes. Toolen complied with the requests and St. Michael's parish assumed responsibility for St. Martin's mission in Auburn. This process did not always occur easily, especially when parish territorial boundaries overlapped and individual churches resisted relinquishing their autonomy.[36]

Opposition to mergers often came from black parishes instead of from whites and was not always based on reasons of racial prejudice. Indeed, as some black defenders of segregated black schools later experienced, combining white and black facilities often led to a sense of loss for the black community. Those institutions, created though they were because of white desires to exclude blacks from public life, had nurtured African American identity and fostered a spirit of group solidarity during tough times. In 1970, for instance, the Shrine of the Holy Cross in Daphne, Alabama—a predominantly black parish with more than four hundred members in 1970—voted, "with only one exception, to keep it open." And in 1993 a Tuscaloosa priest recalled that African Americans had resisted combining with a white parish there because separate facilities gave blacks autonomy that they did not enjoy in an integrated church. "Probably [parish consolidation] was immature because in their own parish of St. Mary Magdalene they were 'top dog' so to speak. They ran the whole parish." Whites accepted African Americans into their parish, but blacks "just didn't have the influence that they had had in their own church and so on so, many Black people were lost through that period to the church."[37]

The South may have managed to postpone radical reform, but the Catholic Church in Alabama and Georgia was not the same institution it had been before the civil rights movement began. Indeed, in 1970 Bishop May claimed that the Diocese of Mobile's record in race relations surpassed that of his native Chicago. He wrote to an Urbana, Illinois, nun that "in our Catholic schools I see a much more constructive situation here than I saw in most cases in Chicago. Almost all our schools are integrated and there has been little difficulty. The same is true of the other institutions of the Diocese for the most part." Problems persisted, however, "especially in housing." But the white community recognized its responsibilities, and "All in all, I believe there is real promise here. I hope we can do our part."[38]

By 1970 the Church had seemingly survived its crisis of authority and institutionalized social concern, with both the Diocese of Mobile and the Archdiocese of Atlanta at least developing plans to solve problems of economic injustice. Officials in both dioceses realized the economic component of segregation. Social justice activism, therefore, dovetailed with efforts to end racial discrimination. In Mobile, for example, Bishop May established a commission for social justice, which listed its first priority as a "challenge to conscience" regarding the nation's racial crisis. "Haunted by the fact that racist attitudes have been and still are accepted as part of our church and national life, this Commission asks for a Christian response to the entire problem." Among other things, the statement urged whites to address blacks with titles of respect (e.g., "Mr." or "Mrs."), called on individual Catholics to adopt in their own businesses the diocesan policy of awarding work contracts only to equal opportunity employers, and invited "all Catholic institutions . . . to find ways to make available to Black people better job opportunities and positions of responsibility." The commission issued the statement—with twenty-eight names attached—"in a spirit of reconciliation with our brothers whom we have offended and alienated by past injustices and with a firm hope in the future that must find us living and working and building together as one people under God."[39]

Some local Catholics charged that the commission's membership did not adequately represent those groups already active in social justice areas in the community. Some activists were conspicuously absent from the commission, omissions that led these critics to question the diocese's commitment to true reform. Sister Judith Ann Pinnell, R.S.M., a nun in Daphne, Alabama, feared the commission would become little more than "a discussion club" that would actually hinder the drive for social justice. Sister Judith questioned whether local blacks—those who would be served by the new diocesan organiza-tion—were familiar with its members. Diane Hampton claimed that the commission "will be unable to function without the knowledge and strategy that only people working with the [poverty] communities can provide." Her suggestions of possible additions to the commission were active in a variety of causes, ranging from urban development to public health.[40]

The commission's initial Statement of Concern elicited favorable response from other Mobilians. Joseph Lanaux Marston, Jr., wrote the bishop that Corpus Christi's parish council was in "unanimous agreement with all parts of the Statement." Marston pledged the par-ish council's unfailing cooperation "to implement all propositions contained in the Statement and to do whatever else is necessary, and within our power, to live in Christian love and unity with all our broth-ers in Christ." The white layman also claimed that the parish council and all parish organizations were "fully integrated with our Black brothers." The interracial group acted in "unity as one people, and we work together as a parish family, under the Fatherhood of God." Ray and Ida Vrazel also praised the statement on behalf of the local Chris-tian Family Movement but expressed fear that the statement's moral force suffered from a lack of sincere priestly interest in social justice is-sues. Sermons that reflected the statement's message "have been either, non-existant [sic] or inadequate." Members of the CFM believed that "most people are followers" and the "hardened non-changer" needed to be taught "that this is a prerequisite of Christianity."[41]

In the South, poverty often accompanied segregation, and the primary concern of social justice commissions in Mobile and Atlanta remained racial discrimination and its concomitant economic ills. In 1971 Bishop May appealed for financial support of Catholic Charities because "the root of much of our poverty in southern Alabama is racial discrimination." Support of Catholic Charities promised to "balance the scales" and end discrimination. In Atlanta archdiocesan officials lob-bied for open housing that did not relegate blacks to the poorest areas of the city. One 1972 report to the archdiocesan pastoral council noted that 45 percent of the city's population (most of whom were black) lived on 16 percent of the land available for residential development. Persistent segregation, moreover, restricted African American move-ment out of low-income environments. The council called for efforts to educate local priests and laity about the problems of open housing. It also encouraged the Georgia Real Estate Commission to enforce the state's laws against racial blockbusting. The federal government had defined the legal parameters of open housing, but the council also insisted that Christians "must take into consideration the moral factor." Christian charity should lead to racial justice "with the realization that all men, women and children share the same human dignity."[42]

This support for social justice activism resulted from the convergence of the civil rights movement and the Second Vatican Council in the 1960s. Those two events disrupted the southern status quo and challenged the episcopal authority of bishops and priests, even as it made this institutionalization of social concern possible. Both Alabama and Georgia wrestled with the implications of conciliar and racial reforms. As a result, the Church in the 1970s was a different institution than it had been in 1945. Conservative and gradualist priests and bishops had lost ground to more progressive forces, and bishops such as Thomas Donnellan and John May recast the southern Church to be more compatible with a new era.

The institutional Church may have achieved some measure of integration, and in the post–civil rights movement modern South, race was—at least on the surface—no longer a central issue. To be sure, forced busing and continuing legal battles over enforcement of the 1964 Civil Rights Act meant that the region had not yet achieved a consensus on race relations. But it had become evident by the 1970s that those issues were not peculiarly southern. Indeed, from Los Angeles to Boston, race riots and forced busing revealed that the South's struggle for the previous decade and a half had been the nation's struggle as well. If the centrality of race no longer separated the South from the rest of the nation, it continued to divide the region's Protestant churches—that is, if they confronted the issue at all. Indeed, as institutions unaffected by federal legislation, churches remained the last unapologetic bastions of racial segregation. Protestant churches located in inner cities either followed their white parishioners to the suburbs or stayed and suffered through declining memberships. Those congregations that stayed often disagreed over their obligations to their urban environments and the African American populations that soon surrounded their churches. Few made inclusiveness an explicit goal, and even more opposed it with a racist passion unaffected by the black freedom struggle.[43] One must be careful, therefore, not to emphasize the Church's racial reform progress so much as to obscure the extent to which race continued to be the primary prism through which whites saw their world and their Church.

The "Tolerable Alien" in the Modern South

✦

The civil rights movement changed the South and the Catholic Church. It linked Catholics to southern culture in a way not previously experienced, even as that culture was undergoing changes from which it would not recover. The black freedom struggle separated southern religion from southern culture and freed southern Protestants to seek common ground with Catholics.[1] A sort of religious pluralism resulted from the shared drama of the black freedom struggle. This pluralism came when many Catholics affirmed the region's secular culture and rose to the defense of racial segregation.

The movement in the 1960s brought divergent paths for the Catholic Church in Alabama and Georgia. In Alabama, Archbishop Toolen was at least a gradualist and proved only moderately supportive of 1960s racial justice goals. Blinded by his own racism and concern over the Church's acceptance by mainstream white society, however, he feared demonstrations and the ways they upset the status quo and the Catholic Church's precarious position therein. Many of his white parishioners agreed with the archbishop on that score. Toolen's initial crisis of authority came with Selma in 1965. He retained control over his own priests and nuns (i.e., kept them from participating); but he could not control those who came from outside the diocese. His episcopal authority had been supplanted by the moral imperatives of the civil rights movement and the Second Vatican Council. For civil rights activists, the Church as the "people of God" proved more morally and ethically compelling than appeals to preconciliar orthodoxy. By the late 1960s, Toolen lost authority over his own priests and nuns as well.

Although not without its own ambivalence and internal divisions, the Archdiocese of Atlanta was more progressive in issues of racial justice. Leadership in civil rights came directly from the hierarchy and prominent lay leaders. Archbishop Hallinan and the archdiocese's white lay leadership fit well with city boosters who sought to project a progressive image. Many of the laity were lawyers and business leaders who understood that peaceful race relations were essential for city growth. This is not to suggest that Catholic proponents of the civil rights movement in Georgia acted out of pragmatic concerns. Indeed, Archbishop Hallinan, Gerard Sherry, and the presidents of lay organizations all evinced sincere conviction that Catholic doctrine should be applied to race relations. All the white laity were not happy, to be sure, but within the parameters of the archdiocese, those disgruntled with racial and liturgical reform became the outsiders from the mainstream Church, while insiders in white southern society.

The end of the 1960s did not bring the end of racial strife, of course. But the South of the early 1970s appeared more diverse, and the mainstream acceptance of the Catholic Church reflected that turnabout. Feeling less embattled, they had become, it would appear, the "tolerable alien." There even appeared to be room for the Catholic moderates and liberals who had been marginalized just a decade before. Indeed, the Second Vatican Council vindicated progressive Catholics like Foley and the Catholic Committee of the South by opening the doors for increased activism. Since the 1960s, this liberalism has become more common—at least among American Catholic bishops. Indeed, the hierarchy absorbed many of the issues of social justice and human rights that activists of the left had embraced. Writing in the late 1990s, historian David J. O'Brien concluded, however, that the hierarchy's identification with a liberal Catholic agenda satisfied very few members of the laity. From the perspective of the Catholic left, the bishops' reform agenda offered inadequate solutions to social problems. From the perspective of the right, in the words of O'Brien, "its social reform proposals seemed unnecessary and its religious stance seemed compromised by undue adaptation to secular culture."[2]

That is, the white laity may not have agreed that interracialism was an appropriate Catholic response to the South's changing racial and social environment. But the bishops gave them little choice within the Church. The reforms of Vatican II encouraged a more activist faith and empowered Catholic liberals to seek out solutions to current social problems. It is difficult to know for certain the nature of the relationship between bishops and laity in Alabama and Georgia in the 1970s. But there is little evidence that their hard line on liberal racial reform softened within the succeeding decade. In fact, race may have ceased to be a primary issue in public debate among Catholic dioceses in the South, but it continued to be a factor in voting well into the 1970s and 1980s. Indeed, in many elections it was the most important factor, even if racial concerns had to be couched in other terms and disguised by other issues.[3]

As race became less overtly important, however, issues of gender and sexuality seized Catholics' and white evangelicals' social and moral imagination. For over a decade, Catholics were the primary opponents of the liberalization of abortion laws. In their minds, their support of racial justice and opposition to legal abortion were consistent social justice positions. It took conservative southern Protestants longer to embrace such thinking. In the 1970s Southern Baptists at least grew increasingly disaffected with modern southern—indeed national— culture. They joined the American evangelical mainstream and in the process followed Catholics into combat in the nation's "culture wars."[4] The nation's conservative realignment has roots in the South and in white opposition to racial reform, but the cultural ecumenism that emerged from it now looks beyond race and regional identity.

Notes

⬥

INTRODUCTION

1. "Trail Blazers in Birmingham," *Catholic Week*, August 24, 1945, p. 7.

2. Charles P. Sweeney, "Bigotry in the South," *Nation*, November 24, 1920: 585–586. On the murder, see Paul M. Pruitt, Jr., "Private Tragedy, Public Shame," *Alabama Heritage* 30 (fall 1993): 24–37; Kay J. Blalock, "The Irish Catholic Experience in Birmingham, Alabama, 1871–1921" (M.A. thesis, University of Alabama at Birmingham, 1989), 89–100. On Black's involvement in the trial, see Roger K. Newman, *Hugo Black: A Biography* (New York: Pantheon Books, 1994), chapter 5; and Virginia Van der Veer Hamilton, *Hugo Black: The Alabama Years* (Baton Rouge: Louisiana State Univ. Press, 1972), 85–93. See Philip Hamburger, *Separation of Church and State* (Cambridge, Mass.: Harvard Univ. Press, 2002), 422–434, for more on Black's anti-Catholicism and the role that anti-Catholicism played in the evolution of contemporary understandings of separation of church and state.

3. On the tension in American history between liberty and coercion, see Gary Gerstle, "Liberty, Coercion, and the Making of Americans," *Journal of American History* 84 (September 1997): 524–558.

4. See Samuel S. Hill, *Southern Churches in Crisis* (Boston: Beacon Press, 1968; New York: Holt, Rinehart, and Winston, 1966). Hill's classic has been reissued with a new introduction and reflection on the state of the field some thirty years later as *Southern Churches in Crisis Revisited* (Tuscaloosa: Univ. of Alabama Press, 1999). See also Samuel S. Hill, "The South's Two Cultures," in *Religion and the Solid South*, ed. Samuel S. Hill (Nashville, Tenn.: Abingdon Press, 1972); John Lee Eighmy, *Churches in Cultural Captivity: A History of the Social Attitudes of Southern Baptists* (Knoxville: Univ. of Tennessee Press, 1972); Barry Hankins, "Southern Baptists and Northern Evangelicals: Cultural Factors and the Nature of Religious Alliances," *Religion and American Culture: A Journal of Interpretation* 7 (summer 1997): 271–298. For a challenge to the cultural captivity thesis, see Beth Barton Schweiger, "The Captivity of Southern Religious History" (unpublished paper presented to Southern Intellectual History Circle, Birmingham, Ala., February 21, 1997); and Beth Barton Schweiger, *The Gospel Working Up: Progress and the Pulpit in Nineteenth-Century Virginia* (New York:

Oxford Univ. Press, 2000). Mark R. Bell recently argued, however, that despite some diversity in the South, cultural captivity is still a viable thesis. See "Continued Captivity: Religion in Bartow County Georgia," *Journal of Southern Religion* 2 (1999).

5. Paul Harvey, *Redeeming the South: Religious Cultures and Racial Identities among Southern Baptists, 1865–1925* (Chapel Hill: Univ. of North Carolina Press, 1997), quotation on 198; and Paul Harvey, *Freedom's Coming: Religious Culture and the Shaping of the South from the Civil War through the Civil Rights Era* (Chapel Hill: Univ. of North Carolina Press, 2005); Mark Newman, *Getting Right with God: Southern Baptists and Desegregation, 1945–1995* (Tuscaloosa: Univ. of Alabama Press, 2001), especially chapters 2, 3, and 9. Also on Southern Baptists' changing attitudes on race, see Alan Scot Willis, *All According to God's Plan: Southern Baptist Missions and Race, 1945–1970* (Lexington: Univ. Press of Kentucky, 2005). The historiography of religion in the civil rights movement is expanding and now includes truly impressive scholarship. See, for example, James F. Findlay, Jr., *Church People in the Struggle: The National Council of Churches and the Black Freedom Movement, 1950–1970* (New York: Oxford Univ. Press, 1993); Michael B. Friedland, *Lift Up Your Voice Like a Trumpet: White Clergy and the Civil Rights and Antiwar Movements, 1954–1973* (Chapel Hill: Univ. of North Carolina Press, 1998); Charles W. Eagles, *Outside Agitator: Jon Daniels and the Civil Rights Movement in Alabama* (Chapel Hill: Univ. of North Carolina Press, 1993); Gardiner H. Shattuck, Jr., *Episcopalians and Race: Civil War to Civil Rights* (Lexington: Univ. Press of Kentucky, 2000); Charles Marsh, *God's Long Summer: Stories of Faith and Civil Rights* (Princeton, N.J.: Princeton Univ. Press, 1997); Peter C. Murray, *Methodists and the Crucible of Race, 1930–1975* (Columbia: Univ. of Missouri Press, 2004).

6. David L. Chappell, *A Stone of Hope: Prophetic Religion and the Death of Jim Crow* (Chapel Hill: Univ. of North Carolina Press, 2004); Marsh, *God's Long Summer,* 3. Also, see Jane Dailey, "Sex, Segregation, and the Sacred after *Brown*," *Journal of American History* 91 (June 2004): 119–144. Dailey argued that the civil rights movement is best thought of as a battle between "competing claims to Christian orthodoxy."

7. On Brownson, see E. Brooks Holifield, *Theology in America: Christian Thought from the Age of the Puritans to the Civil War* (New Haven: Yale Univ. Press, 2003), 482–491, quotation on 489.

8. John T. McGreevy, *Catholicism and American Freedom: A History* (New York: Norton, 2003), chapter 7.

9. "Pastoral Constitution on the Church in the Modern World," in *The Basic Sixteen Documents, Vatican Council II: Constitutions, Decrees, Declarations,* ed. Austin Flannery, O.P. (Northport, N.Y.: Costello, 1996), 165.

10. "Declaration on Religious Liberty," in Flannery, ed., *The Basic Sixteen Documents,* 552.

11. "Dogmatic Constitution on the Church," in Flannery, ed., *The Basic Sixteen Documents,* 14; John T. McGreevy, *Parish Boundaries: The Catholic Encounter with Race in the Twentieth-Century Urban North* (Chicago: Univ. of Chicago Press, 1996), 160.

12. Quoted in William A. Osborne, *The Segregated Covenant: Race Relations and American Catholics* (New York: Herder and Herder, 1967), 78.

13. Newman, *Getting Right with God,* 160–161.

14. On Catholics and segregation, see Dolores Egger Labbé, *Jim Crow Comes to Church: The Establishment of Segregated Catholic Parishes in South Louisiana* (New York: Arno Press, 1978); and Osborne, *The Segregated Covenant*. On the separation of Protestant denominations, see Daniel W. Stowell, *Rebuilding Zion: The Religious Reconstruction of the South, 1863–1877* (New York: Oxford Univ. Press, 1998); Harvey, *Redeeming the South*.

15. McGreevy, *Parish Boundaries*.

CHAPTER 1

1. W. J. Cash, *The Mind of the South*, with a new introduction by Bertram Wyatt-Brown (New York: Vintage Books, 1991; originally published in 1941), first quotation on xlviii, subsequent quotations on 333–334; Gary W. McDonogh, "Constructing Christian Hatred: Anti-Catholicism, Diversity, and Identity in Southern Religious Life," in *Religion in the Contemporary South: Diversity, Community, and Identity*, ed. O. Kendall White, Jr., and Daryl White (Athens: Univ. of Georgia Press, 1995). On anti-Protestantism, see Jay Dolan, "Catholic Attitudes toward Protestants," in *Uncivil Religion: Interreligious Hostility in America*, ed. Robert N. Bellah and Frederick E. Greenspahn (New York: Crossroad, 1987).

2. Eamon Duffy, *The Stripping of the Altars: Traditional Religion in England, c. 1400–c. 1580*, 2nd ed. (New Haven: Yale Univ. Press, 2005).

3. John T. McGreevy, "Thinking on One's Own: Catholicism in the American Intellectual Imagination, 1928–1960," *Journal of American History* 84 (June 1997): 97–131. This appears in revised form as chapter 6 of John T. McGreevy, *Catholicism and American Freedom: A History* (New York: Norton, 2003). See also Mark S. Massa, S.J., "The New and Old Anti-Catholicism and the Analogical Imagination," *Theological Studies* 62 (2001): 549–570.

4. David Tracy, *The Analogical Imagination: Christian Theology and the Culture of Pluralism* (New York: Crossroad, 1981), 408, 413. See also Andrew M. Greeley, *The Catholic Myth: The Behavior and Beliefs of American Catholics* (New York: Collier Books, 1990); Massa, "The New and Old Anti-Catholicism and the Analogical Imagination."

5. *Catechism of the Catholic Church*, (Liguori, Mo.: Liguori Publications, 1994), par. 795, p. 210; Mark A. Noll and Carolyn Nystrom, *Is the Reformation Over? An Evangelical Assessment of Contemporary Roman Catholicism* (Grand Rapids, Mich.: Baker Academic, 2005), 145–147.

6. Tracy, *Analogical Imagination*, 415.

7. Massa, "The New and Old Anti-Catholicism and the Analogical Imagination," 567–568. For an example of Protestant community, see Tracy Elaine K'Meyer, *Interracialism and Christian Community in the Postwar South* (Charlottesville: Univ. Press of Virginia, 1997).

8. McDonogh, "Constructing Christian Hatred: Anti-Catholicism, Diversity, and Identity in Southern Religious Life," 67, 77.

9. On the history of Catholics in the region, see Oscar H. Lipscomb, "The Administration of John Quinlan, Second Bishop of Mobile, 1859–1883," *Records of the American Catholic Historical Society of Philadelphia* 78 (1967): 3–163; Oscar H . Lipscomb,

"The Administration of Michael Portier, Vicar Apostolic of Alabama and the Floridas, 1825–1829, and First Bishop of Mobile, 1829–1859" (Ph.D. diss., Catholic University of America, Washington, D.C., 1963); Fussell Chalker, "Irish Catholics and the Building of the Ocmulgee and Flint Railroad," *Georgia Historical Quarterly* 54 (1970): 507–516; Frank J. Fede, *Italians in the Deep South: Their Impact on Birmingham and the American Heritage* (Montgomery, Ala.: Black Belt Press, 1994); Randall Miller and Jon L. Wakelyn, eds., *Catholics in the Old South: Essays on Church and Culture* (Macon, Ga.: Mercer Univ. Press, 1983); Randall M. Miller, "Catholics in a Protestant World: The Old South Example," in *Varieties of Southern Religious Experience,* ed. Samuel S. Hill (Baton Rouge: Louisiana State Univ. Press, 1988); Rose Gibbons Lovett, *The Catholic Church in the Deep South: The Diocese of Birmingham in Alabama, 1540–1976* (Birmingham, Ala.: The Diocese of Birmingham in Alabama, 1980).

10. "Final Statistic In CCD Census Report Numbers 128,000 Catholics in Diocese," *Catholic Week,* January 17, 1964, p. 1; "CCD Census Report Parish-by-Parish," *Catholic Week,* January 24, 1964, p. 7; Thomas J. Toolen, "My Jubilee Story" [February 1960], Alabama Department of Archives and History, Montgomery, Alabama; Charles E. Nolan, "Modest and Humble Crosses: A History of Catholic Parishes in the South Central Region (1850–1984)," in *The American Catholic Parish: A History from 1850 to the Present,* vol. 1, ed. Jay Dolan (Mahwah, N.J.: Paulist Press, 1987), appendix 4, p. 328. The dioceses in Alabama and Georgia grew and divided during the years covered by this study. In 1945 the Diocese of Mobile and the Diocese of Savannah-Atlanta covered all of their respective states. In 1956 the Church created the Diocese of Savannah and the Diocese of Atlanta out of the Diocese of Savannah-Atlanta. In 1962 Atlanta was elevated to an archdiocese. The Diocese of Mobile became the Diocese of Mobile-Birmingham in 1954, which included portions of west Florida until 1968. In 1969 the Diocese of Mobile-Birmingham separated into two dioceses. Although the Diocese of Mobile was not an archdiocese until 1980, its prelate, Thomas J. Toolen, was given the title "Archbishop ad Personam" by Pope Pius XII in 1954. Therefore, he is referred to throughout most of the book as Archbishop Toolen.

11. "Archdiocese Census Count Shows 43,342," *Georgia Bulletin,* May 30, 1963, p. 1; Questionnaire To Determine Current Religious Resources of Judicatories in Five County Metropolitan Atlanta, Box 021/1, Folder 16, Archives of the Catholic Archdiocese of Atlanta (hereafter ACAA); "Confessional Groups, Membership and Number of Churches Within The State of Georgia in 1968 Compared to National Membership," Box 036/4, Folder 31, ACAA; "Church Membership in Georgia By Denomination In Order of Number of Communicant Members," November 20, 1975, Box 036/4, Folder 31, ACAA; "Diocese of Savannah, Statistical Report," n.d., Box FB-1, A–Ap, Folder, "Apostolic Delegation (2), 1948–1960," Archives of the Catholic Diocese of Savannah, Georgia (hereafter ACDS); Michael J. McNally, "A Peculiar Institution: A History of Catholic Parish Life in the Southeast (1850–1980)," in *The American Catholic Parish: A History from 1850 to the Present,* vol. 1, ed. Jay Dolan (Mahwah, N.J.: Paulist Press, 1987), appendix 2, p. 229.

12. Andrew Michael Manis, *Southern Civil Religions in Conflict: Black and White Baptists and Civil Rights, 1947–1957* (Athens: Univ. of Georgia Press, 1985), 41–49. See chapter 2 in general about Southern Baptists' belief in America's status as a chosen nation.

13. On anti-Catholicism in the nineteenth century, see Ray Billington, *The Protestant Crusade, 1800–1860: A Study of the Origins of American Nativism* (Chicago: Quadrangle Books, 1938); Jenny Franchot, *Roads To Rome: The Antebellum Protestant Encounter with Catholicism* (Berkeley: Univ. of California Press, 1994); and Marie Ann Pagliarini, "The Pure American Woman and the Wicked Catholic Priest: An Analysis of Anti-Catholic Literature in Antebellum America," *Religion and American Culture: A Journal of Interpretation* 9 (winter 1999): 97–128. For the twentieth century, see also Edward Cuddy, "The Irish Question and the Revival of Anti-Catholicism in the 1920s," *Catholic Historical Review* 67 (April 1981): 236–255; Andrew Greeley, *An Ugly Little Secret: Anti-Catholicism In North America* (Kansas City, Mo.: Sheed Andrews and McMeel, 1977); Lynn Dumenil, "The Tribal Twenties: 'Assimilated' Catholics' Response to Anti-Catholicism in the 1920s," *Journal of American Ethnic History* 11 (fall 1991): 21–49; McGreevy, "Thinking on One's Own"; McGreevy, *Catholicism and American Freedom*, chapter 6; Mark S. Massa, S.J., *Anti-Catholicism in America: The Last Acceptable Prejudice* (New York: Crossroad, 2003); Philip Jenkins, *The New Anti-Catholicism: The Last Acceptable Prejudice* (New York: Oxford Univ. Press, 2003). On anti-Catholicism and the Ku Klux Klan in Georgia, see Philip N. Racine, "The Ku Klux Klan, Anti-Catholicism, and Atlanta's Board of Education, 1916–1927," *Georgia Historical Quarterly* 57 (spring 1973): 63–75. On the Klan in Athens, Georgia, see Nancy MacLean, *Behind the Mask of Chivalry: The Making of the Second Ku Klux Klan* (New York: Oxford Univ. Press, 1994). MacLean does not, however, have much to say about anti-Catholicism and the Athens Klan.

14. "Teaching Intolerance to Children," *Catholic Week,* February 2, 1945, p. 4.

15. "Is This Brotherhood?" *Catholic Week,* March 16, 1945, p. 4. On the institutionalization of anti-Catholicism, see Lerond Curry, *Protestant-Catholic Relations in America: World War I through Vatican II* (Lexington: Univ. Press of Kentucky, 1972), particularly chapter 2.

16. Ethan A. Smith, Atlanta, Ga., to Kinchley, December 24, 1948, Hugh Kinchley Collection, ACDS; George J. Gill, "The Truman Administration and Vatican Relations," *Catholic Historical Review* 73 (July 1987): 408–423.

17. Ethan A. Smith, Atlanta, Ga., to Kinchley, December 24, 1948. On the CLA, see Felicitas Powers, R.S.M., "Prejudice, Journalism, and the Catholic Laymen's Association of Georgia," *U.S. Catholic Historian* 8 (summer 1989), 203–204; Richard Reid, K.S.G., "The Catholic Laymen's Association of Georgia," *Missionary* 55 (June 1941): 143–147, ACDS.

18. "Alarm at 'Romish Aspirations,'" clipping from *Bulletin,* September 22, 1951, p. 4, ACDS.

19. "Who Are Our Friends?" *Catholic Week,* April 9, 1949, p. 4. On Birmingham's chapter, see "Birmingham To Be Headquarters Of State Unit of Anti-Catholic POAU," *Catholic Week,* April 9, 1949, p. 1. On Mobile's chapter, see "POAU Unit Being Formed In Mobile," *Catholic Week,* April 23, 1949, p. 1; "'. . . . . and other Americans. . . . ,'" *Catholic Week,* April 9, 1949, p. 4.

20. "What Catholic Editors Are Saying," *Catholic Week,* April 9, 1949, p. 4.

21. "Mobile Catholic Men's Breakfast Club Hears Denunciation of Poau," *Catholic Week,* April 23, 1949, p. 2. See also "Bishop Toolen Urges Support of 'The Catholic

Week' As Diocese Observes Catholic Press Month," *Catholic Week,* February 18, 1949, p. 1.

22. Kinchley to Mr. Ethan A. Smith, Atlanta, Ga., December 29, 1948, Kinchley Collection, ACDS. On *Everson* and *McCollum* see McGreevy, *Catholicism and American Freedom,* 183–185. For a different interpretation, see Peter Irons, *A People's History of the Supreme Court* (New York: Penguin Books, 1999), 344–347, 409–410.

23. Jay P. Dolan, *In Search of an American Catholicism: A History of Religion and Culture in Tension* (New York: Oxford Univ. Press, 2002), 146–157, quotations on 156.

24. Moylan to Kinchley, August 3, 1950; Julian V. Boehm, Atlanta, Ga., to Kinchley, Augusta, Ga., August 1, 1950, Catholic Laymen's Association Collection, ACDS. On the threat of communism, see, for example, Lisle A. Rose, *The Cold War Comes To Main Street: America in 1950* (Lawrence: Univ. Press of Kansas, 1999), 22–38, 117–165; and James T. Patterson, *Grand Expectations: The United States, 1945–1974* (New York: Oxford Univ. Press, 1996), especially chapter 7.

25. Moylan to Kinchley, February 4, 1950, Catholic Laymen's Association Collection, ACDS.

26. On anti-communism and Catholics' place in American culture, see David J. O'Brien, *American Catholics and Social Reform: The New Deal Years* (New York: Oxford Univ. Press, 1968), 96; Charles R. Morris, *American Catholic: The Saints and Sinners Who Built America's Most Powerful Church* (New York: Times Books, 1997), 230; Patrick Allitt, *Catholic Intellectuals and Conservative Politics in America, 1950–1985* (Ithaca, N.Y.: Cornell Univ. Press, 1993), 60–70; Mark S. Massa, S.J., *Catholics and American Culture: Fulton Sheen, Dorothy Day, and the Notre Dame Football Team* (New York: Crossroad, 1999), 91. On communism in the South, see Wayne Addison Clark, "An Analysis of the Relationship Between Anti-Communism and Segregationist Thought in the Deep South, 1948–1964" (Ph.D. diss., University of North Carolina, Chapel Hill, 1976), 74–75; Dan Carter, *Scottsboro: A Tragedy of the American South* (Baton Rouge: Louisiana State Univ. Press, 1969); Matthew Frye Jacobson, *Whiteness of a Different Color: European Immigrants and the Alchemy of Race* (Cambridge, Mass.: Harvard Univ. Press, 1998), 248–256.

27. Bishop Francis E. Hyland, Savannah, Ga., to Most Rev. John B. Montini, S.T.D., Pro-Secretary of State, Vatican City, October 10, 1953, Catholic Laymen's Association Collection, ACDS.

28. "Barden Sees Separation More Important Than Aid," Religious News Service, October 31, 1949, Kinchley Collection, ACDS.

29. Kinchley to Editor, *Morning News,* Savannah, Ga., November 7, 1949, Kinchley Collection, ACDS.

30. "Issue Taken With Heritage Day Attack," *Catholic Week,* November 11, 1950, p. 1; "Heritage Day In Mobile," *Catholic Week,* November 11, 1950, p. 4; "Catholic Spokesmen Hit 'Hate Sermon' At Protestant Event," NC New Service, Mobile, Ala., November 20, 1950, Catholic Laymen's Association Collection, ACDS.

31. Report of the Executive Secretary to the Annual Convention of the Catholic Laymen's Association of Georgia, October 30, 1949; "About Roman Catholics," advertisement in *Morgan County News,* Madison, Ga., January 1949, Catholic Laymen's Association Collection, ACDS; "Report of the Executive Secretary to the Annual

Convention of the Catholic Laymen's Association of Georgia, at Waycross, Georgia," October 26, 1952, Catholic Laymen's Association Collection, ACDS.

32. Ann Taves, *The Household of Faith: Roman Catholic Devotions in Mid-Nineteenth-Century America* (Notre Dame, Ind.: Univ. of Notre Dame Press, 1986), 30–32, 126–127.

33. Kinchley to Mr. P. D. Mathews, Editor and Publisher, *Douglas County (Georgia) Sentinel,* September 16, 1948, Catholic Laymen's Association Collection, ACDS.

34. Kinchley to Mr. J. G. Malphurs, Albany, Ga., July 22, 1950, Kinchley Collection, ACDS.

35. J. G. Malphurs, "Catholics' New Dogma Disputed," Letter to the Editor, *Albany (Georgia) Herald,* n.d., Kinchley Collection, ACDS; Kinchley, Letter to the Editor, *Albany (Georgia) Herald,* n.d., Kinchley Collection, ACDS. Also see Kinchley to Mr. Ethan A. Smith, Atlanta, Ga., December 29, 1948, ACDS.

36. "Is Mary the Mother of God? Is the Doctrine of Immaculate Conception True?" advertisement in Columbus, Ga., *Ledger-Enquirer,* May 20, 1951; see also "Ye Shall Know The Truth," *Ledger-Enquirer,* May 27, 1951; and "What About The Roman Catholic Foundation?" *Ledger-Enquirer,* June 3, 1951, all in Kinchley Collection, ACDS.

37. Kinchley, Letter to the Editor, *Albany (Georgia) Herald,* n.d. For another response to Malphurs, see Morton Wiggins, Jr., "Youth Defends Catholic Dogma," Letter to the Editor, *Albany (Georgia) Herald,* n.d., clippings in Kinchley Collection, ACDS. On the relationship between Mary and Cold War America, see Thomas A. Kselman and Steven Avella, "Marian Piety and the Cold War in the United States," *Catholic Historical Review* 72 (July 1986): 403–424.

38. "Birmingham News Draws Criticism For Acceptance Of Derogatory Advertising," *Catholic Week,* April 1, 1950, p. 1; "Priests Protest Ads Attacking Church," Religious News Service release, April 21, 1950, Catholic Laymen's Association Collection, ACDS. For an example from the laity, see "Muscle Shoals Holy Name Societies Sponsor K.C. Catholic Information Ads In Local Papers," *Catholic Week,* May 5, 1951, p. 6.

39. Monsignor Joseph E. Moylan, Diocese of Savannah, to Hugh Kinchley, Augusta, February 4, 1950, Catholic Laymen's Association Collection, ACDS.

40. Hugh Kinchley, Augusta, Ga., to Monsignor Joseph E. Moylan, July 24, 1950; Moylan to Kinchley, July 25, 1950, Catholic Laymen's Association Collection, ACDS.

41. Monsignor Joseph E. Moylan, Diocese of Savannah, to Hugh Kinchley, Augusta, November 16, 1950, Catholic Laymen's Association Collection, ACDS.

42. John E. Markwalter to Book and Bible House, Decatur, Ga., March 30, 1954; and Markwalter to Members of the Catholic Laymen's Association of Georgia, April 1, 1954, Catholic Laymen's Association Collection, ACDS. On the Protestant reaction to Monk's "revelations," see Franchot, *Roads to Rome.*

43. "Take One—Protestant—Wake Up," *Catholic Week,* January 7, 1949, p. 4; "The Truth And It's [*sic*] Proof Regarding the K.C. 'Oath,'" *Catholic Week,* March 26, 1949, p. 4; Kinchley to Moylan, February 21, 1950, Catholic Laymen's Association Collection, ACDS; "The Truth And It's [*sic*] Proof Regarding the K.C. 'Oath,'" *Catholic Week,* March 26, 1949, p. 4. See also "Rep. Battle Disclaims Any Connection With Alleged K. of C. 'Oath,'" *Catholic Week,* April 2, 1949, p. 1.

44. Edward W. Smith to Monsignor Joseph Moylan, February 20, 1950, Catholic Laymen's Association Collection, ACDS.

45. Edward W. Smith to Monsignor Joseph Moylan, February 20, 1950; and Kinchley to Moylan, February 21, 1950, Catholic Laymen's Association Collection, ACDS; Massa, *Catholics and American Culture,* 21–37, quotation on 35. For other examples of these itinerant "former Catholics," see [Hugh Kinchley or John E. Markwalter], Report of Catholic Laymen's Association, n.d., Kinchley Collection, ACDS; Catholic Laymen Association of Georgia advertisement, appearing in *Savannah Evening Press,* n.d., 1954; and Markwalter to Members of the Catholic Laymen's Association of Georgia, April 1, 1954, Catholic Laymen's Association Collection, ACDS.

46. Kinchley to Malphurs, July 22, 1950. See also Markwalter to Book and Bible House, March 30, 1954; and Markwalter to Members of the Catholic Laymen's Association of Georgia, April 1, 1954.

47. Pastoral letter to "My dear Priests and People," clipping probably from the *Bulletin,* November 26, 1960, in Bishop Hyland Scrapbook, ACAA. See also "Catholics Here Urged to Forgive 'Attacks,'" clipping from *Atlanta Journal,* November 12, 1960, also in Hyland Scrapbook, ACAA. On Kennedy's election in 1960, see Thomas J. Carty, *A Catholic in the White House? Religion, Politics, and John F. Kennedy's Presidential Campaign* (New York: Palgrave Macmillan, 2004).

48. Archbishop Thomas J. Toolen to "Dear Father," December 3, 1963, Toolen papers, Archives of the Catholic Archdiocese of Mobile, Alabama. For an example of Bishop Francis Hyland of Atlanta consoling members of his diocese after the bitter 1960 election, see "Catholics Here Urged to Forgive 'Attacks,'" clipping from *Atlanta Journal,* November 12, 1960, in Bishop Hyland Scrapbook, ACAA; Toolen to Dr. M. J. Fitzgerald, Buena Vista, Ga., February 6, 1965, Toolen papers.

CHAPTER 2

1. Joe and Amy Winters, transcript of interview by Sister Rose Sevenich, O.S.F., September 11, 1992, transcribed by Mr. John J. P. O'Brien, Oral History Project, Box 1, Envelope 2, Archives of the Catholic Diocese of Birmingham in Alabama (hereafter ACDBA).

2. John T. McGreevy, *Parish Boundaries: The Catholic Encounter with Race in the Twentieth-Century Urban North* (Chicago: Univ. of Chicago Press, 1996).

3. "Diocese of Savannah, Religious Report," Box FB-1, A–Ap, Folder, "Apostolic Delegation (2), 1948–1960," ACDS. For examples of the growth of parishes founded in remote areas in which there lived only a few Catholic families, see "History of Holy Family Church, Lanett," *Catholic Week,* September 24, 1965, p. 12; and "History of Parish At Auburn Reflects Growth Of Church," *Catholic Week,* September 23, 1966, p. 13.

4. "Dedication of Holy Spirit Church, Huntsville, Oct. 27," *Catholic Week,* October 22, 1965, p. 11; "Recent Rapid Growth Of Church in Huntsville," *Catholic Week,* October 22, 1965, p. 12; "Final Statistic In CCD Report Numbers 128,000 Catholics in Diocese," *Catholic Week,* January 17, 1964, p. 1; Toolen to Arthur Daly, Lakewood, Calif., January 1, 1962, Toolen papers; Rose Gibbons Lovett, *The Catholic Church in the Deep South: The Diocese of Birmingham in Alabama, 1540–1976* (Birmingham, Ala.: The Diocese of

Birmingham in Alabama, 1980), 126–128. For another example, the Chapel of the Holy Spirit in Winfield, Alabama, see "New Church In Winfield, Ala., Gift of Orth Family," *Catholic Week*, March 20, 1964, p. 1; "It Takes Desire," *Catholic Week*, March 20, 1964, p. 1; Lovett, *Catholic Church in the Deep South*, 128–129; "Church Hopes Grow In Jonesboro Area," *Georgia Bulletin*, November 14, 1963, p. 6; "Dispatches From Some of Georgia Missions," *Georgia Bulletin*, January 11, 1963, p. 2.

5. On the creation of sacred space out of otherwise "profane" places and the necessity of excluding certain groups of people, see David Chidester and Edward T. Linenthal, eds., *American Sacred Space* (Bloomington: Indiana Univ. Press, 1995), especially the editors' introduction and pp. 318–319.

6. "Special Gifts Committee Ready To Start Campaign Saturday," *Catholic Week*, April 25, 1947, p. 6.

7. "Bishop Sheen Keeps Pledge at Tallassee Church," *Montgomery Advertiser*, February 12, 1956; "Bishop Sheen Delivers Church Dedication Talk," *Alabama Journal*, February 13, 1956; see also articles in *Tallassee Tribune*, February 9, 1956; and *Montgomery Advertiser*, February 13, 1956, in Public Information Subject Files—County, Container SG6855, Elmore County, Folder 10 Catholic Church, Alabama Department of Archives and History, Montgomery, Alabama.

8. For nineteenth-century Alabama, see Oscar H. Lipscomb, "Catholic Missionaries in Early Alabama," *Alabama Review* 18 (1965): 124–131.

9. Hugh Kinchley, Augusta, Ga., to Rt. Rev. Monsignor Joseph E. Moylan, Savannah, March 15, 1952, Catholic Laymen's Association Collection, ACDS.

10. Jay P. Dolan, *Catholic Revivalism: The American Experience, 1830–1900* (Notre Dame, Ind.: Univ. of Notre Dame Press, 1978), 91–112.

11. "St. Paul's Mission Given By Paulist Fathers, Oct. 7–21," *Catholic Week*, October 5, 1945, p. 3; "Fr. Silvius To Hold St. Margaret's Mission," *Catholic Week*, March 16, 1945, p. 2; "Saint Catherine's, Mobile, To Observe Mission March 10th," *Catholic Week*, March 1, 1946, p. 2; "Father Broome To Conduct Mission At St. Andrew's," *Catholic Week*, March 7, 1947, p. 7; "Father Maher C.P. Is Mission Speaker," *Catholic Week*, March 2, 1945, p. 2; "Father T. Powers, C.P. Ends Mission Week at St. Aloysius Church," *Catholic Week*, March 4, 1950, p. 5; "Fr. John J. Conway to Conduct Fairhope and Daphne Missions," *Catholic Week*, January 20, 1951, p. 2.

12. "Catholic Rural Life: Discussion Outline," New Orleans Province Institute of Social Order Meeting, Spring Hill College, January 2 and 3, 1948, Loose Folder, "Faculty—Pictures and P.R.," Fr. Albert S. Foley, S.J., Papers, Spring Hill College Archives, Mobile, Alabama. For more on open-air evangelization, especially in rural areas of the South and Midwest, see Douglas J. Slawson, "Thirty Years of Street Preaching: Vincentian Motor Missions, 1934–1965," *Church History* 62 (March 1993): 60–81; Debra Campbell, "Part-Time Female Evangelists of the Thirties and Forties: The Rosary College Catholic Evidence Guild," *U.S. Catholic Historian* 5 (1986): 371–383; Jeffrey D. Marlett, *Saving the Heartland: Catholic Missionaries in Rural America, 1920–1960* (DeKalb, Ill.: Northern Illinois Univ. Press, 2002).

13. "Says 'Unbalanced' Catholic Population—Mostly Urban—Menaces Church's Growth," *Catholic Week*, January 7, 1949; Hugh A. Brimm, "Catholics and Their Two-Hundred-Year Plan for Rural America," *Baptist Standard* 62 (December 7, 1950), 1, 12,

cited in Andrew Michael Manis, *Southern Civil Religions in Conflict: Black and White Baptists and Civil Rights, 1947–1957* (Athens: Univ. of Georgia Press, 1985), 47.

14. "Diocese Support for Students To Priesthood Is Urged By Bishop," *Catholic Week*, April 13, 1945, p. 1.

15. "Dominican Motor Chapel Starts Work In Georgia," n.d.; "The Dominican Motor Chapels Have Very Successful Holy Year Program," Kinchley Collection, ACDS; Ted Ownby, *Subduing Satan: Religion, Recreation, and Manhood in the Rural South, 1865–1920* (Chapel Hill: Univ. of North Carolina Press, 1990), 162, and on lay perceptions of revival meetings, see 144–164.

16. "Street Preaching," *Catholic Week,* September 21, 1945, p. 4.

17. W. J. Cash, *The Mind of the South*, with a new introduction by Bertram Wyatt-Brown (New York: Vintage Books, 1991; originally published in 1941), 51; Miles Richardson, "Speaking and Hearing (in Contrast to Touching and Seeing) the Sacred," in *Religion in the Contemporary South: Diversity, Community, and Identity,* ed. O. Kendall White, Jr., and Daryl White (Athens: Univ. of Georgia Press, 1995), 13–22.

18. Randall M. Miller, "A Church in Cultural Captivity: Some Speculations on Catholic Identity in the Old South," in *Catholics in the Old South: Essays on Church and Culture,* ed. Randall M. Miller and Jon L. Wakelyn (Macon, Ga.: Mercer Univ. Press, 1983), 48–49.

19. Father Henry Thorsen, transcript of interview by Sister Rose Sevenich, O.S.F., transcribed by Mr. John J. P. O'Brien, September 9, 1992, Oral History Project, Box 1, Envelope 8; Father Paul Donnelly, transcript of interview by Sister Rose Sevenich, O.S.F., transcribed by Mr. John J. P. O'Brien, September 25, [n.d.], Oral History Project, Box 1, Envelope 7, ACDBA; "Street Preaching In The Birmingham District," *Catholic Week,* September 21, 1945, p. 5; "St. Anthony's Plans Mission, Oct. 7–14," *Catholic Week,* September, 28, 1945, p. 3.

20. Bishop Joseph A. Durick, interview 1, transcript of interview by Sister Rose Sevenich, O.S.F., October 2, 1992, transcribed by Mr. John J. P. O'Brien, Oral History Project, Box 1, Envelope 11, ACDBA; "Street Preaching In The Birmingham District"; Father Henry Thorsen, interview by Sister Rose Sevenich; Sister Mary Alice Vose, n.d., talk transcribed by Mr. John J. P. O'Brien, Oral History Project, Box 1, Envelope 4, ACDBA. For missions in South Alabama, see "Father Frank Giri Describes Mission Work in South Alabama," *Catholic Week,* January 14, 1949, p. 2; and "Bishop Dedicates 2 Missions Churches In South Alabama," *Catholic Week,* March 5, 1948, p. 1.

21. Alice Slatsky, transcript of interview by Sister Rose Sevenich, O.S.F., transcribed by Mr. John J. P. O'Brien, January 14, 1993, Oral History Project, Box 2, Envelope 13, ACDBA.

22. Joe and Amy Winters, interview by Sister Rose Sevenich, O.S.F.; "1,200 Attend Klan Rally Staged Here," *Montgomery Advertiser,* September 9, 1956; "Montgomery Chosen As Hub of New 6-State KKK Group," *Montgomery Advertiser,* August 24, 1949, Public Information Files—General File, Container SG6966, Folder 962, Alabama Department of Archives and History, Montgomery, Alabama.

23. Annual Reports of North Alabama Missions, Cabinet RG 2.06, North Alabama Missions Folder, Records of the Chancery, Records of Parishes, Statistics, ACDBA; Lovett, *Catholic Church in the Deep South.*

---

24. "Georgia Mission Appeal Sunday," *Georgia Bulletin*, November 7, 1963, p. 1; "St. Luke's Dahlonega—Apostolate In The Mountain Country," *Georgia Bulletin*, November 7, 1963, p. 3; Bishop John L. May to Mr. Thomas Finney, Archdiocesan Chancery Office, New Orleans, November 30, 1970, Bishop May papers, Archives of the Catholic Archdiocese of Mobile, Alabama.

25. Rev. John Horgan, "Catholic Missions of 'The Bible Belt,'" *Catholic Week*, July 9, 1948, p. 1.

26. Dolan, *In Search of an American Catholicism*, 147.

27. Jon W. Anderson, "Catholic Imagination and Inflections of 'Church' in the Contemporary South," in *The Culture of Bible Belt Catholics*, ed. Jon W. Anderson and William B. Friend (New York: Paulist Press, 1995), 88–89.

28. "20,000 Mobile Catholics Honor Christ The King," *Catholic Week*, November 2, 1945, p. 1; Joseph P. Chinnici, O.F.M., *Living Stones: The History and Structure of Catholic Spiritual Life in the United States*, 2nd ed. (Maryknoll, N.Y.: Orbis Books, 1996), 168; Pope Pius XI, *Quas Primas*, December 11, 1925, reprinted in *The Papal Encyclicals, 1903–1939*, ed. Claudia Carlen, I.H.M. ([Wilmington, N.C.]: McGrath, 1981), quotations on 276, 274, 275.

29. See, for example, *St. Anthony's Catholic News*, December 1946, pp. 12–15; "Knights of Columbus—Atlanta Columbus Day Program," *St. Anthony's Catholic News*, October 1952, pp. 8–9; "St. Patrick's Day," *St. Anthony's Catholic News*, March 1947, pp. 25–27; "Fifty Thousand Atlantans Honored St. Patrick on March 17th," *St. Anthony's Catholic News*, May 1956, p. 13, ACAA.

30. On the creation of public sacred space, see Chidester and Linenthal, eds., *American Sacred Space*. For a more traditional view, see Mircea Eliade, *The Sacred and the Profane: The Nature of Religion*, translated by Willard R. Trask (San Diego, Calif.: Harcourt Brace Jovanovich, 1959), 20–65.

31. "'Thanksgiving And Lasting Peace Theme Of Mobile Christ The King Celebration: 18,000 To Attend," *Catholic Week*, October 5, 1945, p. 2; "Father Paul, O.S.B., Speaking At B'ham Christ The King Celebration, Outlined Duties of Catholics to Christ The King," *Catholic Week*, November 2, 1945, p. 6; "Feast of Christ The King Celebrated In Pensacola," *Catholic Week*, November 12, 1948, p. 5; "St. Andrew's Parish Observes Feast of Christ The King With High Mass," *Catholic Week*, November 4, 1950, p. 6.

32. "20,000 Mobile Catholics Honor Christ The King," *Catholic Week*, November 2, 1945, p. 1; "Father Donnelly To Make Address At Pensacola Christ The King Rally," *Catholic Week*, October 29, 1948, p. 7; "Christ's Kingship Over Mankind Described At Birmingham Rally," *Catholic Week*, November 4, 1950, p. 3; Robert C. Broderick, ed., *The Catholic Encyclopedia*, revised and updated edition (Nashville, Tenn.: Thomas Nelson, 1987), 198; see also *Catechism of the Catholic Church*, 346–347.

33. Eamon Duffy, *The Stripping of the Altars: Traditional Religion in England, c. 1400–c. 1580*, 2nd ed. (New Haven: Yale Univ. Press, 2005), 96; Chinnici, *Living Stones*, 68, 78. See also Ann Taves, *The Household of Faith: Roman Catholic Devotions in Mid-Nineteenth-Century America* (Notre Dame, Ind.: Univ. of Notre Dame Press, 1986), 30–32, 126–127.

34. Peter A. Huff, *Allen Tate and the Catholic Revival: Trace of the Fugitive Gods* (Mahwah, N.J.: Paulist Press, 1996), 3.

35. "Thanksgiving and Lasting Peace Theme Of Mobile Christ The King Celebration: 18,000 To Attend," *Catholic Week,* October 5, 1945, p. 2; "Mobile Holy Name Plans To Celebrate Christ The King," *Catholic Week,* September 14, 1945, p. 2; "20,000 Mobile Catholics Honor Christ The King," *Catholic Week,* November 2, 1945, p. 1; "Feast Of Christ The King: Diocese Of Mobile Will Pay Tribute To Christ The King," *Catholic Week,* October 26, 1945, pp. 1, 2; "Scenes From Mobile Christ The King Celebration," *Catholic Week,* November 9, 1945, p. 2; "Florence Christ The King Services Draw Large Crowd," *Catholic Week,* November 2, 1945, p. 3.

36. "20,000 Mobile Catholics Honor Christ the King," *Catholic Week,* November 2, 1945, p. 1; "'Our Beloved America Faces Its Most Critical Hour' Rev. Walter Royer Tells Thousands Celebrating Christ the King," *Catholic Week,* November 2, 1945, p. 7.

37. "Archbishop Stresses Importance of Loyalty to Christ, Nation, At Mobile Christ the King Rally," *Catholic Week,* November 12, 1955, p. 2; "Archbishop Toolen, Bishop Durick Ask United Stand Among Catholics," *Catholic Week,* November 5, 1955, p. 2.

38. "Catholics Told Prayer Needed To Save World," *Catholic Week,* November 4, 1950, p. 2; "Father Donnelly To Make Address At Pensacola Christ the King Rally," *Catholic Week,* October 29, 1948, p. 7; "Heritage Day In Mobile," *Catholic Week,* November 11, 1950, p. 4.

39. "Christ the King Demonstration In Pensacola," *Catholic Week,* October 24, 1947, p. 1; "Father Donnelly To Make Address At Pensacola Christ The King Rally," *Catholic Week,* October 29, 1948, p. 7; "Bishop Urges All Believers To Work For Restoration Of Christ As King," *Catholic Week,* October 29, 1948, p. 3.

40. "20,000 Mobile Catholics Honor Christ the King," *Catholic Week,* November 2, 1945, p. 2; on Catholic compromises with American culture in the twentieth century, see Mark S. Massa, S.J., *Catholics and American Culture: Fulton Sheen, Dorothy Day, and the Notre Dame Football Team* (New York: Crossroad, 1999).

41. Moylan to Kinchley, January 26, 1951, Catholic Laymen's Association Collection, ACDS. Indeed, Mark S. Massa recently argued that is precisely what happened to American Catholics in the middle of the twentieth century. See Massa, *Catholics and American Culture.*

42. "Over 5,000 Hear Father Giri Speak Of The Loyalty Inspired By The Majesty Of Jesus Christ," *Catholic Week,* November 12, 1955, p. 3; "'The 20th Century Has Shown Man Is Inadequate Without God,'" *Catholic Week,* November 9, 1956, p. 2; "Christ Has Never Asked Us To Do What He Had Not Done Himself," *Catholic Week,* November 7, 1958, p. 2; "Sacrifice Separates True Love From Sentimentality, Priest Says," *Catholic Week,* October 31, 1958, p. 3.

43. "A Virtuous, Vigorous Christian Manhood Needed, Renew Society," *Catholic Week,* September 28, 1945, p. 2; Broderick, ed., *Catholic Encyclopedia,* 268.

44. "Montgomery Pays Homage To B.V.M.," *Catholic Week,* May 25, 1945, p. 2; see also "Montgomery Plans Farewell To May To Honor B.V.M.," *Catholic Week,* May 18, 1945, p. 7.

45. "Spiritual Crusade Urged By Bishop Toolen At May Day Demonstrations," *Catholic Week,* May 14, 1948, p. 1; "5000 Crowd Rickwood Field In Honor Of Mother Of God," *Catholic Week,* May 27, 1950, p. 4.

46. Thomas A. Kselman and Steven Avella, "Marian Piety and the Cold War in the United States," *Catholic Historical Review* 72 (July 1986): 411; "Diocese of Mobile

To Pay Tribute To Fatima Statue, Famed 'Pilgrim Virgin,'" *Catholic Week,* February 6, 1948, p. 1; "'Pilgrim Virgin' To Remain In Mobile Diocese Two Weeks," *Catholic Week,* February 13, 1948, p. 1; "Thousands Throng To Venerate 'Pilgrim Virgin' Touring Diocese," *Catholic Week,* February 20, 1948, p. 1.

47. "Mobile Holy Name Men To Pray For Peace At 'Holy Hour Of Reparation,'" *Catholic Week,* March 5, 1948, p. 2.

48. "Archbishop Will Preside At Mary's Day Rally, May 10th," *Catholic Week,* May 1, 1964, p. 2; "Annual Celebration Honoring Mary To Be Held On May 10th," *Catholic Week,* May 1, 1964, p. 4; "Catholic Women Reminded Of Dignity Conferred On Them Through Bl. Virgin," *Catholic Week,* May 8, 1964, p. 8; "'Love Mary; Pray For Peace' Says Archbishop, Fr. Adams," *Catholic Week,* May 15, 1964, p. 2; "Mobile To Celebrate Christ The King Feast On Oct. 25," *Catholic Week,* October 16, 1964, p. 2; "Great Day Coming," *Catholic Week,* November 17, 1972, p. 3; "41st Annual Christ The King Celebration," *Catholic Week,* November 16, 1973, p. 1; on the decline of devotionalism in Pittsburgh, see Timothy Kelly, "Suburbanization and the Decline of Catholic Public Ritual in Pittsburgh," *Journal of Social History* 28 (winter 1994): 311–330; and Timothy Kelly and Joseph Kelly, "Our Lady of Perpetual Help, Gender Roles, and the Decline of Devotional Catholicism," *Journal of Social History* 32 (fall 1998): 5–26.

CHAPTER 3

1. For a history of the Brown decision, see James T. Patterson, *Brown v. Board of Education: A Civil Rights Milestone and Its Troubled Legacy* (New York: Oxford Univ. Press, 2001). On religious people and race, see Mark Newman, *Getting Right with God: Southern Baptists and Desegregation, 1945–1995* (Tuscaloosa: Univ. of Alabama Press, 2001), especially chapters 2 and 9; Gardiner H. Shattuck, Jr., *Episcopalians and Race: Civil War to Civil Rights* (Lexington: Univ. Press of Kentucky, 2000) chapter 3; Michael B. Friedland, *Lift Up Your Voice Like a Trumpet: White Clergy and the Civil Rights and Antiwar Movements, 1954–1973* (Chapel Hill: Univ. of North Carolina Press, 1998), chapter 1. On the reaction to the *Brown* decision, see Michael J. Klarman, "How Brown Changed Race Relations: The Backlash Thesis," *Journal of American History* 81 (June 1994): 81–118; Adam Fairclough, *Race and Democracy: The Civil Rights Struggle in Louisiana, 1915–1972* (Athens: Univ. of Georgia Press, 1995), 164–195; Andrew Michael Manis, *Southern Civil Religions in Conflict: Black and White Baptists and Civil Rights, 1947–1957* (Athens: Univ. of Georgia Press, 1985), chapter 3. On post–World War II political liberalism in Alabama, see William Warren Rogers, Robert David Ward, Leah Rawls Atkins, and Wayne Flynt, *Alabama: The History of a Deep South State* (Tuscaloosa: Univ. of Alabama Press, 1994), chapter 30. On the failure of post–World War II liberalism in the South in general, see Numan V. Bartley, *The New South, 1945–1980* (Baton Rouge: Louisiana State Univ. Press, 1995), chapter 2. On the rise of massive resistance, see Numan V. Bartley, *The Rise of Massive Resistance: Race and Politics in the South during the 1950s,* with a new preface by the author (Baton Rouge: Louisiana State Univ. Press, 1997; originally published 1969).

2. Joan Sage, "The 'Grilling' Story of St. Joan the Bar-Be-Cued and how she got that way!" unpublished memoirs, copy in possession of author, 129.

3. On the civil rights career of Foley, see Carol A. Ellis, "'The Tragedy of the White Moderate': Father Albert Foley and Alabama Civil Rights, 1963–1967" (M.A. thesis, University of South Alabama, 2002).

4. Father Albert S. Foley, "Shadow of the White Camellia: Reminiscences of a Tangle with Terrorists," Sage version, [43–47]. There are two extant versions of Foley's memoirs, both with similar titles. This one was in the possession of the late Ms. Joan Sage, Mobile, Alabama. The other is in the archives of Spring Hill College and is entitled, simply, "In the Shadow of the White Camellias." There is some overlap, but it is possible that these were intended as two volumes (as opposed to two separate versions) of the same memoir. To avoid confusion, in addition to the title, I will refer to each volume according to who has possession of it. That is, each reference will include either Sage version or Spring Hill version.

5. Report by Frederick B. Routh, Assistant Director for State Organization, Southern Regional Council, February 28, 1955, Southern Regional Council Collection, Department of Archives and Manuscripts, Linn-Henley Research Library, Birmingham Public Library, Birmingham, Alabama. These are photocopies of originals from the SRC archives, Atlanta. On LaFarge, see David W. Southern, *John LaFarge and the Limits of Catholic Interracialism, 1911–1963* (Baton Rouge: Louisiana State Univ. Press, 1996), 358; David W. Southern, "But Think of the Kids: Catholic Interracialists and the Great American Taboo of Race Mixing," *U.S. Catholic Historian* 16:3 (summer 1998): 67–93.

6. Foley, "Shadow of the White Camellia: Reminiscences of a Tangle with Terrorists," Sage version, 26, 27, 28, 33–35. He wrote his doctoral dissertation in sociology at the University of North Carolina on race relations in the Archdiocese of Washington, D.C. Albert Sidney Foley, "The Catholic Church and the Washington Negro" (Ph.D. diss., University of North Carolina, Chapel Hill, 1950), 325. On Louisiana, see Fairclough, *Race and Democracy,* especially chapter 2.

7. Foley, "Shadow of the White Camellia: Reminiscences of a Tangle with Terrorists," Sage version, 2, 23.

8. Cyprian Davis, O.S.B., *The History of Black Catholics in the United States* (New York: Crossroad, 1990); Diana L. Hayes and Cyprian Davis, eds., *Taking Down Our Harps: Black Catholics in the United States* (Maryknoll, N.Y.: Orbis, 1998); Albert J. Raboteau, "Minority within a Minority: The History of Black Catholics in America," in *A Fire in the Bones: Reflections on African-American Religious History* (Boston: Beacon Press, 1995). On the history of slavery and Jim Crow within the southern Catholic Church and the lack of any challenge to the southern status quo, see the essays in Randall Miller and Jon L. Wakelyn, eds., *Catholics in the Old South: Essays on Church and Culture* (Macon, Ga.: Mercer Univ. Press, 1983); Michael V. Gannon, *Rebel Bishop: The Life and Era of Augustin Verot* (Milwaukee: Bruce, 1964); Dolores Egger Labbé, *Jim Crow Comes to Church: The Establishment of Segregated Catholic Parishes in South Louisiana* (New York: Arno Press, 1978); and Davis, *The History of Black Catholics.*

9. On religious orders in Alabama and Georgia, see "Passionist Fathers Have Retreat House, 2 Colored Missions," *Catholic Week,* May 9, 1947, p. 33; "Salvatorian Fathers Conduct Mother Mary Colored Mission At Phenix City," *Catholic Week,* May 9, 1947, p. 30-F; "Holy Ghost Fathers Have White, Colored Churches," *Catholic Week,* May 9, 1947, p. 31; "Predominantly Black Parishes," 1970, Bishop John L. May Papers;

"11 Men's Communities In Diocese," *Catholic Week,* April 28, 1972, p. 12-B; "Happy Anniversary!" *Catholic Week,* July 7, 1972, p. 4. For examples of the Edmundites in Alabama, see "Priest's Appeal Supported," *Catholic Week,* March 30, 1945, Section 1, p. 4; "Edmundite Fathers Open Mission Building For Colored In Gadsden," *Catholic Week,* December 9, 1950, p. 3; "All Saints' Church And Playground, Anniston," *Catholic Week,* October 19, 1945, p. 8. On the Josephites, see Stephen J. Ochs, *Desegregating the Altar: The Josephites and the Struggle for Black Priests, 1871–1960* (Baton Rouge: Louisiana State Univ. Press, 1990). On the North Alabama Mission Band, see Father Paul Donnelly, transcription of interview by Sister Rose Sevenich, O.S.F., September 25, 1992, ACDBA. For more on the north Alabama missions, see Toolen to Rev. John A. O'Brien, University of Notre Dame, Notre Dame, Ind., October 7, 1966; Toolen to O'Brien, September 2, 1966, Toolen papers. Annual Reports of North Alabama Missions, Folder, "North Alabama Missions," Cabinet RG 2.06, Records of the Chancery, Records of Parishes, Statistics, ACDBA; Box 052/3, Folder 6, Parishes/Missions, Annual Reports, 1960, ACAA.

10. Mrs. Hattie Bean and Mrs. Ann Taylor, transcription of interview by Sister Rose Sevenich, O.S.F., October 1, 1992, transcribed by Mr. John J. P. O'Brien, Oral History Project, Box 1, Envelope 9, ACDBA; Ochs, *Desegregating the Altar,* 371–373.

11. Quoted in Foley, "Shadow of the White Camellia: Reminiscences of a Tangle with Terrorists," Sage version, 35–36.

12. Hyland to Archbishop Joseph F. Rummel, New Orleans, April 6, 1959, Box 036/6, Folder 49; "Bishop Hyland Confirms Class of 208 Adults," June 22, 1957, newspaper clipping in Bishop Hyland Scrapbook; "Class of 278 Adults Confirmed By Bishop," May 30, 1959, newspaper clipping in Bishop Hyland Scrapbook, ACAA.

13. For confirmation exercises at an African American parish, see "Bishop Toolen Confirms In Selma; Officiates At Patriotic Ceremonies," *Catholic Week,* April 22, 1950, p. 5; Mrs. Earnestine Cotton, transcription of interview by Sister Rose Sevenich, O.S.F., October 1, 1992, transcribed by Mr. John J. P. O'Brien, Oral History Project, Box 1, Envelope 10, ACDBA; Foley, "Shadow of the White Camellia: Reminiscences of a Tangle with Terrorists," Sage version, 38.

14. Foley, "Shadow of the White Camellia: Reminiscences of a Tangle with Terrorists," Sage version, 41; the same story appears in "In the Shadow of the White Camellias," Spring Hill version, [210–213].

15. Mobile Students' Interracial Council, Discussion Outline, Loose Folder, "Materials on Dixie, 1958"; "What To Do In Interracial Week," Foley papers; "Shadow of the White Camellia: Reminiscences of a Tangle with Terrorists," Sage version, 41–41a. On the doctrine of the Mystical Body of Christ, see Pope Pius XII, *Mystici Corporis Christi* [Mystical Body of Christ], June 29, 1943, in *The Papal Encyclicals.*

16. "Interracial Attitude Questionnaire" and "Spring Hill College: Interracial Attitude Survey Summary of Results," Folder, "Race File, 1947– ," Container, Race Relations/Human Rights; Francis J. Corley, S.J., Institute of Social Order, St. Louis, Mo., to Foley, November 27, 1946; Folder, "Race File, 1947– ," Container, Race Relations/Human Rights, Foley Papers.

17. "Shadow of the White Camellia: Reminiscences of a Tangle with Terrorists," Sage version, 41a.

18. Williams quoted in Katherine Martensen, "Region, Religion, and Social Action: The Catholic Committee of the South, 1939–1956," *Catholic Historical Review* 68 (April 1982): 249–267, quotation on 251.

19. Brief vita, Rt. Rev. Monsignor T. James McNamara, V.G., P.A., ACDS. See also "Archbishop Stritch, Five Bishops, Many Priests and Religious, With Hundreds of the Laity, at Convention of Catholic Committee of the South," *Bulletin of the Catholic Laymen's Association of Georgia,* May 27, 1944, p. 4-A. Father Foley attributed the CCS's demise to Bishop Toolen's behind-the-scenes machinations. See Foley to Rev. Oliver Adams, Chickasaw, Ala., November 23, 1977, Loose Folder, "St. Thomas Toolen, Osborne Study," Foley papers.

20. "Tenth Anniversary of Catholic Committee of the South," *Catholic Week,* May 21, 1949, p. 4; A. J. Jackson, "Our Stand: Catholic Committee of the South," *Catholic Week,* February 11, 1949, p. 4. See also "Segregation, Union Membership, Minimum Wage, Management-Labor Harmony Discussed at CCS," *Catholic Week,* May 21, 1949, p. 4.

21. "Race Problem Solution Is Urged At Southern Catholic Convention," *Catholic Week,* January 27, 1951, p. 1; Discussion Outline, Catholic Committee of the South Current Policy Statement On Race, Part I, "The Necessity for a Current Policy Statement," Loose Folder, "Fr. Foley, Personal, 1954–5," Foley papers.

22. Discussion Outline, Catholic Committee of the South Current Policy Statement On Race, Part II, "The Opportuneness of the Current Policy Statement," and Part III, "The Advantages Accruing from the New Policy Statement," Loose Folder, "Fr. Foley, Personal, 1954–5," Foley papers.

23. Foley to Mr. and Mrs. Jerome S. Murray, Annapolis, Md., September 24, 1971, Unlabeled Folder, Container, Foley KKK, Foley papers; Foley, "Shadow of the White Camellia: Reminiscences of a Tangle with Terrorists," Sage version, [48–49]; later in the memoir, Foley wrote that the local Klan started in 1948, [89]. See also "Effort Made Here To Enroll Negro In White School," *Mobile Register,* September 13, 1956, p. 1.

24. Foley, "Shadow of the White Camellia: Reminiscences of a Tangle with Terrorists," Sage version, [50–52]; on Langan's biracial committee, see "Biracial Group Said All-Langan," *Mobile Register,* April 5, 1956, p. 2-A. At the time, Mobile had a commission form of government, and the mayorship rotated among commissioners. This is one reason a Catholic could hold such a prominent citywide public office.

25. Foley, "Shadow of the White Camellia: Reminiscences of a Tangle with Terrorists," Sage version, [52]; "Deputies Probe Cross Burning," *Mobile Press,* October 13, 1956, clipping in Container—Foley KKK, Folder—Cox, Mobile, File, Foley papers.

26. Statement by Father Albert S. Foley, S.J., Ph.D., Professor of Sociology, Spring Hill College, October 13, 1956, Loose Folder, "So. 155. KKK—APA, etc.," Foley papers.

27. "Survey of Attitudes Toward the Ku Klux Klan As A Social Problem," Container—Foley KKK, Folder, KKK Surveys, Foley papers.

28. Albert S. Foley, "KKK in Mobile, Ala.," *America,* December 8, 1956, pp. 298–299; "Responses to Survey of Attitudes Toward the Ku Klux Klan As A Social Problem," Container—Foley KKK, Folder—KKK Surveys, Foley papers.

29. "Responses to Survey of Attitudes Toward the Ku Klux Klan As A Social Problem"; Foley, "Shadow of the White Camellia: Reminiscences of a Tangle with Terrorists," Sage version.

30. Foley, "Shadow of the White Camellia: Reminiscences of a Tangle with Terrorists," Sage version, 8–12, [52, 55–56, 57, 93–98, 99]. The chronology in Foley's memoirs and papers is not always precise. It could be that the advertisement prompted Foley's survey and the efforts to pass the city ordinances. All three are collapsed almost into a single event in Foley's recollection. In his memoirs describing these activities, Foley refers to "we," but it is not clear to whom he is referring. Most likely, he means the Mobile chapter of the Alabama Council on Human Relations.

31. Present Position of the Gulf Klan, Inc. In Mobile, March 8, 1957; Gulf Ku Klux Klan, Top Personnel, March 9, 1957, Folder, "Encounter With The Klan," Container, Foley KKK, Foley papers.

32. Foley, "Shadow of the White Camellia: Reminiscences of a Tangle with Terrorists," Sage version, 18–22; "An Evaluation of a Contemporary Local and Regional Social Problem," Talk: Holy Name Hour: October 20, WKRG Radio Station, 9:30–9:45 P.M., Loose Folder, So. 155, KKK-APA, etc., Foley papers. For Foley's writings on the Klan, see "KKK in Mobile, Ala.," *America,* December 8, 1956, pp. 298–299.

33. Foley, "Shadow of the White Camellia: Reminiscences of a Tangle with Terrorists," Sage version, 13–16, [68–72].

34. Ibid., 23, [59–64], [87]; Foley, "In the Shadow of the White Camellias," Spring Hill version, [222–224]; Joan Sage interview with author, September 18, 1998, and October 22, 1998.

35. Foley, "In the Shadow of the White Camellias," Spring Hill version, [225–227]; Joseph Langan interview with the author, June 29, 1999, audiotape in possession of the author. For Langan's request that Foley and the ACHR mediate the desegregation of downtown, see memo from Foley to Commissioner Langan, Rev. J. M. Lowery, Mr. John LeFlore, and Rev. Robert Hughes, August 24, 1960, John LeFlore Papers, Reel 9, 35A, "Alabama Council on Human Relations, 1955–1971," Archives of the University of South Alabama.

36. In 1963 Foley expanded and revised the report. See Foley, "The Administration of Justice in the State of Alabama, 1958–1963," Loose Folder, "Birmingham, 1963; America Article; Siena Speech; M.L. King's Letter from Birm. Jail," Foley papers; "Rights Group Urges Probing Of Police Power In Alabama," *Mobile Press-Register,* September 10, 1961, clipping in Folder, "Ala. Civil Rights," Container, Race Relations/Human Rights, Foley papers; Sage interview; Sage, "The 'Grilling' Story of St. Joan," 197–199. Also see, for example, Mrs. Moreland G. (Marjorie L.) Smith, Montgomery, Ala., to Foley, March 2, 1961, Folder, "Ala. Civil Rights Cases," Container, Race Relations/Human Rights, Foley papers.

37. "Race Mixers Libel Alabama," *Alabama Journal,* September 11, 1961, p. 4-A, clipping in Folder, "Ala. Civil Rights," Container, Race Relations/Human Rights, Foley papers.

38. Telegram from L. B. Sullivan to Foley, September 8, 1961; Foley's response, September 9, 1961; and Sullivan to Foley, September 11, 1961; memo from Foley to Advisory Committee Members, September 9, 1961; Foley to Berl Bernhard, Director, Civil Rights Commission, Washington, D.C., September 9, 1961; Bernhard to Foley, September 11, 1961, Folder, "Ala. Civil Rights," Container, Race Relations/Human Rights, Foley papers.

39. Robert C. Garrison, Birmingham to Toolen, July 16, 1962; Garrison to Foley, July 13, 1962; Monsignor Philip Cullen to Garrison, July 18, 1962; Cullen to Vincent F. Kilborn, Mobile, July 19, 1962; Cullen to Very Rev. A. William Crandell, S.J., Spring Hill College, July 19, 1962; Crandell to Cullen, July 23, 1962, Toolen papers; Sage, "The 'Grilling' Story of St. Joan," 199.

40. Foley, "Shadow of the White Camellia: Reminiscences of a Tangle with Terrorists," Sage version, [150–181]; Ellis, "'The Tragedy of the White Moderate,'" 58–105; Glenn T. Eskew, *But for Birmingham: The Local and National Movements in the Civil Rights Struggle* (Chapel Hill: Univ. of North Carolina Press, 1997), 222, 380 n. 36. For more on those ministers and the impact of King's letter, see S. Jonathan Bass, *Blessed Are the Peacemakers: Martin Luther King, Jr., Eight White Religious Leaders, and the "Letter from Birmingham Jail"* (Baton Rouge: Louisiana State Univ. Press, 2001).

41. Samuel S. Hill, *Southern Churches in Crisis* (Boston: Beacon Press, 1968; New York: Holt, Rinehart, and Winston, 1966); Samuel S. Hill, "The South's Two Cultures," in *Religion and the Solid South,* ed. Samuel S. Hill (Nashville, Tenn.: Abingdon Press, 1972).

42. "Discrimination and the Christian Conscience," *A Syllabus on Racial Justice,* For Use in the Catholic Schools, Grades 7–12, of the Archdiocese of Atlanta, Box 036/6, Folder 51, ACAA. In 1963, furthermore, Pope John XXIII issued the encyclical *Pacem in Terris* (Peace on Earth), which similarly condemned racial discrimination.

43. Pastoral letter, February 19, 1961, reprinted in *Syllabus on Racial Justice*; Hyland to Hallinan, Charleston, S.C., January 25, 1961; David Murphy, East Wesley Road, Atlanta, Ga., to Hyland, February 19, 1961; (Miss) Mary Bennett to Hyland, February 20, 1961, Box 036/6, Folder 49; "Southern Bishops Carry 'Torch Of Integration,'" clipping from *Register* [n.p.], February 26, 1961, Bishop Hyland Scrapbook, ACAA.

44. Hyland to Very Reverend Monsignor John E. Kelly, Bureau of Information, NCWC, Washington, D.C., Box 036/6, Folder 49, ACAA.

45. See Jay P. Dolan, *The American Catholic Experience: A History from Colonial Times to the Present* (Notre Dame: Univ. of Notre Dame Press, 1992). In addition, underscoring this change was the gradual transformations in Catholic spirituality and devotionalism that had begun in the 1950s, to be replaced by reforms implemented by Vatican II. See Timothy Kelly, "Suburbanization and the Decline of Catholic Public Ritual in Pittsburgh," *Journal of Social History* 28 (winter 1994): 311–330; Timothy Kelly and Joseph Kelly, "Our Lady of Perpetual Help, Gender Roles, and the Decline of Devotional Catholicism," *Journal of Social History* 32 (fall 1998): 5–26; and Dolan, *The American Catholic Experience,* 384–390.

CHAPTER 4

1. On race relations in Atlanta, see Ronald H. Bayor, *Race and the Shaping of Twentieth-Century Atlanta* (Chapel Hill: Univ. of North Carolina Press, 1996); and Gary M. Pomerantz, *Where Peachtree Meets Sweet Auburn: The Saga of Two Families and the Making of Atlanta* (New York: Scribner, 1996).

2. Flannery O'Connor, "The Artificial Nigger," in *The Complete Stories of Flannery O'Connor* (New York: Noonday Press, 1971), 249–270.

3. To Ben Griffith, May 4, 1955, in *The Habit of Being: Letters of Flannery O'Connor*, ed. Sally Fitzgerald (New York: Noonday Press, 1979), 78; Ralph C. Wood, *Flannery O'Connor and the Christ-Haunted South* (Grand Rapids, Mich.: Eerdmans, 2004), especially chapters 3 and 4; Paul Elie, *The Life You Save May Be Your Own: An American Pilgrimage* (New York: Farrar, Straus and Giroux, 2003), 327.

4. L. G. Allain, Horace Bohannon, Charles Goosby, Thomas W. Hines, John Thomas, (Mrs.) Evarie S. Thompson, and (Mrs.) Johnnie Yancey to Hyland, December 11, 1960, Box 036/6, Folder 49, ACAA; news clipping [probably from the *Bulletin*], January 7, 1961, in Bishop Hyland Scrapbook, ACAA. On the 1960 demonstrations, see Pomerantz, *Where Peachtree Meets Sweet Auburn*, 251–264.

5. On New Orleans Archbishop Joseph F. Rummel's earlier vain efforts, see "Catholic Archbishop Backs New Orleans Integration," *New York Times*, July 8, 1959, Proquest Historical Newspapers *New York Times*, 20; "Church Cautions Integration Foes," *New York Times*, February 25, 1956, Proquest Historical Newspapers *New York Times*, 1; Adam Fairclough, *Race and Democracy: The Civil Rights Struggle in Louisiana, 1915–1972* (Athens: Univ. of Georgia Press, 1995), 171–178, 199–204, 324; Michael B. Friedland, *Lift Up Your Voice Like a Trumpet: White Clergy and the Civil Rights and Antiwar Movements, 1954–1973* (Chapel Hill: Univ. of North Carolina Press, 1998), 39–44. For the 1956 pastoral letter condemning segregation, see Archbishop Joseph Francis Rummel, pastoral letter, February 19, 1956, *Catholic Mind* 54 (May 1956), reprinted in *To Redeem a Nation: A History and Anthology of the Civil Rights Movement*, ed. Thomas R. West and James W. Mooney (St. James, N.Y.: Brandywine Press, 1993), 47–48.

6. Proceedings of the Consultors Meeting, October 23, 1957, Box 008/1, Folder 1, ACAA; Bayor, *Race and the Shaping of Twentieth-Century Atlanta*, 224. On southern tactics to resist school integration, see Numan V. Bartley, *The Rise of Massive Resistance: Race and Politics in the South during the 1950s*, with a new preface by the author (Baton Rouge: Louisiana State Univ. Press, 1997; originally published 1969).

7. Hyland to Very Reverend Monsignor John E. Kelly, Bureau of Information, NCWC, Washington, D.C., February 22, 1961; Hyland to Bishop Paul Hallinan, Charleston, S.C., January 25, 1961; Hyland to Hughes Spalding, Atlanta, Ga., March 2, 1961, Box, 036/6, Folder 49, ACAA.

8. Hughes Spalding, Atlanta, Ga., to Hyland, February 22, 1961; Ferdinand Buckley, Atlanta, Ga., to Hyland, February 20, 1961; Henry L. de Give, Atlanta, Ga., to Hyland, February 20, 1961; Irene B. Maslanka, Corresponding Secretary, Atlanta DCCW, to Hyland, February 27, 1961, Box 036/6, Folder 49, ACAA. See also Gladys Gunning, Atlanta, Ga., to Hyland, February 23, 1961; and from David Murphy, Atlanta, Ga., to Hyland, February 19, 1961, in the same folder.

9. (Miss) Mary Bennett to Hyland, February 20, 1961, Box 036/6, Folder 49, ACAA.

10. Betty Tecklenburg Long (Mrs. Leonard L. Long) to Hyland, March 15, 1961, Box 036/6, Folder 49, ACAA. For other opponents, see, for example, anonymous letter to Hyland, n.d., Box 036/6, Folder 49, ACAA.

11. Pastoral letter, February 19, 1961, reprinted in *Syllabus on Racial Justice*; and Hyland to Hallinan, Charleston, S.C., January 25, 1961, Box 036/6, Folder 49; "Southern Bishops Carry 'Torch Of Integration,'" clipping from the *Register* (n.p.), February

26, 1961, Bishop Hyland Scrapbook, ACAA; Hyland to Rev. L. J. Twomey, S.J., Institute of Industrial Relations, New Orleans, April 3, 1961, Box 036/6, Folder 49, ACAA.

12. Pastoral letter from Hyland, April 10, 1961; Hyland to Rev. Michael McKeever, S.M.A., Our Lady of Lourdes Church, Atlanta, Ga., April 13, 1961; and Hyland to Rev. Dennis Walsh, C.R., St. Paul of the Cross Church, Atlanta, Ga., April 14, 1961, Box 036/6, Folder 49, ACAA.

13. Pastoral letter from Hyland, April 10, 1961; Hyland to Bishop Paul J. Hallinan, Charleston, S.C., April 10, 1961, Box 036/6, Folder 49, ACAA.

14. Pastoral letter, February 19, 1961, reprinted in *Syllabus on Racial Justice*; Bayor, *Race and the Shaping of Twentieth-Century Atlanta*, 221–226.

15. Thomas J. Shelley, *Paul J. Hallinan: First Archbishop of Atlanta* (Wilmington, Del.: Michael Glazier, 1989), 116–131, 146–148; sermon quoted in M. Elise Schwalm, R.S.M., ed., "In His Own Words: Paul J. Hallinan, Archbishop of Atlanta, 1962–1968," 13, unpublished manuscript in possession of M. Elise Schwalm. I am grateful to Sister Elise for making the fruits of her hard work available to me.

16. Minutes of Archdiocesan Board of Consultors' Meeting, May 24, 1962, Box 008/1, Folder 2, ACAA; Shelley, *Paul J. Hallinan*, 159–160.

17. Minutes of Archdiocesan Board of Consultors' Meeting, May 24, 1962.

18. Pastoral letter from Hallinan, June 10, 1962, Box 036/6, Folder 50, ACAA; Hallinan at press conference quoted in Shelley, *Paul J. Hallinan*, 160–161.

19. Hallinan's pastoral letter to teachers, *Syllabus on Racial Justice*, i, 2, emphasis in original, Box 036/6, Folder 51, ACAA. On the *Syllabus* in Charleston, see Shelley, *Paul J. Hallinan*, 129–130. On the Archdiocese of New Orleans, see Claude Sitton, "3 Racists Excommunicated By Louisiana Archbishop," *New York Times*, April 17, 1962, Proquest Historical Newspapers *New York Times*, 1; Claude Sitton, "Louisiana Racist Stands Firm," *New York Times*, April 15, 1962, Proquest Historical Newspapers *New York Times*, 62; Claude Sitton, "Louisiana Woman Bids God Forgive Excommunicator," *New York Times*, April 18, 1962, Proquest Historical Newspapers *New York Times*, 1. Also on desegregation of parochial schools, see Claude Sitton, "Catholic Schools Enroll Negroes," *New York Times*, April 14, 1962, Proquest Historical Newspapers *New York Times*, 21; "5 Negroes Enter Catholic School," *New York Times*, August 30, 1962, Proquest Historical Newspapers *New York Times*, 17; "Integration Test Due In Louisiana," *New York Times*, September 4, 1962, Proquest Historical Newspapers *New York Times*, 26; William A. Osborne, *The Segregated Covenant: Race Relations and American Catholics* (New York: Herder and Herder, 1967), 78.

20. *Syllabus on Racial Justice*, 3, 30.

21. Ibid., 5, 33.

22. Ibid., 33–38, 23.

23. "Atlanta Negroes Demand Civil Rights Speed-Up," *Georgia Bulletin*, December 19, 1963; "Recommendations of the Sub-Committee On Proposed Activities for the Ensuing Year," 1964 Annual Report of St. Martin's Council on Human Relations, Box 023/2, Folder 1, ACAA; Hallinan to "Dear Father," September 19, 1963, emphasis in original, Box 023/2, Folder 1; Minutes of Archdiocesan Board of Consultors Meeting, June 27, 1963, Box 008/1, Folder 2, ACAA; Report, St. Martin's Human Relation's Council, 1963–1964 and 1964–1965, June 6, 1965, Box 023/2, Folder 1, ACAA.

24. Report, St. Martin's Human Relation's Council, 1963–1964 and 1964–1965, June 6, 1965.

25. King quoted in Charles Marsh, *The Beloved Community: How Faith Shapes Social Justice from the Civil Rights Movement to Today* (New York: Basic Books, 2005), 45.

26. "What We Are About (Part 1)," *Georgia Bulletin*, January 4, 1963, p. 4; "What We Are About (Part 2)," *Georgia Bulletin*, January 11, 1963, p. 4.

27. See Bayor, *Race and the Shaping of Twentieth-Century Atlanta*, 66–68; and Pomerantz, *Where Peachtree Meets Sweet Auburn*, 308–312.

28. Gerard Sherry, "The 'Wall' of Shame," *Georgia Bulletin*, January 17, 1963, p. 4; "Wall Is Down," *Georgia Bulletin*, March 7, 1963, p. 4.

29. "A Negro Child," *Georgia Bulletin*, September 19, 1963, p. 4; "Court Ruling," *Georgia Bulletin*, May 23, 1963, p. 4.

30. Gerard E. Sherry, "Support The 'March' But . . . ," *Georgia Bulletin*, August 22, 1963, p. 4; Sherry, "Racial Crisis Coming To A Head," *Georgia Bulletin*, June 13, 1963, p. 4. See also Sherry, "The Arrests In Baltimore," *Georgia Bulletin*, July 18, 1963, p. 4; "Calm Is Restored," *Georgia Bulletin*, February 6, 1964, p. 4; Sherry, "Extremism A Virtue," *Georgia Bulletin*, July 30, 1964, p. 4.

31. "Unity of Purpose," *Georgia Bulletin*, May 30, 1963, p. 4. See also "'Patriotic' Racists," *Georgia Bulletin*, July 9, 1964, p. 4; Leonard F. X. Mayhew, "Race Problem Complex," *Georgia Bulletin*, July 4, 1963, p. 4; Mayhew, "Sub-Rational Violence," *Georgia Bulletin*, July 16, 1964, p. 5.

32. "Subsidiary Function," *Georgia Bulletin*, October 31, 1963, p. 4. On the Civil Rights Act, see Numan V. Bartley, *The New South, 1945–1980* (Baton Rouge: Louisiana State Univ. Press, 1995), 370–375; James T. Patterson, *Grand Expectations: The United States, 1945–1974* (New York: Oxford Univ. Press, 1996), 542–547; Robert Weisbrot, *Freedom Bound: A History of America's Civil Rights Movement* (New York: Norton, 1990), 87–90. On the Birmingham movement, see Glenn T. Eskew, *But for Birmingham: The Local and National Movements in the Civil Rights Struggle* (Chapel Hill: Univ. of North Carolina Press, 1997).

33. Wallace quoted in Dan T. Carter, *The Politics of Rage: George Wallace, the Origins of the New Conservatism, and the Transformation of American Politics* (New York: Simon and Schuster, 1995), 217; "The Common Good," *Georgia Bulletin*, February 13, 1964, p. 4.

34. Fred T. Humphrey, Smyrna, Ga., Letter to the Editor, *Georgia Bulletin*, February 20, 1964, p. 6; Andrew Michael Manis, *Southern Civil Religions in Conflict: Black and White Baptists and Civil Rights, 1947–1957* (Athens: Univ. of Georgia Press, 1985).

35. Ferdinand and Marianne Buckley, interview by the author, audiotape recording, Atlanta, Ga., June 18, 2004; Ferdinand Buckley, Atlanta, Ga., Letter to the Editor, *Georgia Bulletin*, April 2, 1964, p. 5. For an opposing view that does not necessarily sympathize with segregationists, see Daniel J. O'Connor, Atlanta, Ga., Letter to the Editor, *Georgia Bulletin*, March 26, 1964, p. 7.

36. "Explanation Of Various Titles In Civil Rights Bill," *Georgia Bulletin*, April 9, 1964, p. 2.

37. Sherry, "Now, Negro Response," *Georgia Bulletin*, July 9, 1964, p. 4. Of course, not all white Atlantans complied. See "Non-Compliance," *Georgia Bulletin*, August 6,

1964, p. 4; "Georgia's Image," *Georgia Bulletin,* July 29, 1965, p. 4. At least two Atlanta landmarks, the Pickrick Restaurant and the Heart of Atlanta Motel, refused to comply. Lester Maddox refused service at his Pickrick Restaurant to three theology students who tried to test the Civil Rights Act's public accommodations section. Maddox eventually closed his restaurant rather than integrate. See Pomerantz, *Where Peachtree Meets Sweet Auburn,* 333–334.

38. On the behind-the-scenes negotiations necessary to insure an interracial banquet, see Pomerantz, *Where Peachtree Meets Sweet Auburn,* 334–340; and Taylor Branch, *Pillar of Fire: America in the King Years, 1963–1965* (New York: Simon and Schuster, 1998), 568–570.

39. Gerard E. Sherry, "Whites, Negroes Join Salute To Dr. King," *Georgia Bulletin,* February 4, 1965, p. 8; Allen quoted in Shelley, *Paul J. Hallinan,* 230; Martin Luther King., Jr., to Hallinan, March 8, 1965, Box 001/2, Folder 7, ACAA; "Remarks of Archbishop Paul J. Hallinan at Civic Dinner Honoring Dr. Martin Luther King, Jr., Atlanta, January 27, 1965," Box 001/6, Folder 42, ACAA.

40. "Between 35–40 Priests At Selma," *Catholic Week,* March 12, 1965, p. 12. See also John T. McGreevy, *Parish Boundaries: The Catholic Encounter with Race in the Twentieth-Century Urban North* (Chicago: Univ. of Chicago Press, 1996), 155–158; Gregory Nelson Hite, "The Hottest Places in Hell: The Catholic Church and Civil Rights in Selma, Alabama, 1937–1965" (Ph.D. diss., University of Virginia, Charlottesville, 2002). On the murder of Jackson, see Branch, *Pillar of Fire,* 593–594. The classic account of the 1965 Selma voting rights demonstrations and the resulting Voting Rights Act is David J. Garrow, *Protest at Selma: Martin Luther King, Jr., and the Voting Rights Act of 1965* (New Haven: Yale Univ. Press, 1978). Also on the Selma movement, see Charles W. Eagles, *Outside Agitator: Jon Daniels and the Civil Rights Movement in Alabama* (Chapel Hill: Univ. of North Carolina Press, 1993); and Sheyann Webb and Rachel Ann Nelson, as told to Frank Sikora, *Selma, Lord, Selma: Girlhood Memories of the Civil-Rights Days* (Tuscaloosa: Univ. of Alabama Press, 1980).

41. See chapter 5.

42. "Archbishop's Notebook," *Georgia Bulletin,* April 1, 1965, p. 2; Monsignor Vincent A. Yzermans, "Wherever They Go, Christians Witness For Christ," interview with Hallinan by Monsignor Vincent A. Yzermans, *Our Sunday Visitor,* Fort Wayne-South Bend Edition, Magazine Section 55 (July 24, 1966), 4–5. The priests of the archdiocese overwhelmingly supported Hallinan's policy. At a 1965 consultors' meeting, fifty-eight voted their approval, six juxta modum, five unfavorable, and three undecided. See Minutes of Archdiocesan Board of Consultors, April 7, 1965, Box 008/1, Folder 3, ACAA.

43. "Archbishop's Notebook," *Georgia Bulletin,* April 1, 1965, p. 2; Leo E. Reichert, Jr., Letter to the Editor, *Georgia Bulletin,* April 8, 1965, p. 8.

44. J. J. Conoley, Jr., Letter to the Editor, *Georgia Bulletin,* April 15, 1965, p. 8.

45. "Contradictions, Tensions Major Hallmark of Selma," *Georgia Bulletin,* March 18, 1965, p. 1; Report, St. Martin's Human Relation's Council, 1963–1964 and 1964–1965, June 6, 1965.

46. Gerard Sherry, "National Shame," *Georgia Bulletin,* March 11, 1965, p. 4; "Contradictions, Tensions Major Hallmark of Selma," *Georgia Bulletin,* March 18, 1965, p. 1.

47. "Southern Catholics' Meet Set On Human Relations Today," *Georgia Bulletin*, July 29, 1965, p. 1; "Social Change and Christian Response Program," *Georgia Bulletin*, July 29, 1965.

48. "Archbishop Hallinan Cites Church In Human Relations," *Georgia Bulletin*, August 5, 1965, p. 1. See also "Race—Frontier and the Market Place," *Georgia Bulletin*, July 29, 1965, p. 1.

CHAPTER 5

1. "Alabama Religious Heads Warn Pro-Segregationists," *Georgia Bulletin*, January 24, 1963, p. 3; "Negro Citizenry Urged To Withdraw Support From Racial Demonstrators," *Catholic Week*, April 19, 1963, p. 1; "Scores Racial Demagoguery in Alabama," *Catholic Week*, May 17, 1963, p. 5. On the religious leaders who signed that statement, see S. Jonathan Bass, *Blessed Are the Peacemakers: Martin Luther King, Jr., Eight White Religious Leaders, and the "Letter from Birmingham Jail"* (Baton Rouge: Louisiana State Univ. Press, 2001).

2. Rev. Roland J.P-M Inkel, Midfield, Ala., Letter to the Editor, *Catholic Week*, May 24, 1963, p. 7; "Bishop Durick Discusses Race Issue Solution," *Catholic Week*, May 31, 1963, p. 1. Besides Inkel's letter, there were two other letters in the same issue that also criticized the Church for its unwillingness to take a firm stance in favor of integration.

3. Sister Carleta Rausch, S.N.D., transcription of interview by Sister Rose Sevenich, O.S.F., February 10, 1993, transcribed by John J. P. O'Brien, Oral History Project, Box 3, Envelope 6, ACDBA.

4. Toolen to My dearly beloved Priests and People, September 17, 1963, Toolen papers. On the bombing, see Taylor Branch, *Parting the Waters: America in the King Years, 1954–1963* (New York: Simon and Schuster, 1988), 889–892; and Taylor Branch, *Pillar of Fire: America in the King Years, 1963–1965* (New York: Simon and Schuster, 1998), 137–138.

5. See, for example, Toolen to Lawrence Cardinal Shehan, Baltimore, April 22, 1965, Toolen papers.

6. Mrs. Mary Hill, transcript of interview by Sister Rose Sevenich, O.S.F., March 9, 1993, transcribed by John J. P. O'Brien; and Mary S. Hill, "Holy Family Elementary School, 1937–1977. A Brief Historical Survey and Comment," Oral History Project, Box 3, Envelope 8, ACDBA.

7. Eddie L. English, Mobile, Ala., to Toolen, September 23, 1963, Toolen papers.

8. Toolen to Rev. Thomas Lorigan, Selma, Ala., September 24, 1963. See also letter from Toolen to English, September 24, 1963, Toolen papers.

9. Joseph I. McHugh, Orrville, Ala., to Toolen, September 29, 1963, Toolen papers. On those so-called "pray-ins," see Charles Marsh, *God's Long Summer: Stories of Faith and Civil Rights* (Princeton, N.J.: Princeton Univ. Press, 1997), chapter 4. For a local example, see Mrs. M. B. Tidwell, Selma, Ala., to Toolen, December 31, 1964; "Three Men Are Held In Connection With Beating of Solder," undated, unidentified newspaper clipping in Toolen papers, 1964; Father Charles F. Auconi, Selma to Toolen, January 2, 1965, Toolen papers.

10. McHugh to Toolen, September 29, 1963, Toolen papers.

11. Toolen to McHugh, October 2, 1963, Toolen papers. Toolen does not say, but the Edmundite causing trouble was probably Rev. Maurice Ouellet, a civil rights activist and head of the Edmundite mission in Selma in the early 1960s. Toolen tolerated the independent priest for a while, but in 1965 ordered him out of the diocese. See Charles W. Eagles, *Outside Agitator: Jon Daniels and the Civil Rights Movement in Alabama* (Chapel Hill: Univ. of North Carolina Press, 1993), 67–68.

12. In Louisiana in 1962, Archbishop of New Orleans Joseph Francis Rummel excommunicated three white Catholics who resisted his order to integrate parochial schools. See Michael B. Friedland, *Lift Up Your Voice Like a Trumpet: White Clergy and the Civil Rights and Antiwar Movements, 1954–1973* (Chapel Hill: Univ. of North Carolina Press, 1998), 43.

13. Charles R. Benboe, Pensacola, Fla., to Toolen, July 10, 1962, Toolen papers.

14. Lawrence McVoy, Pensacola, Fla., to Toolen, July 23, 1962; Willie Collins, Pensacola, Fla., to Toolen, June 30, 1962; see also Dr. Simon William Boyd, D.D.S., Pensacola, Fla., to Toolen, May 18, 1962, Toolen papers.

15. Toolen to Sister Mary Rose, Daughters of Charity, Normandy, Mo., August 4, 1962. For other examples, see Mother Mary Barromea, S.N.D., Covington, Ky., to Toolen, February 10, 1966; and Toolen to Rev. J. B. Tennelly, Washington, D.C., August 29, 1967, Toolen papers.

16. Sister Mary Rose, Marillac Provincial House, St. Louis, Mo., to Toolen, February 11, 1964, Toolen papers.

17. Toolen to Sister Mary Rose, St. Louis, Mo., March 10, 1964, Toolen papers.

18. Transcript of St. Joseph's, Huntsville, video on the forty-third anniversary of founding, transcribed by John J. P. O'Brien, Oral History Project, Box 3, Envelope 4; Isabelle Marrero, *The History of St. Joseph's Catholic Community, 1952–1992*, ACDBA; "Parochial School Degregated [*sic*]," *Georgia Bulletin*, September 12, 1963, p. 2; Rose Gibbons Lovett, *The Catholic Church in the Deep South: The Diocese of Birmingham in Alabama, 1540–1976* (Birmingham, Ala.: The Diocese of Birmingham in Alabama, 1980), 191–192. Father Sterbenz's name was also spelled "Sturbenz" in the *Georgia Bulletin* news story. Since Rose Gibbons Lovett had access to both written records and oral interviews, I have elected to use her spelling. Toolen to Very Rev. John L. May, Extension Society, Chicago, April, 15 1964, Toolen papers.

19. Toolen pastoral letter, April 22, 1964 [to be read April 26, 1964], Toolen papers; "Diocesan Superintendent Announces Procedure For Admission Of All Students," *Catholic Week,* May 1, 1964, p. 1; "Msgr. Stuardi States Policy For Admission to Diocesan High Schools," *Catholic Week,* March 6, 1964, p. 1. On the response to Brown, see, for example, Adam Fairclough, *Race and Democracy: The Civil Rights Struggle in Louisiana, 1915–1972* (Athens: Univ. of Georgia Press, 1995), 234–264; Numan V. Bartley, *The Rise of Massive Resistance: Race and Politics in the South during the 1950s,* with a new preface by the author (Baton Rouge: Louisiana State Univ. Press, 1997; originally published 1969), 77–81; and James T. Patterson, *Brown v. Board of Education: A Civil Rights Milestone and Its Troubled Legacy* (New York: Oxford Univ. Press, 2001), 100.

20. Catherine M. West, Mobile, Ala., to Toolen, April 26, 1964, Toolen papers.

21. Viola Johnson, Marion Junction, Ala., to Toolen, April 30, 1964, Toolen papers.

22. Ibid. On the postwar transformation of American spirituality, see Robert Wuthnow, *The Restructuring of American Religion: Society and Faith since World War II* (Princeton, N.J.: Princeton Univ. Press, 1988); and Robert Wuthnow, *After Heaven: Spirituality in America since the 1950s* (Berkeley: Univ. of California Press, 1998).

23. "Archbishop's Statement On Selma Racial Tension," *Catholic Week*, March 12, 1965, p. 1.

24. "Between 35–40 Priests At Selma," *Catholic Week*, March 12, 1965, p. 12; "Archbishop Toolen Criticizes Presence of Priests, Sisters in Demonstrations," *Catholic Week*, March 19, 1965, p. 1.

25. Toolen to Lawrence Cardinal Shehan, Baltimore, Md., April 22, 1965; Toolen to Daniel Morgan, Huntsville, Ala., January 26, 1966, Toolen papers.

26. See, for example, "Work Is Started On Negro Project In Phenix City," *Catholic Week*, June 15, 1945, p. 5; "Colored Maternity Hospital Will Be Built In Pensacola," *Catholic Week*, November 23, 1945, p. 1; "Citizen Group Backs Plans For Catholic Hospital For Negroes," *Catholic Week*, May 28, 1945, p. 8; "Birmingham To Have Catholic Negro High School and Hospital," *Catholic Week*, June 25, 1948, p. 1; Langan interview with author.

27. Sheyann Webb and Rachel Ann Nelson, as told to Frank Sikora, *Selma, Lord, Selma: Girlhood Memories of the Civil-Rights Days* (Tuscaloosa: Univ. of Alabama Press, 1980), 142, 57, 15.

28. Members of St. Jude and St. John the Baptist Parishes, Montgomery, Ala., to Toolen, March 21, 1965, Toolen papers.

29. Robert Craig, St. Elizabeth's Church, Selma, Ala., to Toolen, November 20, 1965; Chris B. Heinz, Selma, Ala., to Toolen, September 23, 1963, Toolen papers. On Ouellet being the only white supporter of the movement, see J. L. Chestnut, Jr., and Julia Cass, *Black in Selma: The Uncommon Life of J.L. Chestnut, Jr.* (New York: Farrar, Straus and Giroux, 1990), 184.

30. Toolen to Daniel Morgan, Huntsville, Ala., January 26, 1966; Morgan to Toolen, January 16, 1966, Toolen papers; Gregory Nelson Hite, "The Hottest Places in Hell: The Catholic Church and Civil Rights in Selma, Alabama, 1937–1965" (Ph.D. diss., University of Virginia, Charlottesville, 2002), 211–213; Eagles, *Outside Agitator*, 67–68.

31. "Father Mullaney States Policy Involved In Use Of St. Jude's Property," *Catholic Week*, March 26, 1965, p. 1. Indeed, Father Ouellet of St. Elizabeth's often provided the local movement what Taylor Branch calls "fragile sanctuary" for their meetings. See Branch, *Pillar of Fire*, 390–391.

32. Toolen to Mr. W. S. Pritchard, Birmingham, Ala., March 24, 1965; and Pritchard to Toolen, March 19, 1965, Toolen papers.

33. Hite, "Hottest Places in Hell," 284–285.

34. Joseph I. McHugh, Orrville, Ala., to Toolen, September 29, 1963, Toolen papers.

35. Mrs. Madelyn Patterson Burdick, Birmingham, Ala., to Toolen, March 19, 1965, Toolen papers. See also Mr. and Mrs. Edward McCleary, Fort Walton Beach, Fla., to Toolen, March 25, 1965, Toolen papers.

36. "Msgr. Higgins' Column On Dr. King Draws Reaction," *Catholic Week*, July 23, 1965, p. 6; "Red Conspiracy Among Negroes," *Catholic Week*, March 18, 1966, p. 6. On Morrisroe and Jonathan Daniels, who was shot and killed at the same time, see Eagles, *Outside Agitator*.

37. Mrs. James Ainsworth Miller (Dorothea Brown Miller), Montrose, Ala., to Toolen, March 18, 1965, Toolen papers.

38. Joan B. Thyson, Sawyerville, Ala., to Mother Superior, Mary Knoll Sister, Ossinging, N.Y., March 17, 1965; Toolen to Lawrence Cardinal Shehan, Baltimore, Md., April 22, 1965, Toolen papers. On the relationship between segregation and sex, see Jane Dailey, "Sex, Segregation, and the Sacred after *Brown*," *Journal of American History* 91 (June 2004): 119–144.

39. "Archbishop Lauded For His Stand," *Catholic Week*, April 2, 1965, p. 1; Walter F. Gaillard, Mobile, Ala., to Toolen, March 22, 1965, Toolen papers.

40. William J. Ward, Dothan, Ala., to Toolen, March 19, 1965, Toolen papers. For other examples, see The Men's Class of First Methodist Church, Bessemer, Ala., to Toolen, March 24, 1965; Janie Durden, August, Ga., to Toolen, March 18, 1965; State Senator Bill Nichols to Toolen, March 19, 1965, Toolen papers.

41. Peter A. Huff, *Allen Tate and the Catholic Revival: Trace of the Fugitive Gods* (Mahwah, N.J.: Paulist Press, 1996); Burdick to Toolen, March 19, 1965; Joseph P. Myers, Atlanta, Ga., to Toolen, March 19, 1965, Toolen papers.

42. "Archbishop's Notebook," *Georgia Bulletin*, April 1, 1965, p. 2. Hallinan refused to name his correspondents in his newspaper column, and this particular series of correspondence is, according to Hallinan's biographer, in the possession of someone other than the Archives of the Catholic Archdiocese of Atlanta, Georgia.

43. Caroline Krackenberger, Montgomery, Ala., to Toolen, March 22, 1965, Toolen papers.

44. Mrs. R. D. Hawkins, Birmingham, Ala., to Toolen, March 26, 1965; Mrs. Albert E. Taylor, Cherokee, Ala., to Toolen, March 23, 1965, Toolen papers.

45. James R. Jackson, Mobile, Ala., to Toolen, March 23, 1965; Walter Darring, Mobile, Ala., to Toolen, March 21, 1965, Toolen papers.

46. "Editor Says Silence of Christians Allows Abuse of Love, Religion," *Catholic Week*, November 5, 1965, p. 4.

47. Letter to the Editor, Frank Brocato, Birmingham, Ala., *Catholic Week*, November 12, 1965, p. 6; Letter to the Editor, Mrs. Faye W. Tidwell and Mrs. Russell Schmidt, Selma, Ala., *Catholic Week*, November 19, 1965, p. 6. See also Letter to the Editor, Adrian George Daniel, Birmingham, Alabama; and Mrs. E. J. Phillips, *Catholic Week*, November 19, 1965, p. 6.

CHAPTER 6

1. "Freedom Is A Wonderful Thing, But . . . ," *Catholic Week*, February 10, 1967, p. 6.

2. John T. McGreevy, *Parish Boundaries: The Catholic Encounter with Race in the Twentieth-Century Urban North* (Chicago: Univ. of Chicago Press, 1996), 155–158; William A. Osborne, *The Segregated Covenant: Race Relations and American Catholics* (New York: Herder and Herder, 1967).

3. "Official Statement: Admission Policy, Catholic Hospitals in the Archdiocese of Atlanta," *Georgia Bulletin,* March 28, 1963, p. 7; memo from Sister Mary Melanie, R.S.M., Administrator, to Chief Admission Officer and All Employees in the Department of Admissions, July 27, 1965; memo from Sister M. Jacob, Administrator, to Sister M. Geraldine, Nursing Service Director, and Mrs. Marjorie Ray, Supervisor Patient Services Department, June 23, 1966, Box 065/2, Folder 1, ACAA; M. Elise Schwalm, R.S.M., ed., "In His Own Words: Paul J. Hallinan, Archbishop of Atlanta, 1962–1968," 13, unpublished manuscript in possession of M. Elise Schwalm, 15.

4. Robert M. Nash, Chief, Office of Equal Health Opportunity, to Sister Mary Melanie, Administrator, St. Joseph's Infirmary, Atlanta, Ga., June 21, 1966; Nash to Sister Mary Jacob Engelhartd, Administrator, Holy Family Hospital, Atlanta, Ga., Box 065/2, Folder 1; "U.S. Okay Given to 7 Hospitals," *Atlanta Constitution,* June 25, 1966, newspaper clipping in Box 065/2, Folder 1; unsigned letter to Secretary John W. Gardner, Department of Health, Education and Welfare, Washington, D.C., June 21, 1966; and attached Summary, Box 065/2, Folder 1, ACAA.

5. Unsigned letter to Secretary John W. Gardner, Department of Health, Education and Welfare, Washington, D.C., June 21, 1966; and attached Summary, Box 065/2, Folder 1; press release, June 24, 1966, Box 065/2, Folder 1, ACAA.

6. See, for example, "Negro Leader Lauds Attitudes, Actions Toward Racial Harmony," *Catholic Week,* March 22, 1968, p. 8; "Human Relations Council Hears Talk On Negro-White Community," *Catholic Week,* April 5, 1968, p. 9; "Inter-faith Good Friday Services In Town Park," *Catholic Week,* April 19, 1968, p. 3.

7. "Message From Archbishop," *Catholic Week,* April 12, 1968, p. 1; "Archbishop Toolen Backs Dr. King Memorial Rites," *Catholic Week,* April 12, 1968, p. 2; Lipscomb, Chancellor, to Right Reverend Fathers, April 5, 1968, Toolen papers; "Archbishop Toolen Criticizes Presence of Priests, Sisters in Demonstrations," *Catholic Week,* March 19, 1965, p. 1. For other bishops' reactions to King's murder, see "Religious Leaders Mourn Dr. Martin Luther King," *Catholic Week,* April 12, 1968, pp. 1, 7.

8. Rev. Richard T. Sadlier, S.S.J., Mobile, Ala., to Toolen, April 6, 1968; Toolen to Very Rev. George F. O'Dea, S.S.J., Baltimore, Md., May 3, 1969; Toolen to O'Dea, May 26, 1969; O'Dea to Toolen, June 6, 1969; Toolen to O'Dea, June 24, 1969, Toolen papers. In 1965, Toolen managed to have Rev. Maurice Ouellet, S.S.E., reassigned, following Ouellet's alleged participation in the Selma demonstrations contrary to Toolen's direct order. Ouellet denied participating, but left no doubt that he sympathized with the demonstrations. See "Selma, Ala. Pastor Loses His Parish," *Catholic Week,* July 1, 1965, p. 3; and chapter 5.

9. For the argument that the Civil Rights Act of 1964 actually marked an increase in African American activism rather than the apex of the movement, see Timothy J. Minchin, "Black Activism, the 1964 Civil Rights Act, and the Racial Integration of the Southern Textile Industry" *Journal of Southern History* 65 (November 1999): 809–844; and Timothy J. Minchin, *Hiring the Black Worker: The Racial Integration of the Southern Textile Industry, 1960–1980* (Chapel Hill: Univ. of North Carolina Press, 1999).

10. Letter from Toolen to priests and religious of the diocese, May 21, 1968, Toolen papers. See also "Individual Rights of Priests, Religious To Public Protest Backed By Archbishop," *Catholic Week,* May 24, 1968, p. 1; "Archbishop Reiterates Regulations," *Catholic Week,* May 9, 1969, p. 1.

11. Toolen to Sister Robert Ann, Loretta Court, Santa Clara, Calif., May 16, 1968, Toolen papers.

12. Frederick Douglas Richardson, Jr., *The Genesis and Exodus of NOW,* 2nd ed. (Boynton Beach, Fla.: Futura Printing, 1996).

13. John T. Toenes, Mobile, Ala., to Rt. Rev. Thomas Nunan, Catholic Charities, Mobile, January 29, 1969; Toolen to Toenes, February 4, 1969; James. C. Antwerp, Jr., Mobile, to Toolen, February 5, 1969, Toolen papers.

14. James V. Irby, III, to Toolen, March 4, 1969; Toolen to Irby, March 10, 1969, Toolen papers.

15. "93 Are Arrested At Auditorium," *Mobile Press,* May 2, 1969, pp. 1, 8; "Many In March Freed On Bonds," *Mobile Press,* May 3, 1969, pp. 1, 2; "March Halted By Police; 151 Arrested," *Mobile Register,* May 3, 1969, pp. 1, 6; "71 Arrested During Third Protest Try," *Mobile Press-Register,* May 4, 1969, pp. 1, 14.

16. Toolen to Mr. Glenn R. Sebastian, Mobile, May 5, 1969; Toolen to Most Rev. Luigi Raimondi, Apostolic Delegate, Washington, D.C., June 17, 1969; Toolen to Sebastian, Mobile, May 5, 1969, Toolen papers.

17. Wallace Henley, "Showdown for Catholics at Mobile?" *Birmingham News,* May 18, 1969, p. A-12, clipping in Toolen papers; "Priests, Sisters Give Explanation," *Catholic Week,* May 16, 1969, p. 9; memorandum for Monsignor Oscar H. Lipscomb, Chancellor, May 3, 1969, Toolen papers.

18. "Reactions to Mobile Situation," *Catholic Week,* May 16, 1969, p. 9. See also "To The Catholic Christians Of Diocese Of Mobile-Birmingham," *Catholic Week,* May 16, 1969, p. 9; Henley, "Showdown for Catholics at Mobile?"

19. Toolen to Sister Evangelist, Convent of Mercy, County Meath, Ireland, June 12, 1969; Toolen to Miss Sal Devaney, Boyle, Roscommon, Ireland, June 7, 1969; Toolen to Rev. Edward J. Hanrahan, Georgetown University, Washington, D.C., June 9, 1969, Toolen papers; Henley, "Showdown for Catholics at Mobile?"

20. James E. Rice, St. Pius X Parish, Mobile, Ala., to Toolen, July 13, 1969; Petition To Most Reverend Thomas J. Toolen, Bishop, Mobile-Birmingham Diocese; Rice to Toolen, September 4, 1969; Toolen to Rice, September 5, 1969, Toolen papers.

21. "Abbey Announces Amalgamation of Two Tri-Cities Parishes," *Catholic Week,* January 13, 1967, p. 1; "'Newsweek' Abuses Integrity of Archbishop Toolen," *Catholic Week,* February 24, 1967, p. 6. Some of Joyce's friends and fellow activists believed his removal had been orchestrated by Toolen and wrote Toolen and Roettger to complain. See Norman C. McKenna, President, Catholic Interracial Council of Prince George's County, Md., to Toolen, February 12, 1967; McKenna to Right Rev. Gregory Roettger, O.S.B., St. Bernard, Ala., February 12, 1967, Francis X. Walter, Selma Inter-religious Project Files, Folder, "Bryce Joyce Protest," 1044.1.6, Department of Archives and Manuscripts, Linn-Henley Research Library, Birmingham Public Library, Birmingham, Alabama. Toolen had certainly requested of Joyce's superior that the priest be removed whenever possible. See Toolen to Father Gregory Roettger, O.S.B., St. Bernard, Ala., May 6, 1965, Toolen papers.

22. See Rt. Rev. Gregory J. Roettger, O.S.B., St. Bernard, Ala., to Joyce, May 24, 1968; Joyce to Toolen, June 5, 1968; Toolen to Joyce, June 7, 1968, Toolen papers.

23. Toolen to Mrs. Harvey P. Bernard, Decatur, Ala., October 15, 1968, Toolen papers.

24. Toolen to Mr. Ralph Turner, Wilmington, Del., April 4, 1968, Toolen papers.

25. Foust to Bernardin, February 11, 1967; Bernardin to Foust, February 15, 1967; Hallinan to Foust, March 14, 1967, Box 043/3, Folder 2, ACAA. For the "Decree on Ecumenism," see Austin Flannery, O.P., ed., *The Basic Sixteen Documents, Vatican Council II: Constitutions, Decrees, Declarations* (Northport, N.Y.: Costello, 1996), 499–523. On Foust's early questioning of Hallinan's leadership, see, for example, Foust to Hallinan, January 30, 1967, Box 043/3, Folder 2, ACAA.

26. New Parish Experiment, Meeting #2, February 14, 1967, Box 043/3, Folder 2; "Some Reasons for the Establishment of a Non-Territorial Parish and Some Problems Concerning Its Establishment"; "Some General Principles for Discussion Regarding a Parish Community Without Boundaries," Box 043/3, Folder 2; and Foust to Hallinan, March 2, 1967, Box 043/3, Folder 2, ACAA.

27. "'Parish Without Boundaries' Established in Atlanta," June 30, 1967, Religious News Service, Box 043/3, Folder 1, ACAA; Conald Foust, "Parish Without Bounds," *Commonweal*, August 25, 1967, 514–515; Foust, "December, 1967 Report of Community of Christ our Brother," Box 043/3, Folder 2, ACAA. See also Bishop Bernardin to Most Reverend Luigi Raimondi, Apostolic Delegate to the United States, Washington, D.C., April 19, 1968, Box 043/3, Folder 2, ACAA.

28. Bernardin to Raimondi, April 19, 1968. See also memo from Bernardin, April 19, 1968, Box 043/3, Folder 2, ACAA.

29. Memo from Rev. Noel C. Burtenshaw, Chancellor, Archdiocese of Atlanta, May 24, 1968, Box 043/3, Folder 2; Bernardin to Foust, May 26, 1968, Box 043/3, Folder 2, ACAA.

30. Donnellan to Mrs. Kathleen K. Goedecke, Secretary, The Community of Christ Our Brother, December 18, 1968, Box 043/3, Folder 2; Donnellan to Raimondi, December 18, 1968, Box 043/3, Folder 2, ACAA.

31. Toolen to Very Rev. Gerard B. Fredericks, Missionary Servants of the Most Holy Trinity, Silver Spring, Md., May 29, 1965; Toolen to Most Rev. Cletus F. O'Donnell, J.C.D., American Board of Catholic Missions, Madison, Wisc., June 20, 1967; Toolen to Sister Mary Benedicta, O.P., St. Clara's Convent, Sinsinawa, Wisc., April 25, 1967, Toolen papers.

32. Mr. Frank O'Neill, Southern Regional Council, Atlanta, Ga., to Lipscomb, Chancellor, February 27, 1970; Lipscomb to O'Neill, March 16, 1970, Bishop John L. May papers, Archives of the Catholic Archdiocese of Mobile, Alabama. On the persistence of racially separate schools in Montgomery and Selma, see Edward A. Leary, S.S.E., Selma, Ala., to Toolen, May 21, 1969; Monsignor J. Edwin Stuardi, Superintendent of Schools, to Toolen, June 7, 1969; pastoral letter from Bishop John May to priests of the diocese, n.d. [1970], "Comments on the Senate Minutes of Oct. 14"; Father John Crowley, S.S.E., Edmundite Mission Director, Selma, Ala., to Bishop May, March 4, 1970; Meeting with Bishop John L. May Concerning the Future of Catholic Secondary Education in the Montgomery Area, November 9, 1970, Toolen and May papers.

33. "Bishop May Praises Supreme Court Ruling," *Catholic Week*, April 30, 1971, p. 1; "Catholic Schools Today," part of annual report, *Teaching Christ: The Educational Mission of the Church*, supplement in *Catholic Week*, May 26, 1972, p. 3-B. Also see Albert S. Foley, "Mobile, Alabama: The Demise of State Sanctioned Resistance," in

Community Politics and Educational Change: Ten School Systems under Court Order, ed. Charles V. Willie and Susan L. Greenblatt (New York: Longman, 1981).

34. Statement of Most Reverend Thomas A. Donnellan, Archbishop of the Catholic Archdiocese of Atlanta, Press Release, January 11, 1970, Box 036/6, Folder 52, ACAA.

35. "Court Approves Refusals," *Catholic Week,* February 4, 1972, pp. 1, 12.

36. Rev. Joseph F. Konen, C.M., Auburn, Ala., to Toolen, May 3, 1968; Very Rev. Oscar H. Lipscomb, Chancellor, to Konen, June 7, 1968; Toolen to Sister Thomas Veronica, Spaulding College, Louisville, Ky., October 16, 1968; Mr. and Mrs. Gerald V. Flannery, Auburn, Ala., to Parish Council Members, St. Michael's Church, Auburn, Ala., March 27, 1968, Toolen papers. On the problems inherent in such parish consolidation, see, for example, St. Peter Claver Parish Council, October 15, 1968; May, "Comments on the Senate Minutes of October 14, [1970]," Toolen and May papers; "'Two Mobile Churches Unite," *Catholic Week,* February 5, 1971, p. 11. For Georgia, see Michael A. Doyle, Secretary, Archdiocesan Pastoral Council, to Donnellan, May 19, 1970, Box 008/6, Folder 2; and Archdiocesan Pastoral Council, Minutes of Executive Committee Meeting, June 10, 1970, Box 008/6, Folder 3, ACAA.

37. Minutes of the Baldwin County Priests' Association Meeting, May 21, 1970, May papers; Father Michael White, transcription of interview by Sister Rose Sevenich, O.S.F., February 9, 1993, transcribed by Mr. John J. P. O'Brien, Oral History Project, Box 2, Envelope 18, ACDBA.

38. May to Sister Mary Anselm, Mercy Hospital, Urbana, Ill., March 17, 1970, May papers.

39. "Statement of Concern," Social Justice Commission, Mobile, [1970], May papers.

40. Sister Judith Ann Pinnell, R.S.M., Daphne, Ala., to May, March 3, 1970, May papers; Diane E. Hampton, Mobile, Ala., to May, March 2, 1970, May papers. Bishop May defended the composition of the commission on grounds of expedience. See his response to Pinnell (March 5, 1970) and Hampton (March 5, 1970), May papers.

41. Joseph Lanaux Marston, Jr., President, Corpus Christi Parish Council, Mobile, Ala., to May, June 23, 1970; Ray and Ida Vrazel, Mobile, Ala., to May, July 10, 1970, May papers.

42. Bishop John L. May, "For the Record," *Catholic Week,* February 5, 1971, p. 4; "Open Housing in the Metro Atlanta Area," Box 009/1, Folder 9, ACAA; "Open Housing Report," March 12, 1971, Box 009/1, Folder 9. See also Noel C. Burtenshaw, Chancellor, "The Church and Housing," an address to the Christian Council of Metropolitan Atlanta, November 5, 1970, Box 020/5, Folder 2, ACAA. Editors of the *Catholic Week* had endorsed open housing as early as 1966. See "Human Rights, Property Rights," *Catholic Week,* August 19, 1966, p. 4.

43. See Wayne Flynt, *Alabama Baptists: Southern Baptists in the Heart of Dixie* (Tuscaloosa: Univ. of Alabama Press, 1998), 517–529.

CONCLUSION

1. Samuel S. Hill argues that the recent advent of Fundamentalism among southern Protestants (particularly Baptists and Presbyterians) has separated religious and regional identity. An emphasis on doctrinal purity instead of racial or cultural purity

precludes the old "cultural captivity" of southern Protestantism. "Fundamentalism in Recent Southern Culture: Has It Done What the Civil Rights Movement Couldn't Do?" *Journal of Southern Religion* 1 (1998). But see Joel W. Martin's response in the same issue. Martin correctly points out that the success of the civil rights movement made possible the transformation that Hill describes. "All That Is Solid (and Southern) Melts into Air: A Response to Sam Hill's Fundamental Argument Regarding Fundamentalism," *Journal of Southern Religion* 1 (1998).

2. David J. O'Brien, "What Happened to the Catholic Left?" in *What's Left? Liberal American Catholics*, ed. Mary Jo Weaver (Bloomington: Indiana Univ. Press, 1999), 275.

3. Thomas Byrne Edsall, with Mary D. Edsall, *Chain Reaction: The Impact of Race, Rights, and Taxes on American Politics*, with a new afterword (New York: Norton, 1992). On the connection between this and the South's movement into the Republican Party, see Alexander P. Lamis, *The Two-Party South*, 2nd expanded edition (New York: Oxford Univ. Press, 1990); Jack Bass and Walter De Vries, *The Transformation of Southern Politics* (New York: Basic Books, 1976); Dan T. Carter, *The Politics of Rage: George Wallace, the Origins of the New Conservatism, and the Transformation of American Politics* (New York: Simon and Schuster, 1995); Dan T. Carter, *From George Wallace to Newt Gingrich: Race in the Conservative Counterrevolution, 1963–1994* (Baton Rouge: Louisiana State Univ. Press, 1996); Earle Black and Merle Black, *The Rise of Southern Republicans* (New York: Belknap Press, 2002).

4. On Southern Baptists, see Barry Hankins, *Uneasy in Babylon: Southern Baptist Conservatives and American Culture* (Tuscaloosa: Univ. of Alabama Press, 2002). For Catholics, see John T. McGreevy, *Catholicism and American Freedom: A History* (New York: Norton, 2003), especially chapter 9.

Bibliography

✤

MANUSCRIPT COLLECTIONS

Archives of the Catholic Archdiocese of Atlanta, Georgia
Archives of the Catholic Diocese of Savannah, Georgia
Foley, Father Albert S., S.J. Papers. Spring Hill College Archives, Mobile, Alabama
LeFlore, John. Papers. Archives of the University of South Alabama, Mobile, Alabama
May, Bishop John L. Papers. Catholic Archdiocese of Mobile, Alabama
Oral History Project. Archives of the Catholic Diocese of Birmingham in Alabama
Public Information Subject Files, Alabama Department of Archives and History, Montgomery, Alabama
Southern Regional Council Collection and Selma Inter-religious Project Files. Department of Archives and Manuscripts. Linn-Henley Research Library. Birmingham Public Library, Birmingham, Alabama
Toolen, Archbishop Thomas J. Papers. Catholic Archdiocese of Mobile, Alabama

NEWSPAPERS

Catholic Week, 1945–1970
Georgia Bulletin, 1963–1970
Mobile Press, May 1969
Mobile Press-Register, May 1969
Mobile Register, April 1956–September 1956, May 1969

PRINTED PRIMARY SOURCES

Catechism of the Catholic Church. Liguori, Mo.: Liguori Publications, 1994.
Fitzgerald, Sally, ed. *The Habit of Being: Letters of Flannery O'Connor.* New York: Noonday Press, 1979.

Flannery, Austin, O.P., ed. *The Basic Sixteen Documents, Vatican Council II: Constitutions, Decrees, Declarations.* Northport, N.Y.: Costello, 1996.

O'Connor, Flannery. "The Artificial Nigger." In *The Complete Stories of Flannery O'Connor.* New York: Noonday Press, 1971.

Pope Pius XI. *Quas Primas,* December 11, 1925. Reprinted in *The Papal Encyclicals, 1903–1939,* ed. Claudia Carlen, I.H.M. [Wilmington, N.C.]: McGrath, 1981.

Rummel, Joseph Francis. Pastoral Letter, February 19, 1956. *Catholic Mind* 54 (May 1956). Reprinted in Thomas R. West and James W. Mooney, eds., *To Redeem a Nation: A History and Anthology of the Civil Rights Movement* (St. James, N.Y.: Brandywine Press, 1993).

Schwalm, M. Elise, R.S.M., ed. "In His Own Words: Paul J. Hallinan, Archbishop of Atlanta, 1962–1968." Unpublished manuscript in possession of M. Elise Schwalm.

Yzermans, Monsignor Vincent A. "Wherever They Go, Christians Witness For Christ." Interview with Archbishop Paul J. Hallinan by Monsignor Vincent A. Yzermans. *Our Sunday Visitor,* Fort Wayne-South Bend Edition, Magazine Section 55 (July 24, 1966), pp. 4–5.

SECONDARY SOURCE ARTICLES AND CHAPTERS

Anderson, Jon W. "Catholic Imagination and Inflections of 'Church' in the Contemporary South." In *The Culture of Bible Belt Catholics,* edited by Jon W. Anderson and William B. Friend. New York: Paulist Press, 1995.

Bell, Mark R. "Continued Captivity: Religion in Bartow County Georgia." *Journal of Southern Religion* 2 (1999).

Campbell, Debra. "Part-Time Female Evangelists of the Thirties and Forties: The Rosary College Catholic Evidence Guild." *U.S. Catholic Historian* 5 (1986): 371–383.

Chalker, Fussell. "Irish Catholics and the Building of the Ocmulgee and Flint Railroad." *Georgia Historical Quarterly* 54 (1970): 507–516.

Cuddy, Edward. "The Irish Question and the Revival of Anti-Catholicism in the 1920s." *Catholic Historical Review* 67 (April 1981): 236–255.

Dailey, Jane. "Sex, Segregation, and the Sacred after *Brown.*" *Journal of American History* 91 (June 2004): 119–144.

Dolan, Jay. "Catholic Attitudes toward Protestants." In *Uncivil Religion: Interreligious Hostility in America,* ed. Robert N. Bellah and Frederick E. Greenspahn. New York: Crossroad, 1987.

Dumenil, Lynn. "The Tribal Twenties: 'Assimilated' Catholics' Response to Anti-Catholicism in the 1920s." *Journal of American Ethnic History* 11 (fall 1991): 21–49.

Foley, Albert S. "Mobile, Alabama: The Demise of State Sanctioned Resistance." In *Community Politics and Educational Change: Ten School Systems under Court Order,* ed. Charles V. Willie and Susan L. Greenblatt. New York: Longman, 1981.

Gerstle, Gary. "Liberty, Coercion, and the Making of Americans." *Journal of American History* 84 (September 1997): 524–558.

Gill, George J. "The Truman Administration and Vatican Relations." *Catholic Historical Review* 73 (July 1987): 408–423.

Hankins, Barry. "Southern Baptists and Northern Evangelicals: Cultural Factors and the Nature of Religious Alliances." *Religion and American Culture: A Journal of Interpretation* 7 (summer 1997): 271–298.

Hill, Samuel S. "Fundamentalism in Recent Southern Culture: Has It Done What the Civil Rights Movement Couldn't Do?" *Journal of Southern Religion* 1 (1998).

———. "The South's Two Cultures." In *Religion and the Solid South,* ed. Samuel S. Hill. Nashville, Tenn.: Abingdon Press, 1972.

———. "The Story Before the Story: Southern Baptists since World War II." In *Southern Baptists Observed: Multiple Perspectives on a Changing Denomination,* ed. Nancy Tatom Ammerman. Knoxville: Univ. of Tennessee Press, 1993.

Kelly, Timothy. "Suburbanization and the Decline of Catholic Public Ritual in Pittsburgh." *Journal of Social History* 28 (winter 1994): 311–330.

Kelly, Timothy, and Joseph Kelly. "Our Lady of Perpetual Help, Gender Roles, and the Decline of Devotional Catholicism." *Journal of Social History* 32 (fall 1998): 5–26.

Klarman, Michael J. "How *Brown* Changed Race Relations: The Backlash Thesis." *Journal of American History* 81 (June 1994): 81–118.

Kselman, Thomas A., and Steven Avella. "Marian Piety and the Cold War in the United States." *Catholic Historical Review* 72 (July 1986): 403–424.

Lipscomb, Oscar H. "The Administration of John Quinlan, Second Bishop of Mobile, 1859–1883." *Records of the American Catholic Historical Society of Philadelphia* 78 (1967): 3–163.

———. "Catholic Missionaries in Early Alabama." *Alabama Review* 18 (1965): 124–131.

Martensen, Katherine. "Region, Religion, and Social Action: The Catholic Committee of the South, 1939–1956." *Catholic Historical Review* 68 (April 1982): 249–267.

Martin, Joel. "All That Is Solid (and Southern) Melts into Air: A Response to Sam Hill's Fundamental Argument Regarding Fundamentalism." *Journal of Southern Religion* 1 (1998).

Massa, Mark S., S.J. "The New and Old Anti-Catholicism and the Analogical Imagination." *Theological Studies* 62 (2001): 549–570.

McDonogh, Gary W. "Constructing Christian Hatred: Anti-Catholicism, Diversity, and Identity in Southern Religious Life." In *Religion in the Contemporary South: Diversity, Community, and Identity,* ed. O. Kendall White, Jr., and Daryl White. Athens: Univ. of Georgia Press, 1995.

McGreevy, John T. "Thinking on One's Own: Catholicism in the American Intellectual Imagination, 1928–1960." *Journal of American History* 84 (June 1997): 97–131.

McNally, Michael J. "A Peculiar Institution: A History of Catholic Parish Life in the Southeast (1850–1980)." In *The American Catholic Parish: A History from 1850 to the Present,* vol. 1, ed. Jay Dolan. Mahwah, N.J.: Paulist Press, 1987.

Miller, Randall M. "Catholics in a Protestant World: The Old South Example." In *Varieties of Southern Religious Experience,* ed. Samuel S. Hill. Baton Rouge: Louisiana State Univ. Press, 1988.

———. "A Church in Cultural Captivity: Some Speculations on Catholic Identity in the Old South." In *Catholics in the Old South: Essays on Church and Culture,* ed. Randall M. Miller and Jon L. Wakelyn. Macon, Ga.: Mercer Univ. Press, 1983.

Minchin, Timothy J. "Black Activism, the 1964 Civil Rights Act, and the Racial Integration of the Southern Textile Industry." *Journal of Southern History* 65 (November 1999): 809–844.

Nolan, Charles E. "Modest and Humble Crosses: A History of Catholic Parishes in the South Central Region (1850–1984)." In *The American Catholic Parish: A History from 1850 to the Present,* vol. 1, ed. Jay Dolan. Mahwah, N.J.: Paulist Press, 1987.

O'Brien, David J. "What Happened to the Catholic Left?" In *What's Left? Liberal American Catholics,* ed. Mary Jo Weaver. Bloomington: Indiana Univ. Press, 1999.

Pagliarini, Marie Ann. "The Pure American Woman and the Wicked Catholic Priest: An Analysis of Anti-Catholic Literature in Antebellum America." *Religion and American Culture: A Journal of Interpretation* 9 (winter 1999): 97–128.

Powers, Felicitas, R.S.M. "Prejudice, Journalism, and the Catholic Laymen's Association of Georgia." *U.S. Catholic Historian* 8 (summer 1989): 201–212.

Pruitt, Paul M., Jr. "Private Tragedy, Public Shame." *Alabama Heritage* 30 (fall 1993): 24–37.

Raboteau, Albert J. "Minority within a Minority: The History of Black Catholics in America." In *A Fire in the Bones: Reflections on African-American Religious History.* Boston: Beacon Press, 1995.

Racine, Philip N. "The Ku Klux Klan, Anti-Catholicism, and Atlanta's Board of Education, 1916–1927." *Georgia Historical Quarterly* 57 (spring 1973): 63–75.

Richardson, Miles. "Speaking and Hearing (in Contrast to Touching and See-
    ing) the Sacred." In *Religion in the Contemporary South: Diversity, Com-
    munity, and Identity,* ed. O. Kendall White, Jr., and Daryl White. Athens:
    Univ. of Georgia Press, 1995.
Schweiger, Beth Barton. "The Captivity of Southern Religious History." Un-
    published paper presented to Southern Intellectual History Circle, Bir-
    mingham, Alabama, February 21, 1997.
Slawson, Douglas J. "Thirty Years of Street Preaching: Vincentian Motor Mis-
    sions, 1934–1965." *Church History* 62 (March 1993): 60–81.
Southern, David W. "But Think of the Kids: Catholic Interracialists and the
    Great American Taboo of Race Mixing." *U.S. Catholic Historian* 16:3 (sum-
    mer 1998): 67–93.
Sweeney, Charles P. "Bigotry in the South." *Nation,* November 24, 1920, 585–586.

MASTER'S THESES AND DISSERTATIONS

Blalock, Kay J. "The Irish Catholic Experience in Birmingham, Alabama, 1871–
    1921." M.A. thesis, University of Alabama at Birmingham, 1989.
Clark, Wayne Addison. "An Analysis of the Relationship Between Anti-Com-
    munism and Segregationist Thought in the Deep South, 1948–1964." Ph.D.
    diss., University of North Carolina, Chapel Hill, 1976.
Ellis, Carol A. "'The Tragedy of the White Moderate': Father Albert Foley and
    Alabama Civil Rights, 1963–1967." M.A. thesis, University of South Ala-
    bama, 2002.
Foley, Albert Sidney. "The Catholic Church and the Washington Negro." Ph.D.
    diss., University of North Carolina, Chapel Hill, 1950.
Hite, Gregory Nelson. "The Hottest Places in Hell: The Catholic Church and
    Civil Rights in Selma, Alabama, 1937–1965." Ph.D. diss., University of Vir-
    ginia, Charlottesville, 2002.
Lipscomb, Oscar H. "The Administration of Michael Portier, Vicar Apostolic
    of Alabama and the Floridas, 1825–1829, and First Bishop of Mobile, 1829–
    1859." Ph.D. diss., Catholic University of America, Washington, D.C., 1963.

SECONDARY SOURCE BOOKS

Allitt, Patrick. *Catholic Intellectuals and Conservative Politics in America, 1950–
    1985.* Ithaca, N.Y.: Cornell Univ. Press, 1993.
Bartley, Numan V. *The New South, 1945–1980.* Baton Rouge: Louisiana State
    Univ. Press, 1995.
———. *The Rise of Massive Resistance: Race and Politics in the South during
    the 1950s,* with a new preface by the author. Baton Rouge: Louisiana State
    Univ. Press, 1997; originally published 1969.

Bass, Jack, and Walter De Vries. *The Transformation of Southern Politics.* New York: Basic Books, 1976.

Bass, S. Jonathan. *Blessed Are the Peacemakers: Martin Luther King, Jr., Eight White Religious Leaders, and the "Letter from Birmingham Jail."* Baton Rouge: Louisiana State Univ. Press, 2001.

Bayor, Ronald H. *Race and the Shaping of Twentieth-Century Atlanta.* Chapel Hill: Univ. of North Carolina Press, 1996.

Billington, Ray. *The Protestant Crusade, 1800–1860: A Study of the Origins of American Nativism.* Chicago: Quadrangle Books, 1938.

Black, Earle, and Merle Black. *The Rise of Southern Republicans.* New York: Belknap Press, 2002.

Branch, Taylor. *Parting the Waters: America in the King Years, 1954–1963.* New York: Simon and Schuster, 1988.

———. *Pillar of Fire: America in the King Years, 1963–1965.* New York: Simon and Schuster, 1998.

Broderick, Robert C., ed. *The Catholic Encyclopedia,* revised and updated edition. Nashville, Tenn.: Thomas Nelson, 1987.

Carter, Dan T. *From George Wallace to Newt Gingrich: Race in the Conservative Counterrevolution, 1963–1994.* Baton Rouge: Louisiana State Univ. Press, 1996.

———. *The Politics of Rage: George Wallace, the Origins of the New Conservatism, and the Transformation of American Politics.* New York: Simon and Schuster, 1995.

———. *Scottsboro: A Tragedy of the American South.* Baton Rouge: Louisiana State Univ. Press, 1969.

Carty, Thomas J. *A Catholic in the White House? Religion, Politics, and John F. Kennedy's Presidential Campaign.* New York: Palgrave Macmillan, 2004.

Cash, W. J. *The Mind of the South,* with a new introduction by Bertram Wyatt-Brown. New York: Vintage Books, 1991; originally published 1941.

Chappell, David L. *A Stone of Hope: Prophetic Religion and the Death of Jim Crow.* Chapel Hill: Univ. of North Carolina Press, 2004.

Chestnut, J. L., Jr., and Julia Cass. *Black in Selma: The Uncommon Life of J.L. Chestnut, Jr.* New York: Farrar, Straus and Giroux, 1990.

Chidester, David, and Edward T. Linenthal, eds. *American Sacred Space.* Bloomington: Indiana Univ. Press, 1995.

Chinnici, Joseph P., O.F.M. *Living Stones: The History and Structure of Catholic Spiritual Life in the United States,* 2nd ed. Maryknoll, N.Y.: Orbis Books, 1996.

Curry, Lerond. *Protestant-Catholic Relations in America: World War I through Vatican II.* Lexington: Univ. Press of Kentucky, 1972.

Davis, Cyprian, O.S.B. *The History of Black Catholics in the United States.* New York: Crossroad, 1990.

Dolan, Jay P. *The American Catholic Experience: A History from Colonial Times to the Present*. Notre Dame: Univ. of Notre Dame Press, 1992.

———. *Catholic Revivalism: The American Experience, 1830–1900*. Notre Dame, Ind.: Univ. of Notre Dame Press, 1978.

———. *In Search of an American Catholicism: A History of Religion and Culture in Tension*. New York: Oxford Univ. Press, 2002.

Duffy, Eamon. *The Stripping of the Altars: Traditional Religion in England, c. 1400–c. 1580*, 2nd ed. New Haven: Yale Univ. Press, 2005.

Eagles, Charles W. *Outside Agitator: Jon Daniels and the Civil Rights Movement in Alabama*. Chapel Hill: Univ. of North Carolina Press, 1993.

Edsall, Thomas Byrne, with Mary D. Edsall. *Chain Reaction: The Impact of Race, Rights, and Taxes on American Politics*, with a new afterword. New York: Norton, 1992.

Eighmy, John Lee. *Churches in Cultural Captivity: A History of the Social Attitudes of Southern Baptists*. Knoxville: Univ. of Tennessee Press, 1972.

Eliade, Mircea. *The Sacred and the Profane: The Nature of Religion*. Translated by Willard R. Trask. San Diego, Calif.: Harcourt Brace Jovanovich, 1959.

Elie, Paul. *The Life You Save May Be Your Own: An American Pilgrimage*. New York: Farrar, Straus and Giroux, 2003.

Eskew, Glenn T. *But for Birmingham: The Local and National Movements in the Civil Rights Struggle*. Chapel Hill: Univ. of North Carolina Press, 1997.

Fairclough, Adam. *Race and Democracy: The Civil Rights Struggle in Louisiana, 1915–1972*. Athens: Univ. of Georgia Press, 1995.

Fede, Frank J. *Italians in the Deep South: Their Impact on Birmingham and the American Heritage*. Montgomery, Ala.: Black Belt Press, 1994.

Findlay, James F., Jr. *Church People in the Struggle: The National Council of Churches and the Black Freedom Movement, 1950–1970*. New York: Oxford Univ. Press, 1993.

Flynt, Wayne. *Alabama Baptists: Southern Baptists in the Heart of Dixie*. Tuscaloosa: Univ. of Alabama Press, 1998.

Franchot, Jenny. *Roads to Rome: The Antebellum Protestant Encounter with Catholicism*. Berkeley: Univ. of California Press, 1994.

Friedland, Michael B. *Lift Up Your Voice Like a Trumpet: White Clergy and the Civil Rights and Antiwar Movements, 1954–1973*. Chapel Hill: Univ. of North Carolina Press, 1998.

Gannon, Michael V. *Rebel Bishop: The Life and Era of Augustin Verot*. Milwaukee: Bruce, 1964.

Garrow, David J. *Protest at Selma: Martin Luther King, Jr., and the Voting Rights Act of 1965*. New Haven: Yale Univ. Press, 1978.

Greeley, Andrew M. *The Catholic Myth: The Behavior and Beliefs of American Catholics*. New York: Collier Books, 1990.

———. *An Ugly Little Secret: Anti-Catholicism in North America.* Kansas City, Mo.: Sheed Andrews and McMeel, 1977.

Hamburger, Philip. *Separation of Church and State.* Cambridge, Mass.: Harvard Univ. Press, 2002.

Hamilton, Virginia Van der Veer. *Hugo Black: The Alabama Years.* Baton Rouge: Louisiana State Univ. Press, 1972.

Hankins, Barry. *Uneasy in Babylon: Southern Baptist Conservatives and American Culture.* Tuscaloosa: Univ. of Alabama Press, 2002.

Harvey, Paul. *Freedom's Coming: Religious Culture and the Shaping of the South from the Civil War through the Civil Rights Era.* Chapel Hill: Univ. of North Carolina Press, 2005.

———. *Redeeming the South: Religious Cultures and Racial Identities among Southern Baptists, 1865–1925.* Chapel Hill: Univ. of North Carolina Press, 1997.

Hayes, Diana L., and Cyprian Davis, eds. *Taking Down Our Harps: Black Catholics in the United States.* Maryknoll, N.Y.: Orbis, 1998.

Hill, Samuel S., Jr. *Southern Churches in Crisis.* Boston: Beacon Press, 1968; New York: Holt, Rinehart, and Winston, 1966.

———. *Southern Churches in Crisis Revisited.* Tuscaloosa: Univ. of Alabama Press, 1999.

Holifield, E. Brooks. *Theology in America: Christian Thought from the Age of the Puritans to the Civil War.* New Haven: Yale Univ. Press, 2003.

Huff, Peter A. *Allen Tate and the Catholic Revival: Trace of the Fugitive Gods.* Mahwah, N.J.: Paulist Press, 1996.

Irons, Peter. *A People's History of the Supreme Court.* New York: Penguin Books, 1999.

Jacobson, Matthew Frye. *Whiteness of a Different Color: European Immigrants and the Alchemy of Race.* Cambridge, Mass.: Harvard Univ. Press, 1998.

Jenkins, Philip. *The New Anti-Catholicism: The Last Acceptable Prejudice.* New York: Oxford Univ. Press, 2003.

K'Meyer, Tracy Elaine. *Interracialism and Christian Community in the Postwar South.* Charlottesville: Univ. Press of Virginia, 1997.

Labbé, Dolores Egger. *Jim Crow Comes to Church: The Establishment of Segregated Catholic Parishes in South Louisiana.* New York: Arno Press, 1978.

Lamis, Alexander P. *The Two-Party South,* 2nd expanded edition. New York: Oxford Univ. Press, 1990.

Lovett, Rose Gibbons. *The Catholic Church in the Deep South: The Diocese of Birmingham in Alabama, 1540–1976.* Birmingham, Ala.: The Diocese of Birmingham in Alabama, 1980.

MacLean, Nancy. *Behind the Mask of Chivalry: The Making of the Second Ku Klux Klan.* New York: Oxford Univ. Press, 1994.

Manis, Andrew Michael. *Southern Civil Religions in Conflict: Black and White Baptists and Civil Rights, 1947–1957.* Athens: Univ. of Georgia Press, 1985.

Marlett, Jeffrey D. *Saving the Heartland: Catholic Missionaries in Rural America, 1920–1960.* DeKalb, Ill.: Northern Illinois Univ. Press, 2002.

Marsh, Charles. *The Beloved Community: How Faith Shapes Social Justice from the Civil Rights Movement to Today.* New York: Basic Books, 2005.

———. *God's Long Summer: Stories of Faith and Civil Rights.* Princeton, N.J.: Princeton Univ. Press, 1997.

Massa, Mark S., S.J. *Anti-Catholicism in America: The Last Acceptable Prejudice.* New York: Crossroad, 2003.

———. *Catholics and American Culture: Fulton Sheen, Dorothy Day, and the Notre Dame Football Team.* New York: Crossroad, 1999.

McGreevy, John T. *Catholicism and American Freedom: A History.* New York: Norton, 2003.

———. *Parish Boundaries: The Catholic Encounter with Race in the Twentieth-Century Urban North.* Chicago: Univ. of Chicago Press, 1996.

Miller, Randall M., and Jon L. Wakelyn, eds. *Catholics in the Old South: Essays on Church and Culture.* Macon, Ga.: Mercer Univ. Press, 1983.

Minchin, Timothy J. *Hiring the Black Worker: The Racial Integration of the Southern Textile Industry, 1960–1980.* Chapel Hill: Univ. of North Carolina Press, 1999.

Morris, Charles R. *American Catholic: The Saints and Sinners Who Built America's Most Powerful Church.* New York: Times Books, 1997.

Murray, Peter C. *Methodists and the Crucible of Race, 1930–1975.* Columbia: Univ. of Missouri Press, 2004.

Newman, Mark. *Getting Right with God: Southern Baptists and Desegregation, 1945–1995.* Tuscaloosa: Univ. of Alabama Press, 2001.

Newman, Roger K. *Hugo Black: A Biography.* New York: Pantheon Books, 1994.

Noll, Mark A., and Carolyn Nystrom. *Is the Reformation Over? An Evangelical Assessment of Contemporary Roman Catholicism.* Grand Rapids, Mich.: Baker Academic, 2005.

O'Brien, David J. *American Catholics and Social Reform: The New Deal Years.* New York: Oxford Univ. Press, 1968.

Ochs, Stephen J. *Desegregating the Altar: The Josephites and the Struggle for Black Priests, 1871–1960.* Baton Rouge: Louisiana State Univ. Press, 1990.

Osborne, William A. *The Segregated Covenant: Race Relations and American Catholics.* New York: Herder and Herder, 1967.

Ownby, Ted. *Subduing Satan: Religion, Recreation, and Manhood in the Rural South, 1865–1920.* Chapel Hill: Univ. of North Carolina Press, 1990.

Patterson, James T. *Brown v. Board of Education: A Civil Rights Milestone and Its Troubled Legacy*. New York: Oxford Univ. Press, 2001.

———. *Grand Expectations: The United States, 1945–1974*. New York: Oxford Univ. Press, 1996.

Pomerantz, Gary M. *Where Peachtree Meets Sweet Auburn: The Saga of Two Families and the Making of Atlanta*. New York: Scribner, 1996.

Richardson, Frederick Douglas, Jr. *The Genesis and Exodus of NOW*, 2nd ed. Boynton Beach, Fla.: Futura Printing, 1996.

Rogers, William Warren, Robert David Ward, Leah Rawls Atkins, and Wayne Flynt. *Alabama: The History of a Deep South State*. Tuscaloosa: Univ. of Alabama Press, 1994.

Rose, Lisle A. *The Cold War Comes to Main Street: America in 1950*. Lawrence: Univ. Press of Kansas, 1999.

Schweiger, Beth Barton. *The Gospel Working Up: Progress and the Pulpit in Nineteenth-Century Virginia*. New York: Oxford Univ. Press, 2000.

Shattuck, Gardiner H., Jr. *Episcopalians and Race: Civil War to Civil Rights*. Lexington: Univ. Press of Kentucky, 2000.

Shelley, Thomas J. *Paul J. Hallinan: First Archbishop of Atlanta*. Wilmington, Del.: Michael Glazier, 1989.

Southern, David W. *John LaFarge and the Limits of Catholic Interracialism, 1911–1963*. Baton Rouge: Louisiana State Univ. Press, 1996.

Stowell, Daniel W. *Rebuilding Zion: The Religious Reconstruction of the South, 1863–1877*. New York: Oxford Univ. Press, 1998.

Taves, Ann. *The Household of Faith: Roman Catholic Devotions in Mid-Nineteenth-Century America*. Notre Dame, Ind.: Univ. of Notre Dame Press, 1986.

Tracy, David. *The Analogical Imagination: Christian Theology and the Culture of Pluralism*. New York: Crossroad, 1981.

Webb, Sheyann, and Rachel Ann Nelson, as told to Frank Sikora. *Selma, Lord, Selma: Girlhood Memories of the Civil-Rights Days*. Tuscaloosa: Univ. of Alabama Press, 1980.

Weisbrot, Robert. *Freedom Bound: A History of America's Civil Rights Movement*. New York: Norton, 1990.

Willis, Alan Scot. *All According to God's Plan: Southern Baptist Missions and Race, 1945–1970*. Lexington: Univ. Press of Kentucky, 2005.

Wood, Ralph C. *Flannery O'Connor and the Christ-Haunted South*. Grand Rapids, Mich.: Eerdmans, 2004.

Wuthnow, Robert. *After Heaven: Spirituality in America since the 1950s*. Berkeley: Univ. of California Press, 1998.

———. *The Restructuring of American Religion: Society and Faith since World War II*. Princeton, N.J.: Princeton Univ. Press, 1988.

Index